Lecture Notes of the Institute for Computer Sciences, Social Informatics and Telecommunications Engineering   197

More information about this series at http://www.springer.com/series/8197

Jiafu Wan · Kai Lin
Delu Zeng · Jin Li
Yang Xiang · Xiaofeng Liao
Jiwu Huang · Zheli Liu (Eds.)

Cloud Computing, Security, Privacy in New Computing Environments

7th International Conference, CloudComp 2016
and First International Conference, SPNCE 2016
Guangzhou, China, November 25–26, and December 15–16, 2016
Proceedings

 Springer

Editors

Jiafu Wan
South China University of Technology
Guangzhou
China

Kai Lin
Dalian University of Technology
Dalian
China

Delu Zeng
South China University of Technology
Guangzhou
China

Jin Li
School of Computer Science
Guangzhou University
Guangzhou
China

Yang Xiang
Deakin University
Burwood
Australia

Xiaofeng Liao
Southwest University
Chongqing
China

Jiwu Huang
Shenzhen University
Nankai
China

Zheli Liu
Nankai University
Nankai
China

ISSN 1867-8211   ISSN 1867-822X (electronic)
Lecture Notes of the Institute for Computer Sciences, Social Informatics
and Telecommunications Engineering
ISBN 978-3-319-69604-1   ISBN 978-3-319-69605-8 (eBook)
https://doi.org/10.1007/978-3-319-69605-8

Library of Congress Control Number: 2017957850

This Springer imprint is published by Springer Nature
The registered company is Springer International Publishing AG
The registered company address is: Gewerbestrasse 11, 6330 Cham, Switzerland

Preface

In recent years, cloud computing technology has been widely used in many domains, such as manufacture, intelligent transportation system, and finance industry. Examples of cloud services include, but are not limited to, IaaS (Infrastructure as a Service), PaaS (Platform as a Service), and SaaS (Software as a Service). The underlying cloud architecture includes a pool of virtualized computing, storage, and networking resources that can be aggregated and launched as platforms to run workloads and satisfy their service-level agreement (SLA). Cloud architectures also include provisions to best guarantee service delivery for clients and at the same time optimize efficiency of resources of providers. Examples of provisions include, but are not limited to, elasticity through up/down scaling of resources to track workload behavior, extensive monitoring, failure mitigation, and energy optimizations.

The 7th EAI International Conference on Cloud Computing (CloudComp 2016) intended to bring together researchers, developers, and industry professionals to discuss recent advances and experiences in clouds, cloud computing, and related ecosystems and business support. The conference also aims at presenting the recent advances, experiences, and results obtained in the wider area of cloud computing, giving users and researchers equally a chance to gain better insight into the capabilities and limitations of current cloud systems.

CloudComp 2016 was held during November 25–26, 2016, in Guangzhou, China. The conference was organized by the EAI (European Alliance for Innovation). The Program Committee received over 40 submissions from six countries and each paper was reviewed by at least three expert reviewers. We chose 10 papers after intensive discussions held among the Program Committee members. We appreciate the excellent reviews and lively discussions of the Program Committee members and external reviewers in the review process. This year we chose two prominent invited speakers, Prof. Honggang Wang and Prof. Min Chen.

September 2017

Jiafu Wan
Kai Lin
Delu Zeng

CLOUDCOMP 2016 Conference Organization

Steering Committee

Steering Committee Chair

Imrich Chlamtac   CREATE-NET and University of Trento, Italy

Steering Committee Members

Min Chen	Huazhong University of Science and Technology, China
Eliezer Dekel	IBM Research, Haifa, Israel
Victor Leung	University of British Columbia, Canada
Athanasios V. Vasilakos	Kuwait University, Kuwait

Organizing Committee

General Chair

Jiafu Wan   South China University of Technology, China

General Co-chairs

Kai Lin Dalian	University of Technology, China
Delu Zeng	Xiamen University, China

Technical Program Committee Co-chairs

Chin-Feng Lai	National Chung Cheng University, Taiwan
Chi Harold Liu	Beijing Institute of Technology, China
Fangyang Shen	New York City College of Technology, USA

Workshop Chair

Yin Zhang   Zhongnan University of Economics and Law, China

Publicity and Social Media Chair

Houbing Song   West Virginia University, USA

Sponsorship and Exhibits Chair

Shiyong Wang   South China University of Technology, China

Publications Chair

Chun-Wei Tsai   National Ilan University, Taiwan

Local Chair

Yiming Miao   Huazhong University of Science and Technology, China

Website Chair

Mengchen Liu   Huazhong University of Science and Technology, China

Conference Coordinator

Anna Horvathova   European Alliance for Innovation

Technical Program Committee

Houbing Song	West Virginia University, USA
Li Qiu	Shenzhen University, China
Lei Shu	Guangdong University of Petrochemical Technology, China
Yunsheng Wang	Kettering University, USA
Dewen Tang	University of South China, China
Yupeng Qiao	South China University of Technology, China
Leyi Shi	China University of Petroleum, China
Qi Jing	Peking University, China
Caifeng Zou	South China University of Technology, China
Seungmin Rho	Sungkyul University, Korea
Pan Deng	Institute of Software, Chinese Academy of Sciences (ISCAS), China
Feng Xia	Dalian University of Technology, China
Jianqi Liu	Guangdong University of Technology, China
Heng Zhang	Southwest University, China
Chao Yang	Institute of Software, Chinese Academy of Sciences, China
Tie Qiu	Dalian University of Technology, China
Guangjie Han	Hohai University, China
Feng Chen	Institute of Software, Chinese Academy of Sciences, China
Dongyao Jia	University of Leeds, UK
Yin Zhang	Zhongnan University of Economics and Law, China
Qiang Liu	Guangdong University of Technology, China
Fangfang Liu	Institute of Software, Chinese Academy of Sciences, China

Preface

The existing computing models and computing environments have changed immensely due to the rapid advancements in mobile computing, big data, and cyberspace-based supporting technologies such as cloud computing, Internet of Things and other large-scale computing environments. For example, cloud computing is an emerging computing paradigm in which IT resources and capacities are provided as services over the Internet. It builds on the foundations of distributed computing, grid computing, virtualization, service orientation, etc. Cloud computing offers numerous benefits from both the technology and functionality perspectives such as increased availability, flexibility, and functionality. Traditional security techniques are faced many challenges in these new computing environments. Thus, efforts are needed to explore the security and privacy issues of the aforementioned new environments within the cyberspace.

The First EAI International Conference on Security and Privacy in New Computing Environments (SPNCE 2016) intended to bring together researchers, developers, and industry professionals to discuss recent advances and experiences in security and privacy of new computing environments, including mobile computing, big data, cloud computing, and other large-scale computing environments.

SPNCE 2016 was held during December 15–16, 2016, in Guangzhou, China. The conference was organized by the EAI (European Alliance for Innovation). The Program Committee received over 40 submissions from six countries and each paper was reviewed by at least three expert reviewers. We chose 21 papers after intensive discussions held among the Program Committee members. We really appreciate the excellent reviews and lively discussions of the Program Committee members and external reviewers in the review process. This year we chose three prominent invited speakers, Prof. Victor Chang, Prof. Fernando Pérez-González, and Prof. Dongdai Lin.

Imrich Chlamtac
Jin Li
Yang Xiang

SPNCE 2016 Conference Organization

Steering Committee

Imrich Chlamtac	University of Trento, Create-Net, Italy
Jin Li	Guangzhou University, China
Yang Xiang	Deakin University, Australia

Organizing Committee

General Chairs

Jin Li	Guangzhou University, China
Dongqing Xie	Guangzhou University, China

Honorary Chair

Dingyi Pei	Guangzhou University, China

Technical Program Committee Chairs

Yang Xiang	Deakin University, Australia
Xiaofeng Liao	Southwest University, China
Jiwu Huang	Shenzhen University, China

Workshop Chair

Fangguo Zhang	Sun Yat-Sen University, China

Publicity and Social Media Chairs

Zheli Liu	Nankai University, China
Nan Jiang	Jiangxi Jiaotong University, China

Sponsorship and Exhibits Chair

Zhusong Liu	Guangdong University of Technology, China

Publications Chair

Zheli Liu	Nankai University, China

Local Chairs

Chongzhi Gao	Guangzhou University, China
Wenbin Chen	Guangzhou University, China

Web Chair

Chongzhi Gao   Guangzhou University, China

Conference Coordinator

Lenka Oravska   European Alliance for Innovation

Technical Program Committee

Xiaofeng Chen	Xidian University, China
Zheli Liu	Nankai University, China
Tao Xiang	Chongqing University, China
Kim-Kwang Raymond Choo	University of South Australia, Australia
Man Ho Au	Hong Kong Polytechnic University, Hong Kong, SAR China
Xinyi Huang	Fujian Normal University, China
Aniello Castiglione	University of Salerno, Italy
Siu-Ming Yiu	The University of Hong Kong, Hong Kong, SAR China
Joseph C.K. Liu	Monash University, Australia
Xiaofeng Wang	University of Electronic Science and Technology of China, China
Rongxing Lu	Nanyang Technological University, Singapore
Baojiang Cui	Beijing University of Post Telecommunication, China
Aijun Ge	Zhengzhou Information Science and Technology Institute, China
Chunfu Jia	Nankai University, China
Nan Jiang	East China Jiao Tong University, China
Qiong Huang	South China Agricultural University, China
Ding Wang	Peking University, China
Debiao He	Wuhan University, China
Chunming Tang	Guangzhou University, China
Jingwei Li	University of Electronic Science and Technology of China, China
Zhenfeng Zhang	Chinese Academy of Sciences, China
Yinghui Zhang	Xi'an University of Posts and Telecommunications, China
Zhen Ling	Southeast University, China

Contents

SPNCE

CLOUDCOMP

Software Defined Network Routing in Wireless Sensor Network

Junfeng Wang[1], Ping Zhai[1], Yin Zhang[2(✉)], Lei Shi[1], Gaoxiang Wu[3],
Xiaobo Shi[3], and Ping Zhou[3]

[1] School of Information Engineering, Zhengzhou University, Zhengzhou, China
{iewangjf,iepzhai,ielshi}@zzu.edu.cn
[2] School of Information and Safety Engineering,
Zhongnan University of Economics and Law, Wuhan, China
yinzhang@zuel.edu.cn
[3] School of Computer Science and Technology, Huazhong University of Science and
Technology, Wuhan, China
{gaoxiangwu.epic,xiaoboshi.cs,pingzhou.cs}@qq.com

Abstract. Software-Defined Networking (SDN) is currently hot research area. The current researches on SDN are mainly focused on wired network and data center, while software-defined wireless sensor network (WSN) is put forth in a few researches, but only at stage of putting forth models and concepts. In this paper, we have proposed a new SDN routing scheme in multi-hop wireless network is proposed. The implementation of the protocol is described in detail. We also build model with OPNET and simulate it. The simulation results show that the proposed routing scheme could provide shortest path and disjoint multipath routing for nodes, and its network lifetime is longer than existing algorithms (OLSR, AODV) when traffic load is heavier.

Keywords: Software Defined Network (SDN) · Wireless Sensor Network (WSN) · Routing · Multipath

1 Introduction

In wireless sensor network, each node may act as data source & target node, and forwarding node as well. The high dynamic characteristics of wireless link cause poor quality and low stability for link, which poses a challenge to throughput and transmission reliability of wireless sensor network. Otherwise, restricted energy and mobility requirements of node also bring difficulties to design and optimization of routing protocol [1].

Traditional multi-hop wireless routing is divided into active routing and passive routing; active routing such as OLSR [2] is based on broadcast information; in each node, the routing information from that node to all other nodes is saved, so there is so much routing information that requires to be saved in each node, and too much internal storage is occupied; therefore, active routing is not adapted to high dynamic network. As for passive routing such as AODV [3], the

© ICST Institute for Computer Sciences, Social Informatics and Telecommunications Engineering 2018
J. Wan et al. (Eds.): CloudComp 2016, SPNCE 2016, LNICST 197, pp. 3–11, 2018.
https://doi.org/10.1007/978-3-319-69605-8_1

routing is searched with broadcast each time when sending data is required by node; when multiple nodes require sending routing, nodes need broadcasting for many times to search routing; when there are too many links for a node, too much energy is consumed by broadcast.

SDN separates control from data, and open uniform interface (such as Open-Flow) is adopted for interaction. Control layer is responsible for programming to manage & collocate network, to deploy new protocols, and etc. Through central-ized control of SDN, uniform network-wide view may be obtained, and dynamic allocation may be conducted to network resources as per changes in network flow [4]. Currently, the most routing researches for software-defined network are with respect to wired network and data center [5,6]; though software-defined Internet of Things and software-defined wireless sensor network are put forth in a few researches, but only at stage of putting forth models and concepts.

In researches on SDN based on wireless network, the characteristics of wire-less network, such as broadcast characteristics, hidden terminal, node mobility and etc. shall be taken into consideration. OpenFlow Protocol is only applicable to route selection, however, applying more functions such as perceiving a variety of sensor data, sleep, aperiodic data collection and etc. in wireless network node, cannot be realized with OpenFlow Protocol and Standard.

Transforming original sensing node is put forth by some researchers, for instance, the concept of Flow-Sensor and utilization of OpenFlow Protocol between Flow-Sensor and controller is put forth in document [7]. Realization of SDN sensor based on MCUs and FPGAs with super low power consumption is put forth in document [8]. In some researches, the framework of SD-WSN and Sensor OpenFlow Protocol [9] that applies in WSN are put forth; lightweight IP Protocol such as uIP and uIPv6 based on Contiki operating system shall be uti-lized in WSN. From the point of application fields, there are campus WLAN [10], VANET [11], network between mobile base station and base station controller, WSN, MAC laye in WSN, and etc.

The common problem for above researches is that only concepts and simple models are put forth in most researches, and that simulation is not realized or only simple simulation is realized. The description on detailed design and realization algorithms for SDN routing and controller is relatively obscure, and there is no systematic description or realization. In this paper, a novel wireless sensor network routing protocol is proposed, detailed description is conducted to realization process and details of protocol, and model is established with OPNET and simulation verification is conducted to it. The contributions of this document are as follows:

- A WSN routing protocol based on SDN is put forth; the controller has network-wide view and provides single-path routing or multipath routing for other nodes.
- The residual energy of nodes in controller is updated in real time by routing protocol; the shortest path is generated based on energy and hop count.
- The generation method for disjoint multipath from source to target is put forth.

The other parts of this document are arranged as below: routing protocol scheme shall be introduced in Part 2, simulation verification shall be illustrated in Part 3, and Part 4 is summarization to the whole document.

2   Routing Scheme

Exclusive SDN controller node (hereinafter controller for short) is added in network; the broadcast information of controller is reported to each sensing node, normal node sends node information to controller, controller generates the whole network view as per information of normal nodes; when source node requires controller to transmit path, controller calculates the shortest path with Dijkstra algorithm and sends information to source node. The premise of routing design is that nodes in network are not aware of their locations, that controller is located in middle of network and not restricted by energy, and that source node and target node in network are not fixed at certain node.

2.1   Routing Process Design

The flow diagram for routing protocol is shown in Fig. 1, and the specific description is as below:

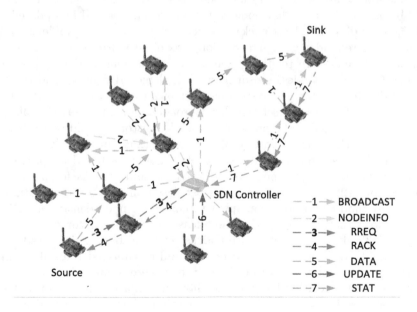

Fig. 1. Schematic diagram of protocol flow

1. Controller broadcasts information to each sensing node, normal node forms the backward path to controller as per broadcast path;

2. Normal node sends node information (residual energy, neighbor nodes) to controller through backward path, and controller establishes network topology picture as per node information received;
3. When source node is to send data without path to target node, it shall send routing information request to controller;
4. Controller calculates the shortest path from source to target (based on hop count and residual energy) as per network-wide view and with Dijkstra algorithm, then sends path information to source node;
5. Source node sends data to target node as per path information;
6. When the change in neighbor node information is discovered by some node, that node would report that change to controller;
7. When there is data receipt at target node, statistical information should be reported to controller periodically.

2.2 Controller Broadcast

In order to clearly define path to controller for nodes in network, firstly controller broadcasts packages. Other nodes establish backward routing as per control package received. After receiving a broadcast package, one node shall check whether it has received that package as per SN, if that broadcast package is new, that node would broadcast it. If that node has received that package, then there would be no broadcast at that node, but the hop count would be updated.

Simply flooding broadcast package in network would cause problems such as rebroadcast & redundancy, signal collision, broadcast storm and etc. Especially when network nodes are relatively dense, these problems would be more outstanding. Generally, wireless sensor network is deployed densely, and there are a lot of redundant nodes, and system bears stronger fault-tolerant performance. If only a part of nodes are selected for rebroadcast on premise that all nodes should receive broadcast, the problem of broadcast storm would be relieved.

At present, there are a variety of researches that aim to solve the problem of broadcast storm, thereinto, there are algorithms based on probability, counter, distance, location, neighbor information and etc. As for probability-based method [12], nodes conduct broadcast based on certain probability; however, this method could not be adapted to change in node density, if the node density is low, the area covered by broadcast decreases. As for counter-based algorithm [13], after the number of broadcast received by a node exceeds a certain threshold, the broadcast at that node would be canceled. This algorithm is not influenced by node density in network, but there is much broadcast delay. As for broadcast algorithm based on neighbor information, a part of nodes are selected for broadcast as per neighbor information. This kind of broadcast algorithm needs neighbor information.

In the algorithm based on neighbor information, the algorithm where MPR nodes are selected by OLSR routing is taken into reference; the neighbors of a part of nodes are selected for broadcast. 1-hop and 2-hop neighbor nodes of some node are utilized in this algorithm.

Tests were conducted for 4 algorithms (3 broadcast methods and full-node broadcast) in simulation scene; the results of performances contrast are shown in Table 1.

Table 1. Performance comparison of four broadcast methods

Method	Number of broadcast	Lifetime(s)	Parameter
All nodes	800	744	
Probability	233	773	p = 0.3
Counter	201	784	Threshold = 3, Wait time = 0.02s
Greedy neighbor	159	798	

There are 800 nodes in total in simulation network, the number of nodes in full-node broadcast is the number of total nodes, while the number of broadcast in the other 3 methods is largely reduced, thereinto, the number in counter method is more than that in greedy neighbor method but less than that in probability method. It can be seen that the less the number of broadcast is, the longer the network lifetime is. What should be noticed is that as for probability method and counter method, if different parameters are set up, the results are different; if the probability set up in probability method is larger, or if the threshold set up in counter method is larger, the number of broadcast is larger. The parameters for probability method and counter method in the table are values with better performance in experiment.

During actual simulation, even greedy neighbor algorithm has multiple redundancies, because overlap exists for greedy neighbor of multiple nodes in transmission distance after multiple hops, and there is still margin for reduction.

Node forms the backward path to controller as per broadcast package received, and sends NODEINFO package along the backward path; if the information of each node is sent separately along the backward path, then midway node could finish sending information of downstream node through sending for many times. In this paper, it is designed that the upstream node shall combine information of all next-hop nodes for sending, after information of downstream node arrives at upstream node.

After a node receives SDN broadcast package, there is certain delay before it sends NODEINFO package; it is designed that the delay time of node is inversely proportional to hop count of the node to controller. The larger the hop count is, the shorter the delay for sending node information package is. Therefore, the information of nodes located at the edge would be reported firstly, and summarization would occur gradually from edge to center. After combination, the relay nodes frequently sending DATA package may be avoided, and energy consumption may be reduced.

After controller receives NODEINFO package, node information shall be saved into array of node information list, and residual energy of node shall be saved into array of residual energy. Thus there is global view at controller, and controller is able to provide routing for other nodes.

2.3   Request and ACK of Node's Routing

If node A is to send data to node B, but there is no routing to node B in routing list, then node A shall send routing request to controller. The information of RREQ package includes: SN, source node, target node and number of path requested. After receiving RREQ package, relay node shall record the backward path to source node. When controller finishes calculating a shortest path or multiple disjoint multi-path routing, it generates RACK package and forwards this package back to source node.

After receiving RREQ package, controller shall operate Dijkstra algorithm of shortest path to calculate the path from source node to target node; here two parameters (hop count and energy) are adopted for measurement. Assume node j is neighbor of node i, and metric function f(j) of node j with respect to node i is shown in Eq. 1.

$$f(j) = \begin{cases} 1 - \frac{E_r(j)}{E_t} & j \text{ is neighbor of i,} \\ 0 & j \text{ isn't neighbor of i.} \end{cases} \tag{1}$$

Thereinto, stands for residual energy of node j, and stands for primary energy of node. The larger the residual energy of node is, the smaller f(j) is, and the higher the possibility where node j is selected as forwarding node is. Thus, Dijkstra may calculate the shortest path as per comprehensive measurement on energy and hop count.

The problem here is that controller needs to know residual energy of node in time; the energy of node may be known at initialization of node, otherwise, residual energy of node may also be collected and estimated by controller as per UPDATE package and statistical package of node.

When source node requests multi-path routing to target node from controller, Dijkstra algorithm shall be invoked for many times as per number of routing requested.

3   Simulation Results

Model is established with OPNET, and simulation is conducted. The contrast among four routing protocols (AODV, OLSR, our SDN routing and GPSR are made, GPSR is introduced as the routing with shortest path for contrast (here the energy consumption when GPSR obtains location information).

3.1   Different Node Density

The contrast among values of energy consumption for each package is as shown in Fig. 2, it can be seen that the energy consumption for each package becomes higher as node density increases. As for SDN routing, the energy consumption is larger due to information exchange between controller and nodes, but the value for SDN routing is smaller than that for OLSR. In traditional routing protocol, the energy consumption for OLSR is higher because the network throughput required to construct routing at preliminary stage is higher. AODV also needs to form routing through broadcast, so its energy consumption for each package is ranked the third; thereinto, GPSR with shortest path does not require broadcast, it only calculates and seeks next-hop forwarding node as per coordinates of neighbor nodes, so its energy consumption is the lowest.

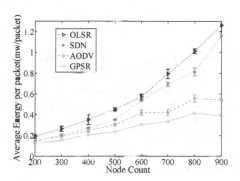

Fig. 2. Contrast on energy consumption and hop count for each package in different network size

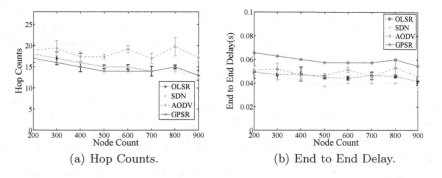

(a) Hop Counts.   (b) End to End Delay.

Fig. 3. Contrast on mean hop count and delay in different network size.

Figure 3 shows the contrast on hop count and delay among different algorithms; it can be seen from the hop count figure that the higher the node density is, the number of forwarding nodes that may be selected is more; one node may select the next-hop node that is more suitable for forwarding, thus the hop count decreases as node density increases. AODV could not provide optimal hop count because it does not have global view; the hop count is higher and unstable as well. However, as for OLSR and SDN, the shortest path could be calculated, thus their hop counts are close to that of GPSR. It can be seen from the delay figure that delay decreases as node density increases. As for each hop of GPSR, time is needed to calculate the next-hop neighbors, so its delay is the longest; because hop count of AODV is higher, so the delay is longer; because SDN is constructed as per the shortest path, and forwarding nodes are put into DATA package that is available for direct reading and forwarding, so the end-to-end delay is the lowest.

4   Conclusion

In this document, a kind of routing protocol where SDN is applied in wireless sensor network is put forth, the protocol put forth is realized with OPNET simulation and contrast is made among this protocol and other algorithms. The simulation results show that with global view, SDN centralized control may provide shortest path and disjoint multipath routing for nodes, and that its network lifetime is longer than existing algorithms (OLSR, AODV) when load reaches a certain value. In the future, deployment of multiple controllers and node mobility will be taken into consideration.

References

1. Chen, M., Ma, Y., Song, J., Lai, C.F., Hu, B.: Smart clothing: connecting human with clouds and big data for sustainable health monitoring. Mob. Netw. Appl. **21**, 1–21 (2016)
2. Clausen, T., Jacquet, P., Adjih, C., Laouiti, A., Minet, P., Muhlethaler, P., Qayyum, A., Viennot, L.: Optimized link state routing protocol (OLSR) (2003)
3. Perkins, C., Belding-Royer, E., Das, S.: Ad hoc on-demand distance vector (AODV) routing, Technical report (2003)
4. Li, Y., Chen, M.: Software-defined network function virtualization: a survey. IEEE Access **3**, 2542–2553 (2015)
5. Chen, M., Hao, Y., Qiu, M., Song, J., Wu, D., Iztok, H.: Mobility-aware caching and computation offloading in 5G ultra-dense cellular networks. Sensors **16**(7), 974 (2016)
6. Chen, M., Qian, Y., Mao, S., Tang, W., Yang, X.: Software-defined mobile networks security. Mob. Netw. Appl. **21**, 1–15 (2016)
7. Mahmud, A., Rahmani, R.: Exploitation of openflow in wireless sensor networks. In: 2011 International Conference on Computer Science and Network Technology (ICCSNT), vol. 1, pp. 594–600. IEEE (2011)
8. Miyazaki, T., Yamaguchi, S., Kobayashi, K., Kitamichi, J., Guo, S., Tsukahara, T., Hayashi, T.: A software defined wireless sensor network. In: 2014 International Conference on Computing, Networking and Communications (ICNC). IEEE, pp. 847–852 (2014)
9. Luo, T., Tan, H.-P., Quek, T.Q.: Sensor openflow: enabling software-defined wireless sensor networks. Commun. Lett. **16**(11), 1896–1899 (2012). IEEE

10. Lei, T., Lu, Z., Wen, X., Zhao, X., Wang, L.: Swan: an SDN based campus WLAN framework. In: 2014 4th International Conference on Wireless Communications, Vehicular Technology, Information Theory and Aerospace & Electronic Systems (VITAE), pp. 1–5. IEEE (2014)
11. Ku, I., Lu, Y., Gerla, M., Ongaro, F., Gomes, R.L., Cerqueira, E.: Towards software-defined vanet: architecture and services. In: 2014 13th Annual Mediterranean Ad Hoc Networking Workshop (MED-HOC-NET), 103–110. IEEE (2014)
12. Cartigny, J., Simplot, D.: Border node retransmission based probabilistic broadcast protocols in ad-hoc networks. In: Proceedings of the 36th Annual Hawaii International Conference on System Sciences, p. 10. IEEE (2003)
13. Levis, P.A., Patel, N., Culler, D., Shenker, S.: Trickle: a self regulating algorithm for code propagation and maintenance in wireless sensor networks. University of California, Computer Science Division (2003)

Efficient Graph Mining on Heterogeneous Platforms in the Cloud

Tao Zhang$^{(\boxtimes)}$, Weiqin Tong, Wenfeng Shen, Junjie Peng, and Zhihua Niu

School of Computer Engineering and Science, Shanghai University,
99 Shangda Road, Shanghai 200444, China
{taozhang,wqtong,wfshen,jjie.peng}@shu.edu.cn, zhniu@staff.shu.edu.cn

Abstract. In this Big Data era, many large-scale and complex graphs have been produced with the rapid growth of novel Internet applications and the new experiment data collecting methods in biological and chemistry areas. As the scale and complexity of the graph data increase explosively, it becomes urgent and challenging to develop more efficient graph processing frameworks which are capable of executing general graph algorithms efficiently. In this paper, we propose to leverage GPUs to accelerate large-scale graph mining in the cloud. To achieve good performance and scalability, we propose the graph summary method and runtime system optimization techniques for load balancing and message handling. Experiment results manifest that the prototype framework outperforms two state-of-the-art distributed frameworks GPS and GraphLab in terms of performance and scalability.

Keywords: Graph mining · GPGPU · Graph partitioning · Load balancing · Cloud computing

1 Introduction

In recent years, various graph computing frameworks [1,3–5] have been proposed for analyzing and mining large graphs especially web graphs and social graphs. Some frameworks achieve good scalability and performance by exploiting distributed computing. For instance, Stratosphere [6] is a representative graph processing framework based on the MapReduce model [7]. However, recent research has shown that graph processing in the MapReduce model is inefficient [8,9]. To improve performance, many distributed platforms adopting the vertex-centric model [5] have been proposed, including GPS [4], GraphLab [2] and Power-Graph [10]. To ensure performance, these distributed platforms require a cluster or cloud environment and good graph partitioning algorithms [1].

Previously, we proposed the gGraph [12] platform which is a non-distributed platform that can utilize both CPUs and GPUs (Graph Processing Units) efficiently in a single PC. Compared to CPUs, GPUs have higher hardware parallelism [15] and better energy efficiency [14]. However, non-distributed platforms are unable to process large-scale graphs by utilizing powerful distributed computing/cloud computing which is widely available. Therefore, in this work, we

© ICST Institute for Computer Sciences, Social Informatics and Telecommunications Engineering 2018
J. Wan et al. (Eds.): CloudComp 2016, SPNCE 2016, LNICST 197, pp. 12–21, 2018.
https://doi.org/10.1007/978-3-319-69605-8_2

focus on developing methods and techniques to build an efficient distributed graph processing framework on hybrid CPU and GPU systems. Specifically, we develop these major methods and techniques: (1) A graph-summary method to optimize graph computing efficiency; (2) A runtime system for load balancing and communication reducing; (3) A distributed graph processing system architecture supporting hybrid CPU-GPU platforms in the cloud. We developed a prototype system called HGraph (that is, graph processing on hybrid CPU and GPU platforms) for evaluation. HGraph is based on MPI (Message Passing Interface), and integrates the vertex-based programming model, the BSP (Barrier Synchronous Parallel) computing model and the CUDA GPU execution model. We evaluate the performance of HGraph with both realworld and synthetic graphs in a virtual cluster on Amazon EC2 cloud. The preliminary results demonstrate that HGraph outperforms evaluated distributed platforms.

The rest of this paper is organized as follows. Section 2 introduces the related work. Section 3 presents the system overview. Section 4 presents the details of the design and implementation. The experiment methodology is shown in Sect. 5 and the result is analyzed in Sect. 6. Section 7 concludes this work.

2   Related Work

The related work can be categorized into graph processing frameworks targeting dynamic graphs and static graphs. The design and architecture of frameworks are fundamentally different depending on the type of the graph.

Realworld graphs are mostly dynamic which are evolving over time. For example, the structure of a social network is ever-changing: vertices and edges change when a user add a new friend or delete an old friend. Frameworks for dynamic graph processing generally adopt the streaming/incremental computing technique in order to handle the variation of the graph and return results in realtime or near realtime. Several work propose to take a snapshot of the graph periodically and then process it based on historical results [16,17]. The graph snapshots they process are complete graphs. In contrast, other frameworks propose to process only the changed portion of graphs in an incremental fashion [18–20]. However, not all graph algorithms can be expressed into the incremental manner, so the applications of such incremental frameworks are limited.

By taking a snapshot of a dynamic graph at a certain time, a dynamic graph can be viewed as a series of static snapshots. Most of the existing graph processing frameworks focus on dealing with static graphs (i.e. snapshots). These frameworks can be grouped into non-distributed ones and distributed ones depending on the number of computing nodes they can control. GraphChi [1], Ligra [11], gGraph [12] and Totem [13] are representative *non-distributed platforms*. The former two platforms are pure-CPU platforms. GraphChi proposed the Parallel Sliding Windows (PSW) method and the compact graph storage method to overlap the computation and I/O to improve performance. Ligra is specifically designed for shared-memory machines. Both gGraph and Totem run on hybrid CPU and GPU systems and achieve better performance and energy efficiency than pure-CPU based platforms. Anyways, non-distributed platforms cannot utilize distributed computing nodes to handle extra-scale graphs. In contrast, the performance of distributed platforms can scale up by utilizing more computing nodes in the cluster. Distributed platforms can be further classified into synchronous platforms and asynchronous platforms according to their computing model. Pregel [5] and GPS [4] are typical *distributed synchronous platforms*. Pregel and GPS adopt the vertex-centric model, in which a vertex kernel function will be executed in parallel on each vertex. GraphLab [2] and PowerGraph [10] are representative *distributed asynchronous platforms*. They follow the asynchronous computing model such that graph algorithms may converge faster. However, research showed that asynchronous execution model will reduce parallelism [12]. Therefore the selection between synchronous and asynchronous model is a trade-off between algorithmic convergence time and performance.

3   System Overview

In this section, we discuss the design principle of the HGraph, followed by a system architecture overview. The detailed optimization techniques of HGraph will be presented in the next section.

3.1   Design Rules

The primary design goals of HGraph include good performance, scalability and programmability.

- HGraph exploits GPU computing for good performance. GPU processors are advantageous for their high throughput [21], energy efficiency [22], and memory bandwidth, and have been widely used in various application domains [15]. HGraph can benefit from GPUs' high throughput to process fine-grained computing tasks in graph processing. In addition, HGraph adopts fully in-memory computing for better performance.
- HGraph utilizes distributed computing in the cloud for good scalability. The computing resource in clouds are elastic which can scale according to users' needs. Since HGraph adopts in-memory computing, we need to ensure that there are enough nodes such that the computing resource (i.e. CPU & GPU processors) and memory resource are adequate.
- HGraph follows the vertex-centric programming model for good programmability. In this model, a specific vertex kernel function for a graph algorithm is executed in parallel on each vertex. Many existing graph processing frameworks [5,11–13] follow this model.

3.2   System Architecture Overview

The system architecture of HGraph is presented in Fig. 1. The master node consists of three major components: a graph partitioner, a task scheduler and a

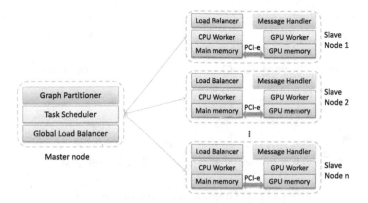

Fig. 1. System architecture of HGraph

global load balancer. The graph partitioner splits the graph into partitions and sends them to slave nodes. The task scheduler maintains a list of pending tasks and dispatches these tasks to slave nodes for execution. The global load balancer is part of the two-level load balancing unit in HGraph. The master node assigns initial load to slave nodes. Then the global load balancer can adjust the load on slave nodes if load imbalance happens during the execution.

In each slave node, there is a CPU worker and a GPU worker, respectively. The discrete GPU communicates with the host CPU through the PCI-e bus. The CPUs and GPUs inside a node work in the Bulk-Synchronous Parallel (BSP) [24] model to execute the update function in the vertex-centric programming model. However, heterogeneous processors (eg. CPUs and GPUs) may take different time for computation. As a result, completed processors need to wait for processors lagging behind before the synchronization, which degrades system performance. The local load balancer is in charge of balancing the load between the CPU and the GPU to solve such issue. The local load balancer and the global load balancer form a two-level load balancer. Finally, there is a massage handler which handles both intra-node and inter-node messages.

4 Design and Implementation

In this section, we present the methods and techniques proposed in this work. The graph summary method is introduced first, followed by the runtime system techniques for load balancing and message handling.

4.1 Graph Summary Method

In the vertex-centric model, partial or all vertices with their edges will be visit once in each iteration for many graph algorithms. Therefore the execution time is proportional to the number of vertices and edges ($O(|V|+|E|)$), and is dominated by the number of edges $|E|$ in most cases since normally $|E|$ is much bigger than

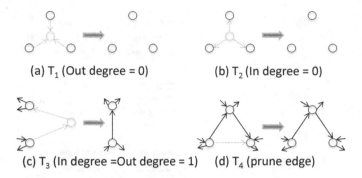

(a) T_1 (Out degree = 0)   (b) T_2 (In degree = 0)

(c) T_3 (In degree =Out degree = 1)   (d) T_4 (prune edge)

Fig. 2. Graph pruning transforms

the number of vertices $|V|$ in graphs. We define four pruning transformations T_i of graph G, as shown in Fig. 2.

T_1 is a transform that removes the vertices and their in-edges whose out-degree equals zero. T_2 is a transform that removes the vertices and their out-edges whose in-degree equals zero. T_3 is a transform that removes the vertices and their out-edges whose in-degree and out-degree both equal 1. T_4 is a transform that removes one edge from a triangle. By applying one of T_i or a series of T_i onto the G, we can get a graph summary G' of smaller size.

$$G' = T_i(G) \tag{1}$$

The selection of T_i depends on algorithms and query conditions. Queries using graph algorithms can be categorized into full queries and conditional queries:

- Full queries: using graph algorithms to identify the maximum, minimum value or all value under certain criteria. For instance, "search for the top 10 vertices with the highest PageRank", or "find out all communities in the graph".
- Partial queries: using graph algorithms to search for some solution. For instance, "search for 10 vertices with PageRank larger than 5", or "find out 10 communities whose sizes are larger than 50".

Accordingly, graph summary G' can be used in two ways:

- As the initialization data: in full query, we can use graph summary G' to initialize G to make graph algorithms converge faster [23].
- As the input for graph algorithms: in partial query, we can directly run graph algorithms on graph summary G' to get results in a shorter time.

The time for pruning vertices and edges to get graph summary is a one-time process, so the time cost can be amortized by later long-running time of iterative graph algorithms. Besides, some graph algorithms have similar algorithmic pattern such that they can share a common graph summary. Therefore, the time cost to produce graph summary can be further amortized.

4.2   Runtime System Techniques

There are two major components in the runtime system: the two-level load balancer and the message handler, as shown in Fig. 1 in Sect. 3. The local load balancer in each slave node exploits the adaptive load balancing method in gGraph [12] to balance the load between CPU processors and GPU processors inside the node. The global load balancer in HGraph is able to adjust the load (eg. number of vertices and edges) on slave nodes to balance their execution time. It calculates the load status of slave nodes based on the monitoring data and tries to migrate appropriate load from heavily loaded nodes to less loaded nodes.

We extended the message handler in gGraph for HGraph's distributed computing. In HGraph, the message handler in each slave node maintains one outbox buffer for every other slave nodes and an inbox buffer for itself. Messages to other slave nodes will be aggregated based on the slave node id and the vertex id using algorithm operators then put into the corresponding outbox buffer. The inbox buffer is used for receiving incoming messages.

5   Experiment Methodology

In this section, we elaborate the graph algorithms, graph data, and the experimental software and hardware settings.

5.1   Graph Algorithms

We use single source shortest path (SSSP), connected components (CC), and PageRank (PR) to evaluate the performance of HGraph, as shown in Table 1.

Single source shortest path finds the shortest path from a given source vertex to all connected vertices. Connected component is used to detect regions in graphs. PageRank is an algorithm proposed by Google to calculate probability distribution representing the likelihood that a web link been clicked by a random user. Their vertex functions are listed in Table 1.

Table 1. Graph Algorithms

Algorithms	Vertex function
SSSP	$v.path \leftarrow min_{e \in inEdges(v)}(e.source.path + e.weight)$
CC	$v.component \leftarrow max_{e \in edges(v)}(e.other.component)$
PR	$v.rank \leftarrow 0.15 + 0.85 \times \sum_{e \in inEdges(v)} e.source.rank$

5.2   Workloads

We use both real-world graphs and synthetic graphs in the RMAT model [25] to evaluate HGraph. The RMAT graphs are generated with parameters $(A, B, C) = (0.57, 0.19, 0.19)$ and an average degree of 16. The graphs are listed in Table 2.

Table 2. Summary of the workloads (Legend: M for million, B for billion)

Abbr.	Graph	|Vertices|	|Edges|	Direction	Type
G1	Twitter 2010	61.6M	1.5B	Undirected	Social
G2	Com-Friendster	65.6M	1.8B	Undirected	Social
G3	Uk-2007-d	106.0M	3.7B	Directed	Web
G4	RMAT29	512.0M	8.0B	Undirected	Synthetic
G5	RMAT30	1.0B	16.0B	Undirected	Synthetic

5.3   Software and Hardware Settings

We developed a system prototype named HGraph on top of MPICH2. We conducted the experiments on Amazon EC2, using 32 g2.2xlarge instances. Each
g2.2xlarge instance consists of 1 Nvidia GPU, 8 vCPU, 15 GB memory and
60 GB SSD disk. Each GPU has 1536 CUDA cores and 4 GB DDR memory.
We compare the performance and scalability of HGraph with two distributed
frameworks GraphLab and GPS.

6   Results and Analysis

In this section, we present the comparison on performance and scalability
of HGraph with GPS and GraphLab. Figure 3 compares the performance of
HGraph, GPS and GraphLab running the CC, SSSP, and PR algorithm. All

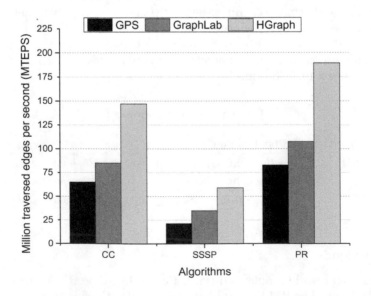

Fig. 3. Performance comparison of platforms

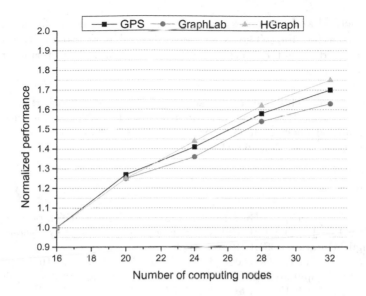

Fig. 4. Scalability comparison of platforms

three platforms are distributed but only HGraph can utilize GPUs in computing nodes and gain additional computing power. The result is the average performance in million traversed edges in one second (MTEPS) on all graphs. In general, platforms achieve better performance in graph analytical algorithms (CC & PR) than in the graph traversal algorithm (SSSP) since CC & PR have higher parallelism than SSSP. HGraph outperforms GPS and GraphLab for two reasons: (1)the graph summary method and the runtime system optimizations; (2) the ability to utilize GPUs for additional power.

Figure 4 compares the scalability of three platforms by increasing the number of computing nodes from 16 to 32 at a step of 4 machines, and calculating the normalized performance. All platforms exhibit significant scalability. HGraph achieves the best scalability while GraphLab achieves the lowest scalability. Adding one or more computing nodes increases the resource including processors, memory and disk I/O bandwidth, and reduces the partitioned workload on each computing node. However, more computing nodes also cause the graph to be split into more partitions, potentially increasing communication messages. HGraph implements the message aggregation technique therefore it is less affected by the increased communications, hence the better scalability.

7   Conclusion

This paper introduces a general, distributed graph processing platform named HGraph which can process large-scale graphs very efficiently by utilizing both CPUs and GPUs in distributed cloud environment. HGraph exploits a graph summary method and runtime system optimization techniques for load balancing and message handling. The experiments show that HGraph outperform two state-of-the-art distributed platforms GPS and GraphLab in terms of performance and scalability.

Acknowledgment. This research is supported by Young Teachers Program of Shanghai Colleges and Universities under grant No. ZZSD15072, Natural Science Foundation of Shanghai under grant No. 16ZR1411200, and Shanghai Innovation Action Plan Project under grant No. 16511101200.

References

1. Kyrola, A., Blelloch, G., Guestrin, C.: GraphChi: large-scale graph computation on just a PC. In: The 10th USENIX Symposium on Operating Systems Design and Implementation (OSDI 12), pp. 31–46 (2012)
2. Low, Y., Bickson, D., Gonzalez, J., Guestrin, C., Kyrola, A., Hellerstein, J.M.: Distributed GraphLab: a framework for machine learning and data mining in the cloud. Proc. VLDB Endow. **5**(8), 716–727 (2012)
3. Shao, B., Wang, H., Li, Y.: Trinity: a distributed graph engine on a memory cloud. In: Proceedings of the 2013 ACM SIGMOD International Conference on Management of Data, pp. 505–516. ACM (2013)
4. Salihoglu, S., Widom, J.: GPS: a graph processing system. In: Proceedings of the 25th International Conference on Scientific and Statistical Database Management, p. 22. ACM (2013)
5. Malewicz, G., Austern, M.H., Bik, A.J., Dehnert, J.C., Horn, I., Leiser, N., Czajkowski, G.: Pregel: a system for large-scale graph processing. In: Proceedings of the 2010 ACM SIGMOD International Conference on Management of data, pp. 135–146. ACM (2010)
6. Warneke, D., Kao, O.: Nephele: efficient parallel data processing in the cloud. In: Proceedings of the 2nd Workshop on Many-task Computing on Grids and Supercomputers, p. 8. ACM (2009)
7. Dean, J., Ghemawat, S.: MapReduce: simplified data processing on large clusters. Commun. ACM **51**(1), 107–113 (2008)
8. Guo, Y., Biczak, M., Varbanescu, A.L., Iosup, A., Martella, C., Willke, T.L.: How well do graph-processing platforms perform? an empirical performance evaluation and analysis. In: 2014 IEEE 28th International Parallel and Distributed Processing Symposium, pp. 395–404. IEEE (2014)
9. Pan, X.: A comparative evaluation of open-source graph processing platforms. In: 2016 17th IEEE/ACIS International Conference on Software Engineering, Artificial Intelligence, Networking and Parallel/Distributed Computing (SNPD), pp. 325–330. IEEE (2016)
10. Gonzalez, J.E., Low, Y., Gu, H., Bickson, D., Guestrin, C.: Powergraph: Distributed graph-parallel computation on natural graphs. In: the 10th USENIX Symposium on Operating Systems Design and Implementation (OSDI 2012), pp. 17–30 (2012)
11. Shun, J., Blelloch, G.E.: Ligra: a lightweight graph processing framework for shared memory. ACM SIGPLAN Not. **48**(8), 135–146 (2013). ACM
12. Zhang, T., Zhang, J., Shu, W., Wu, M.Y., Liang, X.: Efficient graph computation on hybrid CPU and GPU systems. J. Supercomput. **71**(4), 1563–1586 (2015)

13. Gharaibeh, A., Reza, T., Santos-Neto, E., Costa, L.B., Sallinen, S., Ripeanu, M.: Efficient large-scale graph processing on hybrid CPU and GPU systems (2013). arxiv preprint arXiv:1312.3018

14. Zhang, T., Jing, N., Jiang, K., Shu, W., Wu, M.Y., Liang, X.: Buddy SM: sharing pipeline front-end for improved energy efficiency in GPGPUs. ACM Trans. Archit. Code Optim. (TACO) 12(2), 1–23 (2015). Article no. 16

15. Zhang, T., Shu, W., Wu, M.Y.: CUIRRE: an open-source library for load balancing and characterizing irregular applications on GPUs. J. Parallel Distrib. Comput. 74(10), 2951–2966 (2014)

16. Iyer, A.P., Li, L.E., Das, T., Stoica, I.: Time-evolving graph processing at scale. In: Proceedings of the Fourth International Workshop on Graph Data Management Experiences and Systems, p. 5. ACM (2016)

17. Cheng, R., Hong, J., Kyrola, A., Miao, Y., Weng, X., Wu, M., Chen, E.: Kineograph: taking the pulse of a fast-changing and connected world. In: Proceedings of the 7th ACM European Conference on Computer Systems, pp. 85–98. ACM (2012)

18. Murray, D.G., McSherry, F., Isaacs, R., Isard, M., Barham, P., Abadi, M.: Naiad: a timely dataflow system. In: Proceedings of the Twenty-Fourth ACM Symposium on Operating Systems Principles, pp. 439–455. ACM (2013)

19. Wickramaarachchi, C., Chelmis, C., Prasanna, V.K.: Empowering fast incremental computation over large scale dynamic graphs. In: 2015 IEEE International Parallel and Distributed Processing Symposium Workshop (IPDPSW), pp. 1166–1171. IEEE (2015)

20. Zhang, Y., Gao, Q., Gao, L., Wang, C.: Maiter: an asynchronous graph processing framework for delta-based accumulative iterative computation. IEEE Trans. Parallel Distrib. Syst. 25(8), 2091–2100 (2014)

21. Han, S., Lei, Z., Shen, W., Chen, S., Zhang, H., Zhang, T., Xu, B.: An approach to improving the performance of CUDA in virtual environment. In: 2016 17th IEEE/ACIS International Conference on Software Engineering, Artificial Intelligence, Networking and Parallel/Distributed Computing (SNPD), pp. 585–590. IEEE (2016)

22. Jing, N., Jiang, L., Zhang, T., Li, C., Fan, F., Liang, X.: Energy-efficient eDRAM-based on-chip storage architecture for GPGPUs. IEEE Trans. Comput. 65(1), 122–135 (2016)

23. Wang, K., Xu, G., Su, Z., Liu, Y.D.: GraphQ: graph query processing with abstraction refinement scalable and programmable analytics over very large graphs on a single PC. In: 2015 USENIX Annual Technical Conference (USENIX ATC 15), pp. 387–401 (2015)

24. Valiant, L.G.: A bridging model for parallel computation. Commun. ACM 33(8), 103–111 (1990)

25. Chakrabarti, D., Zhan, Y., Faloutsos, C.: R-MAT: a recursive model for graph mining. SDM 4, 442–446 (2004)

Correlation-Aware Virtual Machine Placement in Data Center Networks

Tao Chen[1], Yaoming Zhu[1], Xiaofeng Gao[1], Linghe Kong[1], Guihai Chen[1], and Yongjian Wang[2(✉)]

[1] Shanghai Key Laboratory of Scalable Computing and Systems,
Department of Computer Science and Engineering,
Shanghai Jiao Tong University, Shanghai 200240, China
{tchen,grapes_islet,linghe.kong}@sjtu.edu.cn,
{gao-xf,gchen}@cs.sjtu.edu.cn
[2] Key Laboratory of Information Network Security of Ministry of Public Security,
The Third Research Institute of Ministry of Public Security, Shanghai, China
wangyongjian@stars.org.cn

Abstract. The resource utilization (CPU, memory) is a key performance metric in data center networks. The goal of the cloud platform supported by data center networks is achieving high average resource utilization while guaranteeing the quality of cloud services. Previous work focus on increasing the time-average resource utilization and decreasing the overload ratio of servers by designing various efficient virtual machine placement schemes. Unfortunately, most of virtual machine placement schemes did not involve the service level agreements and statistical methods. In this paper, we propose a correlation-aware virtual machine placement scheme that effectively places virtual machines on physical machines. First, we employ Neural Networks model to forecast the resource utilization trend according to the historical resource utilization data. Second, we design correlation-aware placement algorithms to enhance resource utilization while meeting the user-defined service level agreements. The results show that the efficiency of our virtual machine placement algorithms outperform the previous work by about 15%.

Keywords: Virtual machine · Prediction · Correlation · Placement

1 Introduction

As the rapid development of cloud technology, data center networks (DCNs), the essential backbone infrastructure of cloud services such as cloud computing, cloud storage, and cloud platforms, attract increasing attentions in both academia and industry. Cloud data centers attempts to offer an integrated platform with a pay-as-you-go business model to benefit tenants at the same time, which is gradually adopted by the mainstream IT companies, such as Amazon EC2, Google Cloud Platform and Microsoft Azure. The multi-tenant and on-demand cloud service platform is achieved through virtualization on all shared resources

© ICST Institute for Computer Sciences, Social Informatics and Telecommunications Engineering 2018
J. Wan et al. (Eds.): CloudComp 2016, SPNCE 2016, LNICST 197, pp. 22–32, 2018.
https://doi.org/10.1007/978-3-319-69605-8_3

and utilities, such as CPU, memory, I/O and bandwidth, in which various tenants buy virtual machines (VMs) within a certain period of time to run their applications [2]. Owing to multi-tenant demands, all kinds of workloads physically coexist but are logically isolated in DCNs, including data-intensive and latency-sensitive services, search engines, business processing, social-media networking, and big-data analytics. Elastic and dynamic resource provisioning is the basis of DCN performance, which is achieved by virtualization technique to reduce the cost of leased resources and to maximize resource utilization in cloud platforms. Therefore, the effectiveness of virtualization becomes essential to DCN performance.

Originally, the design goal of a DCN is to meet the peak workloads of tenants. However, at most time, DCNs are suffering from high energy cost due to low server utilization. A lot of servers are running with low workloads while consuming almost the same amount of energy as servers with high workloads. The cloud service providers have to spend more money on cooling bills to keep the servers in normal running. They aim to allocate resources in an energy-effective way while guaranteeing the Service Level Agreements (SLAs) for tenants.

A lot of literatures focus on enhancing the average utilization without violating SLAs. Some researchers focus on fair allocation schemes. Bobroff et al. [3] proposed a dynamic VM placement system for managing service level agreement (SLA) violations, which forecasts the future demand and models the prediction error. However, their approach only deals with single VM prediction, does not take correlation into consideration. Meng et al. [12] argued that VM should not be done on VM-by-VM basis and advocated joint-VM-provisioning, which can achieve 45% improvements in terms of overall utilization.

In this paper, we propose a correlation-aware virtual machine placement scheme that effectively places virtual machines on physical machines. First, we employ Neural Networks model to forecast the resource utilization trend according to the historical resource utilization data. Second, we design correlation-aware placement algorithms to enhance resource utilization while meeting the user-defined service level agreements. The simulation results show that the efficiency of our virtual machine placement scheme outperforms the previous work by about 15%.

The rest of the paper is organized as follows. Section 2 introduces the related work about resource demand prediction and virtual machine placement. Section 3 proposes the correlation-aware virtual machine placement system. Section 4 concludes this paper.

2   Related Work

2.1   Resource Demand Prediction

By appropriate prediction schemes, it is probable to mitigate hot spots in DCNs. Demand prediction methods will provide us early warnings of hot spots. Hence, we can adopt measures to ease the congestions in DCNs and allocate resource in a way that guarantee the performance of applications for tenants. The demand prediction methods usually fall into time series and stochastic process analyses.

The ARIMA model is often used to predict time series data. [3] forecasts the future demand and models the prediction error. However, their approach only deals with single VM prediction, does not take correlations between VMs into consideration. [11] accurately predicts the future VM workloads by seasonal ARIMA models. [13] employs SARMA model on Google Cluster workload data to predict future demand consumption. [14] uses a variant of the exponentially weighted moving average (EWMA) load predictor. For workloads with repeating patterns, PRESS derives a signature for the pattern of historic resource utilization, and uses that signature in its prediction. PRESS uses a discrete-time Markov chain with a finite number of states to build a short-term prediction of future metric values for workloads without repeating pattern, such as CPU utilization or memory utilization [7]. In [8], Markov chain model is applied to capture the temporal correlation of VM resource demands approximately.

2.2 Virtual Machine Placement

Virtual Machine Placement (VMP) is a problem involving mapping virtual machines (VMs) to physical machines (PMs). A proper mapping scheme can result in less PMs required and less energy cost. A poor resource allocation scheme may require more PMs and may induce more service level agreement (SLA) violations. Bobroff et al. [3] proposed a dynamic VM placement system for managing service level agreement (SLA) violations. They presented a method to identify servers which benefit most from dynamic migration. Meng et al. [12] argues that VM sizing should not be done on VM-by-VM basis and advocates joint-VM-provisioning which can achieve 45% improvements in terms of overall utilization. They first introduced a SLA model that map application performance requirements to resource demand requirement. Kim et al. [9] proposed a novel correlation-aware virtual machine allocation for energy-efficient datacenters. Specifically, they take correlation information of core utilization among virtual machines to consideration. Wang et al. [15] attempt to explore particle swarm optimization (PSO) to minimizing the energy consumption. They design an optimal VMP scheme with the lowest energy consumption. In [10], authors propose a VMP scheme which minimizes the energy consumption of the data center by consolidating VMs in a minimum number of PMs while respecting the latency requirement of VMs.

3   Correlation-Aware Virtual Machine Placement

3.1   System Architecture

We propose a correlation-aware virtual machine placement system for data center networks (DCNs) that predicts the future resource demand (utilization) of requests and minimize the number of physical machines (PMs) to meet the demand while considering the correlations between virtual machines (VMs) and satisfying a user-defined server level agreement (SLA) at the same time.

The system architecture is shown in Fig. 1, which includes three key components: monitor, predictor and controller. Tenants submit resource requests to the cloud platform. The cloud platform allocates the resources (VMs) for the requests. VMs are usually hosted on PMs in DCNs. Monitor module records the historical utilization data of VMs and transmit it to Predictor module. The predicted data generated from Predictor is delivered to Controller modular that makes a strategic decision for VM placement problem. An new VM placement strategy happens periodically every 100 time slots (a resource demand data recorded at a time slot).

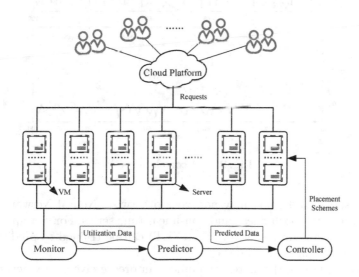

Fig. 1. Placement system architecture.

Traditionally, a VM placement scheme considers one VM at a time. In [12], the authors argued that the anti-correlation between VMs can be utilized. Their approach only picks two VMs at a time and allocate as less resource as possible for VMs. However, it is possible that three VMs that negatively correlate with each other, as shown in Fig. 2. Hence, we can do joint-provisioning of any number of VMs without SLA violations. The overall capacity allocated for VM 1, VM 2 and VM 3 under joint-provisioning is about 70% of a PM while the traditional VM placement needs to allocate about 85% capacity for these three VMs.

3.2 Prediction

In [16], the authors applied ARIMA and GARCH model to forecast the trend and volatility of the future demand. ARIMA performs well when an initial differencing step can be applied to remove non-stationarity. However, ARIMA is a

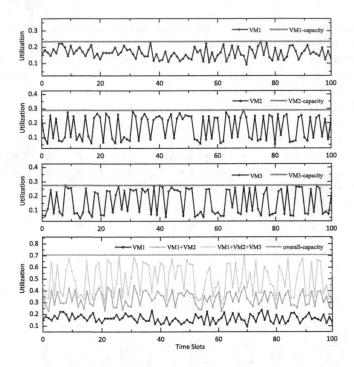

Fig. 2. VM correlation.

linear time series model and may not work otherwise. Neural Networks can be applied to predicted both linear and non-linear time series. For example, nonlinear autoregressive neural network (NARNET) can be trained to predict a time series from historical demand data.

Let NARNET(ni, nh) denotes a nonlinear autoregressive neural network with ni inputs and nh outputs. Such a model can be described as

$$U_i(t) = F(U_i(t-1), U_i(t-2), \dots) + \varepsilon \tag{1}$$

where U_t is the variable of interest, and ε is the error term. We can the use this model to predict the value of U_{t+k}.

The performance of NARNET(10, 20) is shown in Fig. 3. The simulation results shows that NARNET can predict future resource demand accurately.

3.3 Virtual Machine Placement Algorithms

In this subsection, we present correlation-aware virtual machine placement algorithms. The allocated resource for VMs should match the future resource demand to achieve high resource utilization of PMs while meeting user-defined SLAs. Table 1 summarizes the main symbols used in this paper.

We use two performance metrics, overload ratio $\overline{o}$ and average resource demand $\overline{D}$, to evaluate the effectiveness of our proposed VM placement algorithms. The former is the ratio of the number of time slots when the actual

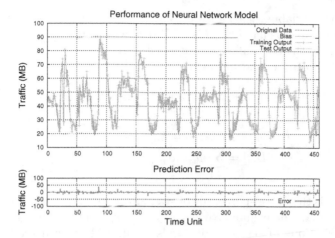

Fig. 3. Performance of NARNET.

Table 1. Main symbols and descriptions

Symbol	Description
$V = \{v_1, \cdots, v_n\}$	Set of VMs
$S = \{s_1, \cdots, s_m\}$	Set of PMs
N_{PM}	Number of used PMs for placement
D_m	Sum of resource demands in PM m
C	Capacity of a PM
$\bar{o}$	Overload ratio
$\overline{D}$	Average resource demand (utilization)
ϵ	User-defined SLA

resource demand of a PM is higher than its capacity over all the time slots $\times$ N_{PM}. The latter is the average resource utilization of PMs over all the time slots. The objective of algorithms is to achieve low overload ratio $\bar{o}$ and high average resource utilization $\overline{D}$. We monitor resource demand (e.g., CPU, memory) of each VM and predict conditional mean μ and the conditional variance σ. We also calculate the correlations ρ between different VMs placed on the same PMs according to resource demand time series data.

We can formulate the correlation-aware VM placement problem as follows.

$$\min N_{PM} \tag{2}$$

$$s.t. \ \Pr(D_m > C) < \epsilon, \ \forall m, \tag{3}$$

$$\sum_m x_{mn} = 1, \ \forall n, \tag{4}$$

$$x_{mn} \in \{0, 1\}, \ \forall m, \ \forall n. \tag{5}$$

The binary variable x_{mn} indicates VM n is hosted on PM m or not. D_m denotes the resource demand of VMs on PM m. C means the capacity of a PM. $\epsilon > 0$ is a small constant, called *user-defined SLA*.

Equation (3) can be transformed to:

$$C \geqslant E[D_m] + c_\epsilon(0,1)\sqrt{var[D_m]}$$

$$E[D_m] = \mu_1 x_{m1} + \mu_2 x_{m2} + \ldots + \mu_n x_{mn},$$
$$var[D_m] = \sum_{i,j} \rho_{ij}\sigma_i\sigma_j x_{mi}x_{mj}.$$

where $c_\epsilon(0,1)$ is the $(1-\epsilon)$-percentile of standard normal distribution with mean 0 and variance 1. For example, when $\epsilon = 2\%$, $c_\epsilon(0,1) = 2.06$. $E[D_m]$ is the sum of expectations of resource demands of all VMs placed on PM m, and $var[D_m]$ is the variance of the workload with correlations between VMs taken into consideration.

After problem formulation, we will present our algorithms to the VM placement problem. The first algorithm is *Correlation-Aware First-Fit* algorithm. The algorithm is similar to first-fit algorithm in solving the bin-packing problem, which is shown in Algorithm 1.

Algorithm 1. Correlation-aware First-Fit VM Placement Algorithm

---

Input: Historical resource demand data of VMs from the monitor.
Output: A VM placement scheme with a user-defined SLA.

```
1  foreach VM n do
2  |    foreach PM m do
3  |    |    Add VM n to PM m;
4  |    |    x_mn = 1;
5  |    |    if E[D_m] + c_ε(0,1)√var[D_m] < C then
6  |    |    |    break;
7  |    |    else
8  |    |    |    Remove VM n from PM m;
9  |    |    |    x_mn = 0;
10 |    |    end
11 |    end
12 end
```

Algorithm 1 is a first-fit algorithm which will place a certain VM into the first PM that can hold it with a certain probability less than a user-defined SLA. Since this problem is very similar to first-fit algorithm of bin packing problem, we can easily reach the inequality the number of PMs used by first-fit described above is no more than $2\times$ optimal number of PMs. If we first sort the VMs by the size, then this is very similar to first fit decreasing algorithm in bin packing problem. It has been shown to use no more than $\frac{11}{9}\mathbf{OPT} + 1$ bins (where $\mathbf{OPT}$ is the number of bins given by the optimal solution).

The second algorithm is *Correlation-Aware Best-Fit* algorithm, as shown in Algorithm 2. The main idea is: each packing is determined in a search procedure

Algorithm 2. Correlation-Aware Best-Fit VM Placement Algorithm

Input: Historical resource demand data of VMs from the monitor.
Output: A VM placement scheme with a user-defined SLA.
1 **foreach** *VM n* **do**
2   Try to place VM n on every PM, and finally chose the PM m with the least slack to place;
3     $x_{mn} = 1$;
4   **if** $E[D_m] + c_\epsilon(0,1)\sqrt{var[D_m]} < C$ **then**
5   break;
6   **else**
7   Remove VM n from PM m;
8         $x_{mn} = 0$;
9   **end**
10 **end**

that tests all possible subsets of items on the list which fit the bin capacity. We will choose the subset with the least slack to fill the bin. If the algorithm finds a subset that fills the bin completely, the search is stopped, for there is no better packing possible.

We compare our VM placement algorithms with the following benchmark algorithms:

Random. It is based on the idea of randomly place VMs to PMs according the peak value in historical resource demand data without making any predictions and considering correlations between VMs.

Constant variance (CV). This algorithm predicts the future demand of VMs while not taking correlations between VMs into consideration [16].

3.4 Evaluation

The resource demand (utilization) data is generated by the method in [1]. We put 384 VMs on 128 PMs. We first generate 200 resource demand traces with different mean and variation. Each trace contains a list of 400 historical resource demand data (400 time slots). We will use the first 100 data to train the neural network model and the remaining data to compare our correlation-aware placement algorithms with previous proposed algorithms. We normalize the capacity of a PM as 100%.

As shown in Table 2 and Fig. 4, when the user-defined SLA becomes larger, there are more PMs that achieve average resource utilization. There is a trade-off between resource utilization and SLA guarantee, and we should think twice before we make the decision under different scenarios.

As shown in Fig. 5, the resource utilizations of PMs are different under the four algorithms with user-defined SLA 5%. The random algorithm randomly place VMs to PMs according to the peak value in the historical data. Hence, the average resource utilization of PMs is the lowest among the four algorithm and the number of used PMs are the largest. The constant variance algorithm assumes the variance of VM i is constant which is apparently not the case in the real world. Correlation-aware first-fit and best-fit algorithms outperforms

Table 2. Number of used PMs, the overload ratio ($\overline{o}$), and average resource utilization of PMs ($\overline{D}$) in different time slots under different user-defined SLAs.

	Time Slots 100–200			Time Slots 200–300			Time Slots 300–400		
$\epsilon = 2\%$	N_{PM}	$\overline{o}$	$\overline{D}$	N_{PM}	$\overline{o}$	$\overline{D}$	N_{PM}	$\overline{o}$	$\overline{D}$
FF	95	0.76%	66.87%	96	0.69%	66.17%	96	0.69%	66.15%
BF	95	0.72%	66.87%	96	0.63%	66.17%	96	0.71%	66.15%
CV	128	0.007%	49.63%	128	0%	49.63%	128	0%	49.61%
$\epsilon = 5\%$	N_{PM}	$\overline{o}$	$\overline{D}$	N_{PM}	$\overline{o}$	$\overline{D}$	N_{PM}	$\overline{o}$	$\overline{D}$
FF	90	2.22%	70.58%	91	1.74%	69.81%	92	1.73%	69.03%
BF	90	2.27%	70.58%	91	1.84%	69.81%	92	1.72%	69.03%
CV	96	2.4%	66.17%	96	2.74%	66.17%	96	2.95%	66.15%
$\epsilon = 10\%$	N_{PM}	$\overline{o}$	$\overline{D}$	N_{PM}	$\overline{o}$	$\overline{D}$	N_{PM}	$\overline{o}$	$\overline{D}$
FF	85	6.36%	74.74%	87	4.9%	73.02%	86	5.32%	73.84%
BF	85	6.63%	74.74%	87	4.9%	73.02%	86	5.32%	73.84%
CV	96	2.65%	66.17%	96	2.65%	66.17%	96	2.95%	66.15%
Random	128	6.02%	52.5%	128	5.74%	52.37%	128	5.94%	52.48%

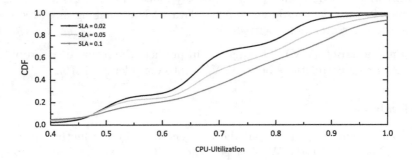

Fig. 4. Correlative-aware algorithms with different user-defined SLAs.

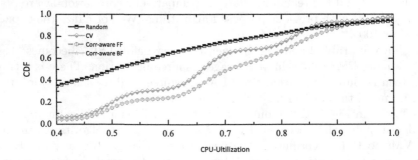

Fig. 5. Resource utilization with user-defined SLA 5%.

the other two algorithms. There are more PMs with high resource utilization and reduces the total number of used PMs. Tough the resource utilizations of PMs are almost the same, the best-fit algorithm costs more than the first-fit algorithm due to the test of placing a VM on every PM.

4   Conclusion

In this paper, we proposed a correlation-aware virtual machine placement system that effectively places virtual machines on physical machines. First, we employ Neural Networks model to predict the resource utilization trend according to the historical resource utilization data. Second, we presented two correlation-aware placement algorithms to enhance resource utilization while meeting the user-defined service level agreements. The simulation results show that the efficiency of our virtual machine placement scheme outperforms the previous work by about 15%.

Acknowledgement. This work has been supported in part by the China 973 Project (2014CB340303), China NSF Projects (Nos. 61672353, 61472252, 61672349 and 61303202), the Opening Project of Key Lab of Information Network Security of Ministry of Public Security (the Third Research Institute of Ministry of Public Security) (Grant no. C15602). The authors also would like to thank Wei Wei and Bo Cao for their contributions on the early versions of this paper.

References

1. Ajiro, Y., Tanaka, A.: Improving packing algorithms for server consolidation. In: International CMG Conference, vol. 253 (2007)
2. Buyya, R., Yeo, C.S., Venugopal, S., Broberg, J., Brandic, I.: Cloud computing and emerging IT platforms: vision, hype, and reality for delivering computing as the 5th utility. Future Gener. Comput. Syst. **25**(6), 599–616 (2009). Elsevier
3. Bobroff, N., Kochut, A., Beaty, K.: Dynamic placement of virtual machines for managing SLA violations. In: IFIP/IEEE International Symposium on Integrated Network Management (IM), pp. 119–128. IEEE Press (2007)
4. Cao, B., Gao, X., Chen, G., Jin, Y.: NICE: network-aware VM consolidation scheme for energy conservation in data centers. In: IEEE International Conference on Parallel and Distributed Systems (ICPADS), pp. 166–173. IEEE Press (2014)
5. Clark, C., Fraser, K., Hand, S., Hansen, J.G., Jul, E., Limpach, C., Warfield, A.: Live migration of virtual machines. In: USENIX Proceedings of the 2nd Conference on Symposium on Networked Systems Design & Implementation (NSDI), pp. 273–286. USENIX Association (2005)
6. Ghorbani, S., Schlesinger, C., Monaco, M., Keller, E., Caesar, M., Rexford, J., Walker, D.: Transparent, live migration of a software-defined network. In: ACM Symposium on Cloud Computing (SOCC), pp. 1–14. ACM (2014)
7. Gong, Z., Gu, X., Wilkes, J.: Press: predictive elastic resource scaling for cloud systems. In: International Conference on Network and Service Management (CNSM), pp. 9–16. IEEE Press (2010)

8. Han, Z., Tan, H., Chen, G., Wang, R., Chen, Y., Lau, F.: Dynamic virtual machine management via approximate Markov decision process. In: IEEE International Conference on Computer Communications (INFOCOM), pp. 1–9. IEEE Press (2016)

9. Kim, J., Ruggiero, M., Atienza, D., Lederberger, M.: Correlation-aware virtual machine allocation for energy-efficient datacenters. In: Proceedings of the Conference on Design, Automation and Test in Europe, pp. 1345–1350. EDA Consortium (2013)

10. Khalilzad, N., Faragardi, H.R., Nolte, T.: Towards energy-aware placement of real-time virtual machines in a cloud data center. In: IEEE High Performance Computing and Communications (HPCC), pp. 1657–1662. IEEE Press (2015)

11. Lin, H., Qi, X., Yang, S., Midkiff, S.: Workload-driven VM consolidation in cloud data centers. In: Parallel and Distributed Processing Symposium (IPDPS), pp. 207–216. IEEE Press (2015)

12. Meng, X., Isci, C., Kephart, J., Zhang, L., Bouillet, E., Pendarakis, D.: Efficient resource provisioning in compute clouds via VM multiplexing. In: International Conference on Autonomic Computing, pp. 11–20. ACM (2010)

13. Qiu, C., Shen, H., Chen, L.: Probabilistic demand allocation for cloud service brokerage. In: IEEE International Conference on Computer Communications (INFOCOM), pp. 1–9. IEEE Press (2016)

14. Song, W., Xiao, Z., Chen, Q., Luo, H.: Adaptive resource provisioning for the cloud using online bin packing. IEEE Trans. Comput. **63**(11), 2647–2660 (2014). IEEE Press

15. Wang, S., Liu, Z., Zheng, Z., Sun, Q., Yang, F.: Particle swarm optimization for energy-aware virtual machine placement optimization in virtualized data centers. In: Parallel and Distributed Systems (ICPADS), pp. 102–109. IEEE Press (2013)

16. Wei, W., Wei, X., Chen, T., Gao, X., Chen, G.: Dynamic correlative VM placement for quality-assured cloud service. In: IEEE International Conference on Communications (ICC), pp. 2573–2577. IEEE Press (2013)

17. Wood, T., Shenoy, P., Venkataramani, A., Yousif, M.: Black-box and gray-box strategies for virtual machine migration. In Proceedings of the 4th USENIX conference on Networked systems design & implementation (NSDI) pp. 17–17. USENIX Association (2007)

18. Wood, T., Ramakrishnan, K.K., Shenoy, P., Van der Merwe, J., Hwang, J., Liu, G., Chaufournier, L.: CloudNet: dynamic pooling of cloud resources by live WAN migration of virtual machines. IEEE/ACM Trans. Netw. (TON) **23**(5), 1568–1583 (2015)

19. Xu, F., Liu, F., Liu, L., Jin, H., Li, B., Li, B.: iAware: making live migration of virtual machines interference-aware in the cloud. IEEE Trans. Comput. (TOC) **63**(12), 3012–3025 (2014)

20. Ye, K., Jiang, X., Huang, D., Chen, J., Wang, B.: Live migration of multiple virtual machines with resource reservation in cloud computing environments. In: IEEE International Conference on Cloud Computing (CLOUD), pp. 267–274. IEEE Press (2011)

Connectivity-Aware Virtual Machine Placement in 60 GHz Wireless Cloud Centers

Linghe Kong[1(✉)], Linsheng Ye[1], Bowen Wang[1], Xiaofeng Gao[1], Fan Wu[1], Guihai Chen[1], and M. Shamim Hossain[2]

[1] Shanghai Key Laboratory of Scalable Computing and Systems,
Department of Computer Science and Engineering,
Shanghai Jiao Tong University, Shanghai 200240, China
linghe.kong@sjtu.edu.cn

[2] College of Computer and Information Sciences, King Saud University,
Riyadh 11543, Saudi Arabia

Abstract. Benefiting from the 60 GHz technology, physical machines in advanced cloud centers are connected by not only the conventional wired links but also the wireless communications. The 60 GHz *millimeter-wave* (mmWave) introduces valuable advantages into cloud centers including flexibility, scalability and high rate. Nevertheless, mmWave is constrained by directional communications, i.e., a wireless link is connected if and only if two directional antennas face to each other. This constraint introduces a new problem in cloud service: the *virtual machine* (VM) placement should consider the real-time connectivity if communications are required between VMs. Otherwise, rotating the antenna costs additional delay, resulting in performance degradation. To address this problem, we propose a novel *connectivity-aware VM placement* (CAVMP) specialized for 60 GHz wireless cloud center. The core of CAVMP is to dynamically place VMs in order to improve the utilization and avoid overloads while taking the connectivity state into account. We build a 2-rack cloud to measure the connectivity feature of mmWave communications. In addition, we conduct extensive simulations to evaluate CAVMP. Performance results demonstrate that CAVMP significantly outperforms existing VM placement schemes in wireless cloud center.

1 Introduction

Recent years, both industry and academia pay great attention to cloud computing. In industrial field, plenty of cloud centers are built all over the world to provide promising cloud services such as Amazon EC2, Microsoft Azure and Alibaba Cloud. In academic field, many efforts have been contributed on cloud computing from different directions, e.g., FairCloud [12] and ElasticSwitch [13].

With the development of 60 GHz *millimeter-wave* (mmWave) technology, wireless cloud centers [4] are available from lab to market, in which racks are able to transmit data by wireless communications. Compared with the conventional wired links, wireless communications show three merits. (i) The topology

© ICST Institute for Computer Sciences, Social Informatics and Telecommunications Engineering 2018
J. Wan et al. (Eds.): CloudComp 2016, SPNCE 2016, LNICST 197, pp. 33–43, 2018.
https://doi.org/10.1007/978-3-319-69605-8_4

is flexible by adjusting the direction of wireless transmission; (ii) Getting rid of the complex cabling system, the cloud center is easily scalable by deploying directional antenna by putting antennas on racks' roofs. (iii) The 60 GHz band has up to 7 GHz channel bandwidth. With a suitable modulation, the data rate can easily achieve multi-gigabit level. It is promising that using wireless communications as a complementary for wired links in cloud centers.

However, different from the omni-directional transmissions in conventional WiFi, mmWave communications require directional transmissions due to its high attenuation in the air. Field test [6] shows a 7-degree and 15-m communication range of the mmWave device in real prototype. During data transmissions, it is required that the antennas in two mmWave transceivers face to each other. In addition, rotating the mmWave antenna introduce extra delay no matter by motor or beamforming. This feature causes a new problem, connectivity awareness, in *virtual machine* (VM) placement in cloud computing for minimizing the time consumption on antenna adjustment.

In cloud centers, VM placement is a fundamental problem, which dynamically allocates the resources of physical machines (PMs) including CPU and memory according to the applications. Inappropriate VM placement results in over-provision or under-provision issues. The over-provision wastes unnecessary energy and resource. And the under-provision degrades the performance.

Great efforts have been contributed in VM placement in literature. In [1], the VM placement is developed to manage the service level agreement (SLA) violations. Then, [8] proposes the joint-VM-provisioning, which considers the correlation among VMs. Furthermore, MPT [14] is designed to combine the utilization ratio as well as the energy efficiency. Communication traffic are considered in [7]. These works optimize different metrics for VM placement. However, none of them involves in the connectivity.

In this paper, we propose a new *connectivity-aware VM placement* (CAVMP) scheme that dynamically allocates the VMs according to the connectivity state to enhance the utilization of cloud center. There are four major components in CAVMP. First, the *resource monitor* senses the real-time utilization and connectivity state. Second, based on the sensory and historical results, the *utilization estimator* predicts the future utilization of existing VMs because the utilization of these VMs is time-varying. Third, the *VM requestor* reports the request of new VMs from users. Fourth, the *strategy manager* makes the decision on new VM placement and antenna adjustment.

The contributions of this work are three-fold:

- To the best of our knowledge, this is the first work to study the problem of connectivity-aware VM placement in 60 GHz wireless cloud center.
- To tackle this problem, we propose a novel scheme, named CAVMP. In this scheme, the connectivity tracking is newly added into the resource monitor module; ARIMA and GARCH models are adopted to estimate the future utilization and its volatility; and a new algorithm is developed to make the decision of VM placement.

– We build a wireless cloud prototype including 2 racks equipped with mmWave devices. Based on the communication features, we conduct extensive simulation to evaluate CAVMP. Performance results demonstrate that CAVMP improves up to 8% average utilization ratio while reducing 95% time consumption on antenna adjustment, compared with the state-of-the-art scheme.

2   Preliminary of 60 GHz Wireless Cloud Center

In cloud computing, 60 GHz mmWave communication technology is exploited to supplement the wired links, which has the following advantages:

First, the topology of wireless cloud is flexible by rotating antennas. The wireless cloud Flyways [6] was implemented as an incremental overlay network to the wired cloud. The mmWave devices HXI with horn antenna are placed on top of racks to generate wireless links as shown in Fig. 1(a). Then, Zhou et al. [16] proposed 3D Beamforming to establish the indirect link between two racks by reflecting the signal using the ceiling as shown in Fig. 1(b). Both Flyways and 3D Beamforming can adjust their antenna directions to change the topology.

Second, it is not easy to expand a wired cloud center due to the complicated cabling workload, which wastes huge amount of time and manpower. However, the wireless cloud center is able to get rid of the cabling procedure and easy to be scaled up. In addition, the cloud center can decease the construction and maintenance cost without wired cables.

Third, mmWave communication also enables high-speed data transmissions, which satisfies the transmission requirements of cloud centers. The 60 GHz spectrum was set as unlicensed band by the FCC in 2001 and the available 7 GHz channel bandwidth supports multi-gigabit wireless communications.

However, the limitation of mmWave is its directional transmission, so that two mmWave devices are connected only if their antenna beams can cover each other. Hence, when one device needs to link a new device, the antenna directions need to be adjusted, which leads to additional time consumption.

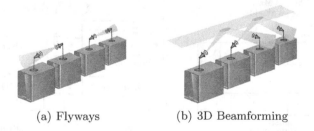

(a) Flyways   (b) 3D Beamforming

Fig. 1. Illustrations of directional transmissions in existing wireless clouds.

3   Design of Connectivity-Aware VM Placement

The objective of the virtual machine placement is to improve the average utilization of physical machines (PMs). Without considering the limitation of directional transmission, existing VM placement schemes cannot perform well in 60 GHz cloud center. Since some applications require data transmission among multiple VMs, (i) the performance will dramatically degrade if there is no link establishment; (ii) the utilization ratio will be reduced if time is consumed on antenna adjustment. To address this new problem in wireless cloud, we plan to construct a new *connectivity-aware VM placement* (CAVMP) scheme.

3.1   Design Overview

The idea of CAVMP is to place VMs according to the connectivity state. It is better that dependent VMs (data exchange are required among them) are placed in two already connected PMs to minimize the time for antenna adjustment.

In the system, we assume that there are thousands of PMs in the wireless cloud; a rack is composed of multiple PMs; VM placement happens periodically every Δt; the time consumption of antenna adjustment cannot be ignored, which is proportional to the given angle speed; the duration of updated period exceeds the interval Δt so that the VM placement keeps pace with the demand changes.

We design the architecture of CAVMP as shown in Fig. 2. CAVMP has four key modules: resource monitor, utilization estimation, VM requestor, and strategy manager.

First, the *resource monitor* tracks the utilization (including CPU, memory, and storage) of all PMs and the real-time connectivity state.

Second, the historical and real-time utilization are fed into the *utilization estimator* to predict the future utilization of existing VMs in the next Δt time. The estimator predicts not only the expected demand, but also the volatility, which indicates the fluctuating degree of the demand.

Third, the *VM requestor* gets the new VM requests from users and translates these information into utilization request and link dependency.

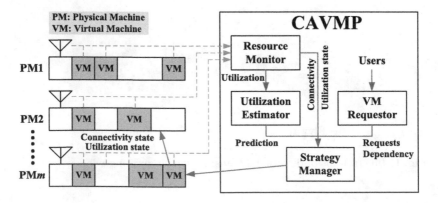

Fig. 2. System architecture of CAVMP.

Finally, the *strategy manager* takes the results from all other modules as inputs, and figures out the placement strategy scheme about where each VM should be placed. The final output is a binary matrix $X_{(t+1)} = [x_{mn}]$ for the placement in the next time slot.

In the following subsections, we introduce four components in details.

3.2 Resource Monitor

The resource monitor collects the states of existing VMs in PMs, including three kinds of data: utilization state, connectivity state, and deployment matrix.

Utilization state. For a VM n during $[t, t+\Delta t)$, the utilization state is denoted by U_t^n, which includes the real-time computing and storage resources. The resource monitor collects the utilization every Δt and log all history.

Connectivity state. The resource monitor also collects the real-time antenna directions in order to imply the connectivity state, denoted by $C_t = [c_{ij}]$, where $c_{ij} = 1$ indicates that rack i and j are connected by 60 GHz mmWave.

Deployment matrix. The resource monitor collects the real-time VM deployment in PMs, which is denoted by $X_t = [x_{mn}]$, where $x_{mn} = 1$ indicates that VM n is placed on PM m.

The transmission area of a 60 GHz mmWave transceiver can be expressed as a cone model with the transmission range λ and the transmission angle α as shown in Fig. 1(a). With the transmission area, the locations of all antennas, and the height of ceiling, the connectivity state can be calculated.

3.3 Utilization Estimator

The resource consumption of existing VMs in PMs are dynamic. This module is used to estimate the future utilization. Conventional works usually exploit the average utilization or historical data as inputs to operate the VM placement scheme. However, we propose to predict not only the expectation of the future utilization, but also its variance as an fluctuation indicator. Benefitting from this variance, the quality assurance can be taken into account, whose goal is:

$$Pr\{L_m > R_m\} < \epsilon, \forall m \tag{1}$$

where ϵ is a small positive constant, R_m is the capacity of PM m, and L_m is the load of PM m. To achieve SLA, this Equation should be satisfied.

Based on the historical data and the real-time monitor results, we leverage the *AutoRegressive Integrated Moving Average* (ARIMA) model [3] to estimate the mean of future utilization and the *Generalized AutoRegressive Conditional Heteroskedasticity* (GARCH) model [2] to estimate the variance.

ARIMA-based mean estimation. Let U_t^n as the utilization of VM n during $[t, t+\Delta t)$ and L as the lag operator, where $LU_t^n = U_{t-1}^n$. Then, the lag difference ∇ is expressed by

$$\begin{cases} L^d U_t^n = U_{t-d}^n, \\ \nabla^d U_t^n = \nabla(\nabla^{d-1} U_t^n), \end{cases} \tag{2}$$

where $d \geq 1$ and $\nabla^0 = 1$.

In order to eliminate the impact of periodicity, we define $\nabla_j U_t^n = U_t^n - U_{t-j}^n$. Hence, the stationary time series of utilization can be formulated by ARIMA(p, q) model. Using the classic Box-Jenkins methodology, the values of p and q are easily to be determined. Thus, the mean and k-step-ahead prediction of U_t^n can be determined.

GARCH-based variance estimation. Besides the mean estimation, the variance estimation is significant to optimize the VM placement. We leverage the advanced GARCH(p, q) model to estimate the standard deviation by

$$Z_{i\tau} = \sqrt{h_{i\tau}} e_\tau, \tag{3}$$

and

$$h_{i\tau} = \gamma_{i0} + \sum_{j=1}^{P} \gamma_{ij} Z_{i\tau-j}^2 + \sum_{j=1}^{Q} \beta_{ij} h_{i\tau-j}, \tag{4}$$

where $e_\tau \sim \mathcal{N}(0, 1)$, $Z_{i\tau}$ is a zero-mean, Gaussian process, and $h_{i\tau}$ is the time-varying conditional variance. Based on training, parameters in Eq. (4) can be decided using method proposed in [3]. Thus, the GARCH process can forecast the conditional variance.

3.4   VM Requestor

In a cloud center, new requests of VMs are always proposed by users. These VMs need to be added into PMs. The VM requestor module delivers the new VMs information from users to the Strategy Manager module, including the number of new VMs and their dependency.

Number of new VMs. A user requires computing and storage resources from cloud center, which are described by several VMs. We assume that all VMs have the same utilization at the beginning. Thus, all new requests could be transformed into the number of new VMs.

Dependency. Partial VMs need to work together for one user's application, so links are required for these VMs, which is so-called dependency in this paper. The dependency is denoted by D, where D is a $n \times n$ matrix and $D_{ij} = 1$ implies that VM i and j is dependent.

3.5   Strategy Manager

To achieve high utilization without SLA violations, the strategy manager needs to match the future demand. In addition, to minimize the delay of antenna adjustment, the strategy manager needs to consider the connectivity state.

Three performance metrics are adopted to evaluate the effectiveness of the proposed strategy manager:

- Overload ratio V. This is the ratio of time periods where the reserved resource is lower than the actual demand over all the periods.
- Average utilization $\overline{U}$. This is the average utilization of the allocated resource over all the periods.

– Average delay of antenna adjustment $\overline{T}$. This is the average time consumed by adjusting the antennas' directions over all the periods.

Our objective is to keep a low overload ratio V while achieving a high average utilization $\overline{U}$ and a low average adjustment time $\overline{T}$. To fulfill our goal, the resource monitor collects the utilization of each VM and the connectivity statement. The utilization estimator predicts the mean μ, the variance σ, the correlation ρ and their historical data. With μ, σ, ρ and the connectivity state C_t, the strategy manager determines the VM placement without violating SLA.

Based on the above analysis, we formulate the VM placement problem as follows:

$$
\begin{cases}
\text{Objective } \min \ (L_{max} - L_{min}) \\
\text{Subject to } Pr(L_m > R_m) < \epsilon \\
\quad \sum_{i=1}^{m} \sum_{j=1}^{n} |c_{ij(t+1)} - c_{ijt}| < \varepsilon \\
\quad x_{mn} \in \{0,1\} \\
\quad \sum_{i=1}^{n} x_{mi} = 1
\end{cases}
\tag{5}
$$

where ε is a small positive value. Suppose that L follows a normal distribution. Hence, $Pr(L_m > R_m) < \epsilon$ can transform to

$$
R_m \geq E[L_m] + c_p(\mu, \sigma^2)\sqrt{var[L_m]},
\tag{6}
$$

where $c_p(\mu, \sigma^2)$ follows the normal distribution with mean μ and variance σ, $E[L_m]$ is the sum of expectations of utilization of all the hosted VMs and $var[L_m]$ is the variance of the workload.

Based on the problem formulation, we design our CAVMP algorithm using the modern portfolio theory as the following pseudo-code.

Algorithm 1. CAVMP Algorithm

Input: C_t, X, μ_t, σ, U, D
Output: VM placement strategy
1 Sort PM by load in increasing order;
2 Sort new VM by utilization in decreasing order;
3 **foreach** new VM n **do**
4   **foreach** PM m **do**
5   **if** $\sum_{i=1}^{m} \sum_{j=1}^{n} |c_{ij(t+1)} - c_{ijt}| < \varepsilon$ **then**
6   **if** $E[L_m] + c_p(\mu, \sigma^2)\sqrt{var[L_m]} < R_m$ **then**
7   Place new VM n to PM m;
8   Adjust the position of PM m in PM list to ensure increasing order;
9                 $R_m = R_m - E[L_m] - c_p(\mu, \sigma^2)\sqrt{var[L_m]}$;
10                 $x_{mn} = 1$;
11   **break**;

The CAVMP algorithm places a VM with large U into the PM with small load that can hold the requirement of both SLA violation and connectivity state. Although CAVMP cannot guarantee an optimal solution due to multiple constraints but it is still efficient to find a better solution than existing solutions. Since VM placement problem is polynomial time many-to-one reducible to multiple knapsack problem, which is a known NP-optimization problem, the proposed CAVMP provides a greedy-like solution for this NP problem with tolerant approximation errors and time complexity $O(mn)$.

4   Performance Evaluation

In this section, we build a 2-rack prototype of 60 GHz wireless cloud center and evaluate the time consumption of antenna adjustment. Based on the time consumption, we conduct simulations to evaluate the performance of CAVMP.

4.1   Prototype and Field Test

To measure the transmission feature of 60 GHz wireless cloud center, we build a prototype of mmWave radio as shown in Fig. 3. This radio is supported by the liftable and rotatable cranks, so its height and direction could be arbitrarily adjusted by motor. The radio frontend consists of an mmWave transceiver to provide 4 Gbps-bitrate transmission in 60 GHz band and a customized cylinder metal waveguide as the antenna to form the signal into a beam. Then, the beam can be considered as the cone model with the angle α.

We conduct field test of a pair of such radios by HD video transmission as shown in Fig. 3. The transmission angle α is nearly 9° and the communication range is about 13 m. Especially, we vary the distance between two radios with a step of 1 m and the 4 Gbps communication link is maintained without obvious lag from 1 to 10 m. The rotation speed is 60°/s and the lift speed is 0.5 m/s.

Fig. 3. The prototype of mmWave radios are equipped on the racks in cloud center.

4.2   Simulation

Then, we evaluate the proposed CAVMP algorithm by extensive simulations. We randomly generate 1000 utilization traces with different means and variations. All these utilization traces are not independent, thus their placement requires

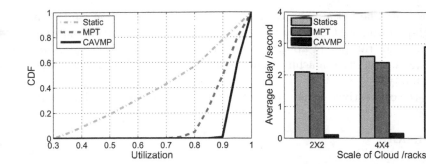

Fig. 4. CDF of resource utilization.   **Fig. 5.** Delay of antenna adjustment.

some communications among VMs. The connectivity state is also randomly generated in a 8 × 8-rack cloud center. Each trace or state contains 500 historical data. We use the first 200 traces to train the time series model and the remaining data to test our algorithm and compare with existing algorithms.

In Fig. 4, we compare CAVMP with two VM placement algorithms Static and MPT about the cumulative distribution function (CDF) of utilization. Static is always provisioning for the peak. Static allocates resources based on historical data without any prediction. MPT is a state-of-the-art VM placement algorithm with the correlation among VMs. However, it does not consider the directional transmission of mmWave antenna. As shown in the figure, Static has the most machines running with low utilization. Since Static is not predictive and dynamic, it cannot respond to time-varying demand well. The result of MPT shows that almost all the VMs is running with utilization larger than 80%. CAVMP performs better than Static algorithm and improves about 8% compared with MPT. This result demonstrates the proposed CAVMP can achieve a high resource utilization in 60 GHz wireless cloud center.

The comparison on average delay of antenna adjustment is shown in Fig. 5. We find that CAVMP significantly outperform the other two algorithms, which is always close to zero due to the connectivity-aware design. In contrast, Static and MPT algorithms only consider the utilization and ignore the connectivity state, so their average delays are usually larger than 2 s. Moreover, with the increase of size, the dependency of connectivity is more complicated. Hence, the trend of delay increases with the size.

5   Related Work

The related work can be classified into two categories:

Network performance prediction: The volatility prediction in bandwidth reservation is proposed in [10] to build an auto-scaling system that dynamically books the minimum bandwidth resources from multiple data centers for the VoD provider in [11]. In [15], the robust dynamic approach is designed to periodically identifies bandwidth allocation to virtual networks.

VM placement: Clark et al. [5] present the design, implementation, and evaluation of high-performance OS migration built on top of the Xen virtual machine monitor. A fast and transparent application migration system is proposed in [9]. And the traffic-aware virtual machine placement is studied in [7] to improve the network scalability.

However, the connectivity-aware solution is still a vacancy in VM placement.

6   Conclusion

In this paper, we investigate the connectivity-aware VM placement solution for 60 GHz wireless cloud center. Time series prediction techniques and algorithm design are combined to provide better performance in minimizing the delay of antenna adjustment and maximizing the resource utilization. We build a prototype and evaluate CAVMP using extensive simulations. Performance results show that the effectiveness of CAVMP.

Acknowledgment. This research was supported by China 973 Project 2014CB340303, NSFC Grant Nos. 61672349, 61303202, 61672353, and 61472252.

References

1. Bobroff, N., Kochut, A., Beaty, K.: Dynamic placement of virtual machines for managing SLA violations. In: IFIP/IEEE IM (2007)
2. Bollerslev, T.: Generalized autoregressive conditional heteroskedasticity. J. Econom. **31**(3), 307–327 (1986)
3. Box, G.E., Jenkins, G.M., Reinsel, G.C., Ljung, G.M.: Time Series Analysis: Forecasting and Control. Wiley, Hoboken (2015)
4. Chen, M., Jin, H., Wen, Y., Leung, V.: Enabling technologies for future data center networking: a primer. IEEE Netw. **27**(4), 8–15 (2013)
5. Clark, C., Fraser, K., Hand, S., Hansen, J.G., Jul, E., Limpach, C., Warfield, A.: Live migration of virtual machines. In: USENIX NSDI (2005)
6. Halperin, D., Kandula, S., Padhye, J., Bahl, P., Wetherall, D.: Augmenting data center networks with multi-gigabit wireless links. In: ACM SIGCOMM Computer Communication Review, vol. 41, no. 4, pp. 38–49 (2011)
7. Jiang, J.W., Lan, T., Ha, S., Chen, M., Chiang, M: Joint VM placement and routing for data center traffic engineering. In: IEEE INFOCOM (2012)
8. Meng, X., Isci, C., Kephart, J., Zhang, L., Bouillet, E., Pendarakis, D.: Efficient resource provisioning in compute clouds via VM multiplexing. In: ACM ICAC (2010)
9. Nelson, M., Lim, B.H., Hutchins, G.: Fast transparent migration for virtual machines. In: USENIX Annual (2005)
10. Niu, D., Li, B., Zhao, S.: Understanding demand volatility in large VoD systems. In: ACM NOSSDAV (2011)
11. Niu, D., Xu, H., Li, B., Zhao, S.: Quality-assured cloud bandwidth auto-scaling for video-on-demand applications. In: IEEE INFOCOM (2012)
12. Popa, L., Kumar, G., Chowdhury, M., Krishnamurthy, A., Ratnasamy, S., Stoica, I.: FairCloud: sharing the network in cloud computing. In: ACM SIGCOMM (2012)

13. Popa, L., Yalagandula, P., Banerjee, S., Mogul, J.C., Turner, Y., Santos, J.R.: ElasticSwitch: practical work-conserving bandwidth guarantees for cloud computing. ACM SIGCOMM Comput. Commun. Rev. **43**(4), 351–362 (2013)
14. Wei, W., Wei, X., Chen, T., Gao, X., Chen, G.: Dynamic correlative VM placement for quality-assured cloud service. In: IEEE ICC (2013)
15. Zhang, M., Wu, C., Yang, Q., Jiang, M.: Robust dynamic bandwidth allocation method for virtual networks. In: IEEE ICC (2012)
16. Zhou, X., Zhang, Z., Zhu, Y., Li, Y., Kumar, S., Vahdat, A., Zheng, H.: Mirror mirror on the ceiling: flexible wireless links for data centers. ACM SIGCOMM Comput. Commun. Rev. **42**(4), 443–454 (2012)

Ethical Trust in Cloud Computing Using Fuzzy Logic

Ankita Sharma[1](✉) and Hema Banati[2]

[1] Jagannath University, Jaipur, Rajasthan, India
Ankita.sharma@jimsindia.org
[2] Department of Computer Science, University of Delhi, New Delhi, India
banatihema@hotmail.com

Abstract. Cloud computing, today, has gained wide acceptance by business enterprises across the globe. With growing popularity of cloud computing and a considerable amount of research already conducted on the fundamental issue of trust in the cloud, researchers are now focused on determining the linkage between ethics and trust. Ethical issues in cloud depend on the particular application and current circumstances. The paper proposes a novel technique of computing ethical trust placed on a service provider. The approach takes into consideration various factors which affect trust and ethics; as qualitative inputs through a customized interface. The accepted inputs are fuzzified and using a special set of designed rules, an ethical trust value is computed. The resultant output is subsequently de-fuzzified using the centroid method The calculated degree of ethical trust can help in ascertaining the significance of a service provider and is therefore of great utility in the area of cloud computing.

Keywords: Cloud · Ethics · Trust · Fuzzy systems

1 Introduction

In today's dynamic and competitive business world, cloud computing has proved to be a boon to commercial enterprises. Cloud computing includes a set of resources that are allocated as a when on demand. Cloud computing is a collection of various resources which provided to the customer via the internet. Cloud computing has made it possible for the users to get in use of all the virtual resources with the help of internet. An example of cloud services is Google Engine, Oracle Cloud, Office 365. But nowadays as cloud computing is growing it is leading to severe security issues and because of this, the trust factor comes into picture [14]. Cloud computing comprises of three layers i.e. Infrastructure, Platform, and Application. IAAS means Infrastructure as a service; PAAS means Platform as a service; SAAS means Software as a service The SaaS layer in the cloud helps the customer to run an application of their choices such as Inventory Management and Customer Relations Management. Software as a Service (SaaS) also expels the need to install the software on the system and provides the advantage to run the software as an application on the customer's own computer which in turn simplifies the maintenance and support of the software on the customer's end. PaaS stands for Platform as a Service. To make use of this service an organization must have a good

© ICST Institute for Computer Sciences, Social Informatics and Telecommunications Engineering 2018
J. Wan et al. (Eds.): CloudComp 2016, SPNCE 2016, LNICST 197, pp. 44–55, 2018.
https://doi.org/10.1007/978-3-319-69605-8_5

number of computing experts. This service is popular amongst the developers who need to test their services in multiple platforms such as various versions of Windows, Mac, Linux operating systems. IaaS stands for Infrastructure as a Service. This service is most suitable for large businesses only as the customer is expected to manage both the hardware and the software that run on this hardware. So instead of purchasing the servers, software's, data space the client's buys the resources as a complete outsourced service.

It saves the cost of carrying out business, but, of late cloud computing domain is flooded with issues of ethics and trust. Trust is defined as a generation of a feeling of assurance or confidence, of one party onto another party who are somewhat bounded by certain terms and conditions. It is this element of *bounded* which ensures the process of building trust between two parties. An example of trust for a cloud vendor includes sending a trusted employee to the customer's site with the assurance that *this* trusted employee will be able to handle the technical problems reported by the customer. Here, the trust is implied in the *technical domain* of the *said* employee. The trust factor is based on evidence and subjective logics and is further used for the evaluation of security issues based on historical data. [12] A practice, which is specially drafted by business units to ensure that the trust is adequately implied is ethics and is this implication has aptly demonstrated the principles of ethics. For example, ethics for a cloud computing vendor includes an organization-wide *policy*, and *practice* of the policy of never divulging the details of *confidential data* of a client to another third party, except, as specified by the policy in its exceptions clause. For example, an exception could be to provide details to government authorities or tax authorities.

Evaluating Trust for a cloud computing service is a complex task as it is a qualitative concept. The current research work aims to address the issue of trust on cloud computing and also to provide an effective mechanism to evaluate services of cloud provider based on trust and ethics. For a reliable cloud provider, a mechanism needs to be devised which effectively ensures clients that service provider is trustworthy and its services will be efficiently followed with ethics. There have been several models proposed for calculating trust e g. Trust Management Model for Cloud Computing Environment [15]. This model analyzes the properties of trust in a cloud environment. It follows the approach that the value of trust was evaluated based on the uncertainty of each by computing the decay function, number of positive interactions, reputation factor and satisfaction level for the collected information But the model does not address the issue of Ethics. In give name [17] the authors have explained security, privacy, accountability, audit ability as factors affecting user's trust in cloud computing but again have not accounted for ethics in the same. The service models of cloud computing are being introduced in [12] and the authors have talked about security as the main concern which acts as a hurdle from cloud computing being used widely. Without ethics trust becomes uncertain, because ethics provides integrity in a way of services provided, so the advantage of our model is that it is considering the factors which affect trust and ethics altogether, taking those factors into consideration ethical trust index is calculated. Higher the Value of this index, more the reliable is a service provider.

Worth mentioning is the fact that the issue of trust was already in vogue since the advent of cloud computing technology, on account of the fact of placing confidential data to another party, but the question of ethics has slowly made its way in the cloud arena [8] Ethical trust is the implementation of a feeling of assurance or confidence between the client and server following some principles.

Also, further fuzzy set logic is developed that explains the human perception in a better manner. An approach is developed that devises the major aspects of trust and ethics relationship between cloud providers and users. All the dimensions of trust and ethics are represented with a fuzzy framework and degree of ethical trust is calculated [7].

This paper proposes a distinct method to calculate the ethical trust value in a cloud computing service provided by a vendor. The structure of the paper is as follows. Section 2 identifies the various factors that impact the calculation of ethical trust. Section 3 outlines the approach used for computing the ethical trust value followed by the prototype of the tool developed. Section 4 is based on the experimentation and results of the ethical trust index calculated summarizing up by the conclusion in Sect. 5.

2 Parameters for Calculating Ethical Trust

In this paper, we identify the parameters which can affect the ethical trust evaluation of IaaS.

2.1 Control

Cloud computing supports the outsourcing of data to third party service providers. All the information is locally stored in the cloud. Therefore the user places his computation and data on machines which are not directly under control. So a majority of users or customers claim their control over the data [2].

Also, the organizations suffer a huge loss of by providing direct control of data. The risks associated with cloud computing include the following unauthorized access to data, corruption of data, any kind of failure in the infrastructure [6]. So because of the above factors, there comes a contradiction between the outside data and in between the organization. This process is referred to as de-parameterization of data: "removal of a boundary between an organization and the outside world." This further affects not only the border of the organization's IT infrastructure, but also the organization's accountability fades out eventually [6]. In a large organization, it becomes difficult to correct the consequences created by a single person.

2.2 Division of Responsibility

The responsibility of data is divided between the customer and the service provider and none of them is in a good position to represent them [2]. This eventually leads to a problem in ethical computing which is referred as "Division of Responsibility". This division of work at times leads to many undesirable consequences and no one can be held responsible for the same. In cloud computing whenever a specific service delivered to a user depends on it depends on a large number of factors of the other system. Cloud computing typically makes use a service-oriented architecture (SOA) in which all the services are combined into large applications which are further provided to the end users. Therefore this complex structure of cloud makes it difficult to determine who is responsible in case something undesirable happens. Hence the problem of many hands working together still persists.

2.3 Accountability

The data majorly the personal data that is to be stored in the cloud should be managed properly. It should be made sure that the users and the consumers both should be able to manage the data on the cloud. If a problem appears anytime, they should be able to determine which of them is responsible [2]. For the cloud user, the risk of privacy in cloud computing can be greatly reduced if the organizations providing cloud computing services combines the contractual terms and private policies to create an accountability in the form of transparent, enforceable commitments that are responsible data handling [1]. It should be taken care what all is being recorded and to who all the particular record is made available to.

There are few key elements which provide the provision of accountability within the cloud:

(1) Transparency
(2) Assurance
(3) User Trust
(4) Responsibility.

2.4 Privacy

Many of the companies providing cloud services store huge terabytes of data which might include personal information which is further stored in data centers in countries all around the world. Privacy becomes a major issue in this case [5]. All the privacy concerns are taken care by the governments, researchers, users, and providers of cloud services. Moreover majorly whenever there is a discussion about the ethical issue, cloud privacy is the main concern but on the other hand it is difficult to explicitly describe the concerns [3]. In general the basic aim to constrain the access to personal data which helps in prevention to acquire data and put a stop to the illegal use of information related to other persons [3]. So as the data is no more stored locally the control over the data now comes in the hands of the cloud service provider. The consumers of cloud have to completely trust the cloud provider that their data is safe and will not be leaked to the outside world. Also different service providers have different options in terms of privacy and the consumer will never be clear with which service provider they are dealing with. Both reasons imply that to consumers it will not always be clear what they can expect from service providers in the cloud concerning privacy [7].

The parameters outlined above do not have crisp values. They are qualitative in nature as they are based on the subjectivity of the user opinion. Specifying a numeric quantity for a subjective concept is difficult and introduces a degree of imprecision, or uncertainty. To handle this, this contribution employs fuzzy logic. It proposes a distinct method of ethical trust calculation keeping in consideration the subjective nature of the various influencing factors, explained above.

3   Evaluating Ethical Trust with Fuzzy Interface

This section presents an algorithm which takes into consideration the factors affecting trust on cloud (listed above) as inputs. Since these inputs are qualitative in nature, hence they are appropriately transformed into numerical values by applying triangular member functions and subsequently defuzzified through the centroid method.

Figure 1 presents the various stages of the fuzzy logic applied for trust index evaluation.

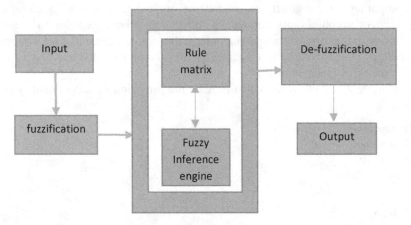

Fig. 1.   Fuzzy logic controls analysis flow.

The initial qualitative input is accepted from the user, where the user specifies the required degree of the considered parameters viz. the control, division of responsibility, accountability and privacy in the service being considered. These values are then fuzzified by using membership functions for predefined input in this paper utilizes the triangular member function for the same.

A triangular MF is defined by three input parameters {a, b, c} as follows:

$$\text{triangle}(x; a, b, c) = \begin{cases} 0, & x \le a. \\ \frac{x-a}{b-a}, & a \le x \le b. \\ \frac{c-x}{c-b}, & b \le x \le c. \\ 0, & c \le x. \end{cases}$$

By using min and max, we can have an alternative expression for the preceding equation:

$$\text{triangle}(x; a, b, c) = \max\left(\min\left(\frac{x-a}{b-a}, \frac{c-x}{c-b}\right), 0\right)$$

Our chosen input parameters can have range of values between low, medium and high, Fig. 2 is depicting fuzzified of input values using triangular input function.

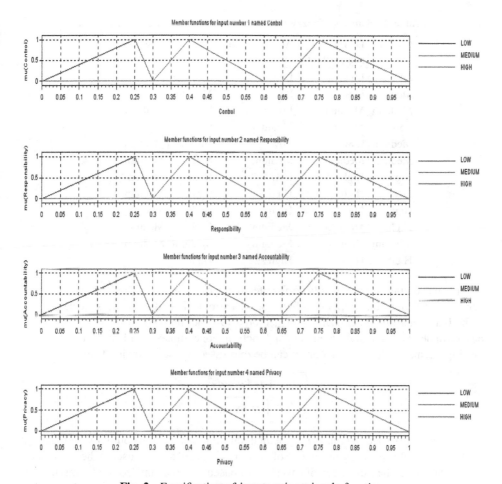

Fig. 2. Fuzzification of inputs using triangle function

The fuzzified input is then processed through the rule matrix (Table 1) which comprises of specifically designed rules. These are as follows:

1. If Control is LOW and Responsibility is LOW and Accountability is LOW and Privacy is LOW then TrustEthicsIndex is LOW.
2. If Control is LOW and Responsibility is MEDIUM and Accountability is MEDIUM and Privacy is LOW then TrustEthicsIndex is LOW.
3. If Control is MEDIUM and Responsibility is MEDIUM and Accountability is LOW and Privacy is HIGH then TrustEthicsIndex is MEDIUM.
4. If Control is MEDIUM and Responsibility is MEDIUM and Accountability is MEDIUM and Privacy is MEDIUM then TrustEthicsIndex is MEDIUM.
5. If Control is HIGH and Responsibility is HIGH and Accountability is HIGH and Privacy is HIGH then TrustEthicsIndex is HIGH.

Table 1. Samples of fuzzy rules for ethical trust evaluation of IaaS

Control	Division of responsibility	Accountability	Privacy	Degree of ethical trust
Low	Low	Low	Low	Low
Medium	Low	Low	Medium	Low
Medium	Medium	Low	High	Medium
Low	Medium	Medium	Low	Low
Medium	Low	Low	High	Medium
Medium	Medium	Medium	Medium	Medium
High	High	Low	High	Medium
Low	High	High	Low	Medium
High	Low	High	High	Medium
High	Medium	Medium	High	Medium
Medium	High	Medium	Medium	Medium
High	High	High	High	High

The final output is subsequently de-fuzzifed using centroid method to find a single crisp value which defines the output of a fuzzy set. Centroid Method is the most widely used methods amongst all the defuzzification methods [19, 20]. This method provides a center of the area under the curve of the membership function. For complex membership functions, it puts high demands on computation. It can be expressed by the following formula

$$z_0 = \frac{\int \mu_i(x)x\,dx}{\int \mu_i(x)\,dx}$$

where z_0 is de-fuzzified output, u_i is a membership function and x is output variable.

This final value provides the degree of the ethical trust of a single user in the respective service. However the trust index of a user is not based on a one time computation of trust degree. It needs to take in account the experience of the user in the relevant field and the level of expertise of the user. Thus the trust index for a single user is computed as below

$$\textbf{Ethical trust Index } (\textbf{T}) = (\textbf{U} \times \textbf{E}) + \textbf{O}$$

where U is Degree of Ethical trust calculated above using fuzzy logic.

And E is the experience of a user and significance of this factor, higher level of experience a user has more will be the values assigned, more experience also means User is more familiar with usage of cloud computing services. Experience of user can have following sample values in Table 2 below:

Table 2. Sample values of experience factor for ethical trust evaluation of IaaS

Experience of user	Value assigned
>1	0.1
1–3 years	0.5
3–8 years	0.75
8–10 years above	1.0

Table 3. Sample values of ownership factor for ethical trust evaluation of IaaS

Ownership of user	Value assigned
Trainee/non-IT staff	0.1
Developers/testers	0.4
Manager level users	0.8
Admin user	1.0

O is the ownership level of the user. Ownership is related to the rights allocated to a user. Higher the authority higher the rights of a user. For example Admin User and Manager level User will have the highest rights, they will have most of the or all of the rights to access all the cloud services so eventually they can provide better feedback of services used. The only exception to this factor is their level of experience, if user is not experienced with usage of cloud services even though he has all the access then his experience factor will be having low value.

Ownership can have different values based on user access level. Table 3 is showing sample values of Ownership factor:

For n number of users in the system, ethical trust index can be calculated as follows:

$$T = \frac{\sum (Un \times En) + On}{n} \quad \text{(For multiple users where is n } > 0)$$

The Ethical trust index is calculated and the normalized value of the ethical trust index will vary between 0 and 1 as depicted in Fig. 3.

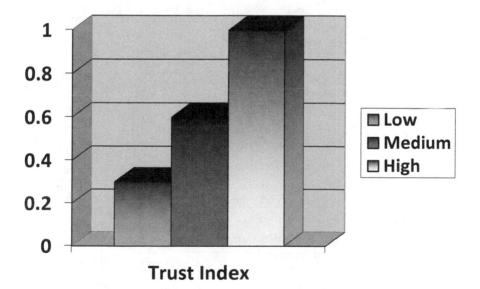

Fig. 3. Sample values of trust index

4 Experimentation and Results

A prototype based on the above approach has been developed using 64 bit Java SE Development toolkit update 60 and also using jFuzzyLogic open source library on the following configuration of hardware:Intel i5 5th Gen processor 2.7 GHz CPU speed, with 8 GB of RAM and with 1 TB HDD. It accepts as input the parameters: Control, Division of responsibility, Accountability and Privacy in form of rating gathered for a cloud provider.

The interface developed is simplistic in nature as it prompts the user for each of parameter. Depending on the user requirement of each parameter a qualitative input is provided in the form of three values Low, Medium, and High. Limitation of possible three values for each parameter is kept to minimize possible fuzziness in user's inputs. All the calculations are backend through a set of rules and the user is simply provided on the click of Calculate button, a precise index of the ethical trust. The calculated value is not reflected back as a qualitative value, to ensure dynamism in the interpretation of the value. A value of 0.75 might be acceptable as **"high"** under certain conditions for some users rather than a value of 0.85. Thus the users are free to decide their own range of Low, medium and High ethical trust values.

The model can be extended with more parameters and a wider range of inputs to fine tune the output result. The significant issue is the generation of a quantitative value for a qualitative concept.

The screenshots below presents some sample screens of the designed interface.

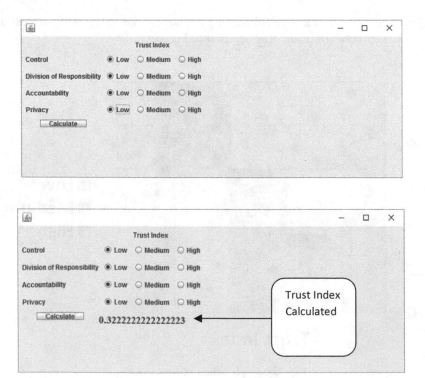

Trust Index

Control	○ Low ● Medium ○ High	
Division of Responsibility	○ Low ● Medium ○ High	
Accountability	○ Low ● Medium ○ High	
Privacy	○ Low ● Medium ○ High	

Calculate   0.7239427860696521

Trust Index

Control	● Low ○ Medium ○ High	
Division of Responsibility	○ Low ● Medium ○ High	
Accountability	○ Low ● Medium ○ High	
Privacy	● Low ○ Medium ○ High	

Calculate   0.32571585903083716

Trust Index

Control	○ Low ● Medium ○ High	
Division of Responsibility	○ Low ● Medium ○ High	
Accountability	○ Low ○ Medium ● High	
Privacy	● Low ○ Medium ○ High	

Calculate   0.7184210526315792

Trust Index

Control	○ Low ○ Medium ● High	
Division of Responsibility	○ Low ○ Medium ● High	
Accountability	○ Low ○ Medium ● High	
Privacy	○ Low ○ Medium ● High	

Calculate   0.85

This application takes all these inputs as a fuzzy set and de-fuzzify them using centroid algorithm [13] and based upon the rules in Table 2 it calculates the Trust Index. The prototype above assumes a Trust index between value 0 to 0.40 is low and from 0.50 to 0.75 is medium and in between 0.75 to 1.0 is high. More high the trust index more reliable the services are.

5 Conclusion

This paper proposes a distinct approach to compute a quantitative value of f ethical trust for cloud computing services. The approach recognizes the fuzzy nature of the significant factors which affect the trust on cloud providers and computes a distinct degree of ethical trust pertaining to each user, the aggregate Trust index is subsequently obtained by taking in consideration this degree of ethical trust per user along with the experience of each user and ownership of each user. The calculated ethical trust index is distinctive in nature as it quantifies the hitherto qualitative concept of trust and ethics. Such a measure can significantly affect the market presence of the cloud provider in all situations. The prototype implementation of the algorithm provides an insight into the calculation procedure, which works by accepting inputs as factors which affect ethical trust on the cloud. Higher values of this index represent high ethical trust and lower values represent low ethical trust. The calculated ethical trust index values can be suitably customized and enhanced by considering more factors, in future.

References

1. Pearson, S., Charlesworth, A.: Accountability as a way forward for privacy protection in the cloud. In: Jaatun, M.G., Zhao, G., Rong, C. (eds.) CloudCom 2009. LNCS, vol. 5931, pp. 131–144. Springer, Heidelberg (2009). https://doi.org/10.1007/978-3-642-10665-1_12
2. Haeberlen, A.: A case for the accountable cloud. SIGOPS Oper. Syst. Rev. **44**, 52–57 (2010). http://doi.acm.org/10.1145/1773912.1773926
3. van den Hoven, J.: Information technology, privacy and the protection of personal data. In: Information Technology and Moral Philosophy, pp. 301–321 (2008)
4. Timmermans, J., et al.: The ethics of cloud computing. In: Academia.edu (2010)
5. Nelson, M.: The cloud, the crowd, and public policy. Issues Sci. Technol. (2009). http://www.issues.org/25.4/nelson.html
6. Paquette, S., et al.: Identifying security risks associated with the governmental use of cloud computing. Gov. Inf. Q. (2010). ISSN 0740-624X
7. Alhamad, M., et al.: A trust-evaluation metric for cloud applications. Int. J. Mach. Learn. Comput. **1**(4) (2011)
8. Buyya, R.: Market-oriented cloud computing: vision, hype, and reality of delivering computing as the 5th utility. In: CCGRID 2009 Proceedings of the 2009 9th IEEE/ACM International Symposium on Cluster Computing and the Grid (2009)
9. Zeller, M., et al.: Open standards and cloud computing: Kdd-2009 panel report, pp. 11–18 (2009)
10. Chen, Y., et al.: What's New About Cloud Computing Security? (2010)
11. Capurro, R.: Privacy. An intercultural perspective. Ethics Inf. Technol. **7**, 37–47 (2005)

12. Shaikha, R., Sasikumar, M.: Trust model for measuring security strength of cloud computing. Proc. Comput. Sci. **45**, 380–389 (2015). International Conference on Advanced Computing Technologies and Applications (ICACTA)
13. Wang, Y.: Centroid defuzzification and the maximizing set and minimizing set ranking based on alpha level sets. Comput. Ind. Eng. 228–236 (2008)
14. Sharma, R., Trivedi, R.K.: Cloud computing–security issues, solution and technologies. Int. J. Eng. Res. **3**(4), 221–225 (2014)
15. Prajapati, S.K., et al.: Trust management model for cloud computing environment. In: Proceedings of the International Conference on Computing. Communication and Advanced Network - ICCCAN 2013 (2013)
16. Sharma, A., Banati, H. A framework for implementing trust in cloud computing. In: Proceedings of the International Conference on Internet of things and Cloud Computing. ACM DL (2016)
17. Ko, R.K.L., Jagadpramana, P., Mowbray, M., Pearson, S., Kirchberg, M., Liang, Q., Lee, B. S.: TrustCloud: a framework for accountability and trust in cloud computing. In: 2nd IEEE Cloud Forum for Practitioners. IEEE (2011)
18. Subashini, S., Kavitha, V.: A survey on security issues in service delivery models of cloud computing. J. Netw. Comput. Appl. (2010). Elsevier
19. Sugeno, M.: An introductory survey of fuzzy control. Inf. Sci. (1985)
20. Lee, C.: Fuzzy logic in control systems: fuzzy logic controller, parts I and II. IEEE Trans. Syst. Man Cybern (1990)

Answer Ranking by Analyzing Characteristic of Tags and Behaviors of Users

Qian Wang[1], Lei Su[1(✉)], Yiyang Li[1], and Junhui Liu[2]

[1] School of Information Engineering and Automation,
Kunming University of Science and Technology, Kunming 650093, China
ml8288793132@163.com, s28341@hotmail.com
[2] School of Software, Yunnan University, Kunming 650091, China

Abstract. The quality of the ranking answer is good or bad, directly affects the high quality answers for users in the community question answering system. Learning method by sorting, establish the answer ranking model, is a research hotspot in community question answering system. The characteristics of tags and behavior of users, often have a direct relationship with the answer to the users' expectations. In this paper, ListNet is used as the ranking method which selects Neural Networks as the model and Gradient Descent as the optimization method to structure ListNet ranking model which blends in characteristics of tags and behaviors of user. Then, the ranking mode is utilized to finish experiment combining the answers feature space, and the result of experiment shows that the ListNet ranking model can improve effect of answers ranking obviously which blends in the characteristics of tags and behaviors of users.

Keywords: Community question answering system · User tags · Behavioral characteristics · ListNet · Gradient descent · Feature space

1 Introduction

With the rapid development of the question and answer services which are based on community, the Community-based Question Answering service has become a new knowledge-sharing model [1], social network. It is inconvenient for users to choose web pages from a large number of returned web pages through keyword matching by traditional search engines. However, the community question answering is an open, interactive network platform, which uses the collective wisdom of the network users, through the participation of users and provides a direct answer to the question, it provides a new way and platform for the sharing of the internet knowledge, and also brings new vitality life for answering technology. The community question answering system [2] develops rapidly with the mainstream of Baidu know and Yahoo! in recent years.

The answer ranking is an important issue to be solved in community question answering [3]. The effect of the answer ranking directly affects the quality of community question answering system and the users' experience. In order to return the best answer directly to users, you must choose the best answer from a number of answers. In answer ranking model, the answer of the most consistent with the users' needs will be put in the front row, so as to locate the target knowledge directly for users. So, the

© ICST Institute for Computer Sciences, Social Informatics and Telecommunications Engineering 2018
J. Wan et al. (Eds.): CloudComp 2016, SPNCE 2016, LNICST 197, pp. 56–65, 2018.
https://doi.org/10.1007/978-3-319-69605-8_6

performance of the answer ranking model is very important, its accuracy directly determines the performance of the entire community question answering system. Therefore, it is worthy of study the sort of the answer ranking in the community question answering.

At present, ranking learning has attracted the interest of many scholars and has become a research hotspot of scholars. There have been many methods have achieved very good results in practice, such as the LambdaRank method proposed by Burges in 2006 [4]; list rank method based on the ListNet proposed by Cao in 2007, directly sequencing the whole return list [5]; the RankCosine method proposed by Qin in 2008, which is based on the level of query to construct the loss function, with the method of Boosting to optimize [6]. As for the answer ranking in community question answering system, the characteristics of the community that is the tags and behavior of users, which makes great effect on the answering ranking. For example, the level and experience value of respondents, areas of expertise, respondent's adoption rate and approval rate, the keywords to answer question and other user tags features that the respondents concerned, reflects the senior level of the person who answers the question, Further to say, it reflects the credibility of the answer provided. Generally speaking, the higher level of the respondents, the higher value of experience, the higher rate of adoption and the higher approval rate, the higher quality of the questions answered. The category of the question often being answered, the score of the respondents answered questions and the tourists together with other users' behavior have great impact on the credibility of the answers, directly responses to the answers with respect to issues related to the degree of matching, and further reflects the answer can be taken. Therefore, the characteristic of tags and behavior of users and other community features blend in the answers feature space to improve the effect of the answer ranking is worthy of study and realization.

In this paper, the characteristic of tags and behaviors of users blend in the answers feature space, combined with ListNet rank learning method to construct ranking model so as to improve the effectiveness of answer system in community question answering. Finally, the ranking mode is utilized to finish experiment combining the answers feature space, and the result of experiment show that the ListNet ranking model can improve effect of answers ranking obviously which blend in the characteristics of tags and behaviors of user.

The rest of this paper is organized as follows. Section 2 focuses on the characteristic of tags and behaviors of users blend in the answers feature space and the feature extraction; Sect. 3 presents the sorting method of ListNet in the community question answering ranking method; Sect. 4 reports on the classification experimental and results analysis based on the domain of "Baidu know"; Finally, Sect. 5 gives a summarize of the main study of the paper.

2 Factors Affecting the Ranking of Answers

There are many factors that affect the performance of the answer ranking in community question answering system, such as the similarity, the density and frequency of the query and the candidate answer.

In the community question answering, the level of respondents, the field of the respondents interest, the rate of adoption and the approval of the respondents, the questions and answers the experience value, answer the questions the focus of keywords, the score of the respondents and tourists, which attribute to the tags and users' behavior, they are important supporting elements for answer ranking and important factors to affect the answer ranking in community question answering system. Therefore, it is necessary to consider the effect of the tag and behavior of the user in the order of the ranking answer. The following details are the content of the two aspects.

2.1   User Tags

User tags include the level of the respondents, the professional field of the respondents, the rate of adoption and the approval of residents, the experience value and problem on keywords for answer. When the user answers the questions in the community question answering, there will be other relevant users, ask questions or tourists who have related knowledge needs will give their votes, scores or adopt or not. When a user answers a lot of questions, some of the answers will be adopted, so the rate of approval and adoption reflect the degree of the authority of the user. When a user takes some activities in a certain period of time in CQA, there will be relevant experience value, the more frequent activities, the more questions answered, the more experience value will be. So user tags reflect the community attitudes and the quality of answers, which is an important factor affecting the rank of the answer, it is very necessary to integrate users tags into the answer ranking model.

2.2   User Behavior

User behavior includes the score of the questions, as well as score of questions by tourists and the category of the questions and so on. In CQA System, for one particular issue, there will be a lot of other answers which provided by other users, the quality of these answers or credibility may be good or bad, the questioner will give the score or vote according to their own needs and the professional degree of the answer, and users with the same or similar knowledge needs will give the score or vote in the same way, the scoring or voting reflects the credibility of the answers to the corresponding problems. If a user often answers a question or a question of a particular field, then the user is likely to be good at this area or field in CQA and his answer to this question is of relatively high reliability. Therefore, the user behavior also reflects the quality of the relevant answers, which is an important factor that affects the rank of answer, so, the characteristic of tags and behaviors of users and other community features blend in the answers feature space to improve the effect of the answer ranking is worthy of study and implementation.

2.3   Method of Feature Extraction

The tags and behavior of users have an important effect for the effect of answer ranking in CQA. Therefore, in order to improve the ranking accuracy of the process, it is worth studying the importance of community characteristics. This thesis relies on the platform of the Baidu know to collect the answers to the problems by hand, while the characteristics of tags and behaviors of users were extracted so as to be blended in the answers feature space.

Word similarity computing is a basic research topic of natural language and widely used in natural language processing, information retrieval, text classification, automatic response, the meaning of the word row discrimination and machine translation field and other areas. It has attracted more and more researchers attention [10, 11] called "hit the extended version of Tongyicicilin [7, 8]".

In order to solve the problem of sparse matrix, this thesis introduces the method of calculating the semantic extension of words based on the synonyms Clilin method proposed by Liu and Wang [8, 9]. This method analyzed Clilin hierarchical structure, and combined the semantic with lexical chain extension and proposed a relatively novel text keyword extraction method based on the semantic relation between the word [9].

According to the hierarchical structure of the tree, all the words in the dictionary are divided into 3 levels, including 12 larger categories, 97 middle categories, and 1400 small classes [10]. All kinds of the small classes in the word forest contain a lot of words and each of them is divided into a number of words according to the meaning and the relevance of the word [10]. The words and expressions in each word group are divided into many lines according to the distance and the relevance of the word meaning. The same line of words is not the same word meaning, that is, the word meaning has a strong correlation [10]. The thesaurus is classified by hierarchical system, and the whole dictionary has 5 layers of structure. With the delicate classification of meaning step by step, the number of words in each category is very small to fifth layers, many of the words in the classification can't be classified again, that is, the atomic word group, atomic class or atomic node [10].

The semantic extension of words include two parts: word similarity and word correlation calculation. Word similarity calculation is based on the synonyms word Lin encoding distance to the two words semantic similarity calculation. Its main idea is to determine the two words in the word forest belong to which layer of branches. Then according to the semantic distance of the two words to calculate the similarity between the two words, which, the closer of semantic distance between two words, the higher word similarity they are.

The formula for calculating the similarity of words is as follows:

$$sim(w_1, w_2) = d \cdot \left(\frac{n - k + 1}{n} \right) \cdot \cos \left(n \cdot \frac{\pi}{180} \right) \qquad (2.1)$$

In this formula, $sim(w_1, w_2)$ is semantic similarity $(0 < sim < 1)$. d is coefficient. The two word similarity calculation decided by the needs of the encoding branch. n is the total number of nodes in the branch layer. k is the distance between branches.

Then calculate the words in the semantic relevancy. Make use of the semantic relation between the words in the "a synonym in the word", and calculate the relevance degree of the two words by means of statistical methods. Firstly, find out the correlation calculation of the word w_1 and w_2 and the corresponding encoding code1 and code2 in "a synonym in the word forest", if the coding code1 is equal to code2, and two codes' bit 8 is marked as "#", then these two words correlation degree is 1; if the coding code1 is equal to code2, but the two code s' bit 8 is marked as "=", then the two words correlation degree is 0.85; otherwise, we must calculate out the times of the two words appear at the same time and the times of them appear alone, then statistical information is substituted into the formula to calculated correlation degree between the two words. The formula for calculating the correlation of words is as follows:

$$\text{rel}(w_1, w_2) = \frac{count(w_1, w_2)}{\min(count(w_1), count(w_2))} \tag{2.2}$$

In this formula, $count(w_1, w_2)$ is the number of the w_1 and w_2 both appears in the question. $count(w_1)$ and $count(w_2)$ is the number of the w_1 and w_2 appears alone in the question. $\min(count(w_1), count(w_2))$ is the w_1 and w_2 minimum number of occurrences alone.

3   Attribute Reduction Based on List Net Sort Method

The rank learning has three category methods: based on PointWise, PairWise and List-Wise. And ListNet is a rank method based on ListWise. Cao came up with the method of the feedback corresponding to the entire list of search rank [11]. ListNet rank model is used Neural Network as a model ω, based on the probability of the entire arrangement of the feedback list $p_s(\pi)$ and Partition Function $f\left(x_j^{(i)}\right)$, and use Gradient Descent as an optimization method. Through continuous training, so that the loss of function is the best and then output the sort model. Arranged probability formula is as follows:

$$p_s(\pi) = \prod_{j=1}^{n} \frac{\varphi(s_{\pi(j)})}{\sum_{k=j}^{n} \varphi(s_{\pi(k)})} \tag{3.1}$$

$\phi()$ is an increasing function and constant greater than 0. For example, linear function $\varphi(x) = \alpha x, a > 0$, Exponential function $\varphi(x) = exp(x)$, this thesis chooses the Exponential function. π is a list of retrieve and feedback query. $S_{\pi}(j)$ is the score of the goal scoring function of the arrangement for the first chapter of the document score. Because of the low efficiency of a ranked list of the entire sorting list, we only calculate the first k article document at present; that is, $Top(k)$ is the Probability Model. Here is the formula:

$$p_s(\wp_k(j_1, j_2, \cdots, j_k)) = \sum_{\pi \in \wp_k(j_1, j_2, \cdots j_k)} p_s(\pi) = \prod_{t=1}^{k} \frac{exp(s_{j_t})}{\sum_{l=t}^{n} exp(s_{j_l})} \tag{3.2}$$

In this formula $\wp_k(j_1, j_2, \ldots, j_k)$ is a permutation of the previous K document. The paper chooses $k = 1$. Then the probability model becomes:

$$p_s(\wp_1(j_1)) = \frac{exp(s_j)}{\sum_{1}^{n} exp(s_{j_1})} \tag{3.3}$$

The Loss Function of ListNet ranking method is as follows:

$$L(y^{(i)}, z^{(i)}(f_\omega)) = - \sum_{\forall g \in \wp_k} P_{y^{(i)}}(g) \log(p_{z^{(i)}(f_\omega)}(g)) \qquad (3.4)$$

In this formula, Permutation probability is a neural network model of the rank function or scoring function. Its formula is as follows:

$$f_\omega(x_j^{(i)}) = \langle \omega, x_j^{(i)} \rangle \qquad (3.5)$$

Here $<.>$ is Inner product. ListNet is used as the ranking method which selects Gradient Descent as the optimization method and Gradient descent calculation formula is:

$$\Delta\omega = \frac{\partial L(y^{(i)}, z^{(i)}(f_\omega))}{\partial \omega} = - \sum_{\forall g \in \wp_k} \frac{\partial p_{z^{(i)}(f_\omega)}(g)}{\partial \omega} \frac{P_{y^{(i)}}(g)}{p_{z^{(i)}(f_\omega)}(g)} \qquad (3.6)$$

In the process of ranking model repeated training, using Gradient Descent method to continuously optimize the loss function, until the order of the model's loss function is optimal. The pseudo-code of ListNet learning method is shown in Fig. 1.

ListNet learning method

Input: training set $\{(x^{(1)}, y^{(1)}), (x^{(2)}, y^{(2)}), ..., (x^{(m)}, y^{(m)})\}$
   Parameters settings: steps T, learning rate η
   Initialization parameters ω
   For $t = 1$ to T do
     For $t = 1$ to m do
       Put list of documents query $x^{(i)}$ of i $q^{(i)}$ to the neural network combining gradient descent ω
       calculation corresponding scores list $z^{(i)}(f_\omega)$
     Use (3.6) calculation Gradient $\Delta\omega$
     Update gradient $\omega = \omega - \eta \times \Delta\omega$
    End for
      End for
Output Neural Network Model

Fig. 1. The pseudo-code of ListNet

4 Experiment Results and Analysis

This section is to verify the rank results of a list ranking method that blend in the characteristics of tags and behaviors of users. The experimental data is from Baidu know, collected a total of 150 questions and 1499 answers, the question category covers 10 small classes, and marked annotation of the degree of correlation between the answers and questions. These 10 sub-classes are: the use of mobile phones, health care, the common sense of life, the employment, fitness, outdoor sports, holiday tourism, flowers, birds, fish and insects, and pediatric traumatology.

Experiments adopted 10-fold cross-validation method, divide the 150 questions and 1499 answers corpus according to the proportion into test set T_1 and training set T_2. Here, the Proportion of T_1 is 20, the Proportion of T_2 is 80. That is to say, take 30 questions and 300 answers for the test set, the remaining 120 questions and 1199 answers for the training set. In order to verify the effect of the combination of user tags and behavior feature, we will put each relevant answer and the characteristics of tags and behavior of users blended in answer feature space, in the training and testing phases of answer ranking model, the steps of List Net is set to 1500 and learning rate is 0.00001.

4.1 The Comparison of Different Ranking Methods

This thesis chooses the rank of ListNet method as the answer method in the CQA system, with the extended version of tongyicicilin based on hit word similarity computing as a method of data processing [11]. In order to make the experiment more sufficient, the experiments were carried out 50 and 136 dimensional feature space respectively, and used five kinds of ring methods including ListNet and NDCG evaluation, MAP evaluation and P@1 evaluation of the 3 evaluation methods to compare. The result of answering sorting in different sorting methods, different dimensions of the feature space and different evaluation indicators of the answers in community question answering system are shown in Table 1.

Table 1. The result of different sorting method dimension and evaluation index

Dimensions	Evaluation indexes	Ranking method				
		RankNet	RankBoost	AdaRank	LambdaRank	ListNet
50	NDCG	0.7063	0.6808	0.6941	0.6998	0.7114
	MAP	0.8190	0.7956	0.7958	0.8488	0.8483
	P@1	0.7633	0.7000	0.5667	0.7867	0.7900
136	NDCG	0.6925	0.6977	0.6779	0.6977	0.7094
	MAP	0.8216	0.8224	0.7958	0.8417	0.8341
	P@1	0.7800	0.8333	0.5667	0.7500	0.8367

From Table 1 we can be see, as for the RankNet ranking method, RankBoost ranking method and AdaRank ranking method through NDCG evaluation methods, MAP evaluation methods and P@1 evaluation method for answer ranking results evaluation, ListNet ranking methods have better sorting effect in 50 and 136 dimensions feature space experiments. As for LambdaRank ranking method, in the case of MAP evaluation is slightly better than the ListNet method, but there is also an obvious gap between ListNet in the NDCG evaluation and P@1 evaluation method. In general, whether it is in the 50dimensional feature space or in the 136 dimensional feature space, with the NDCG evaluation methods, MAP evaluation methods and P@1 evaluation methods the evaluation results show that ListNet ranking method performed better and more valid than other ranking methods in community question answering system answers ranking task.

4.2 The Rank Method Blend in Tags and Behavior of User

In this section, the characteristics of tags and behavior of users are blended in the feature space to improve the effect of the answer to the question in CQA systems. In order to verify the validity of characteristics of the tags and behavior of the user in the CQA system, different ranking method are used. That is, RankNet ranking method, RankBoost ranking method, LambdaRank ranking method, AdaRank ranking method and ListNet ranking method and different feature space dimensions 50, 59,136 and 145 dimensional are used to do experiment. At the same time, with different evaluations such as NDCG evaluation methods, MAP evaluation methods, and P@1 evaluation methods to evaluate the results of the ranking. After the characteristics of the tags and behavior of user blended in 50 and 136 dimensional feature space turn to 59 and 145 dimensional feature space. The result of the experiment is shown in Tables 2 and 3.

Table 2. The result of 50 and 59 dimensional feature space

Rankting method	Evaluation					
	NDCG		MAP		P@1	
	Unfused feature	Fusion features	Unfused feature	Fusion features	Unfused feature	Fusion features
RankNet	0.7063	0.7103	0.8190	0.8629	0.7633	0.8100
RankBoost	0.6808	0.6808	0.7956	0.7956	0.7000	0.7000
AdaRank	0.6941	0.6941	0.7958	0.7958	0.5667	0.5667
LambdaRank	0.6998	0.7134	0.8488	0.8359	0.7867	0.7667
ListNet	0.7114	0.8041	0.8483	0.8889	0.7900	0.9000

Table 3. The result of 136 and 145 dimensional feature space

Ranking method	Evaluation					
	NDCG		MAP		P@1	
	Unfused feature	Fusion features	Unfused feature	Fusion features	Unfused feature	Fusion features
RankNet	0.6925	0.7315	0.8216	0.8300	0.7800	0.8133
RankBoost	0.6977	0.6977	0.8224	0.8224	0.8333	0.8333
AdaRank	0.6779	0.6779	0.7958	0.7958	0.5667	0.5667
LambdaRank	0.6977	0.7097	0.8417	0.8257	0.7500	0.7767
ListNet	0.7094	0.7503	0.8341	0.8723	0.8367	0.8867

Tables 2 and 3 show that each dimension feature space, the characteristics of tags and behavior of user blended in the feature space, and there is no obvious improvement, and there is even a sign of decline for RankBoost ranking method, AdaRank ranking methods and AdaRank ranking methods. However, as for the RankNet ranking method and ListNet ranking method with the characteristics of the tags and behavior of user characteristics, the ranking effect is significantly improved. And it can also be seen that the ListNet ranking method is far better than the RankNet ranking method. For example, the characteristics of tags and behavior of user blend in the 50 dimensional feature space, the result of RankNet ranking method in NDCG evaluation method, MAP evaluation method and P@1 evaluation methods increase respectively for 0.004, 0.0439 and 0.0467; however, ListNet increase for respectively 0.0927, 0.0406 and 0.11; the characteristics of tags and behavior of user blend in the 136 dimensional feature space, the result of RankNet ranking method in NDCG evaluation method, MAP evaluation method and P@1 evaluation methods increase respectively 0.039, 0.0084 and 0.0333; but the characteristics of the tags and behavior of the user, the result of ListNet ranking method increase respectively 0.0409, 0.0382 and 0.05. After the characteristics of the tags and the behavior of the user blend in the answers feature space, the result of the ListNet ranking method in the community question answering system is still better than other methods, and compared with other methods, the ranking effect is more obviously than other methods. So, the experiment proves that the ListNet ranking method is effective in the community question answering system again, and it is quite obvious that the result of answer ranking with the characteristics of tags and behavior of user blend in the feature space.

5   Conclusion

This paper, mainly introduces the answer list ranking method of the characteristics of the tags and the behavior of the user in the community question answering system, with the characteristics of the tags and behavior of the user blended in the answering feature space to improve the answer ranking accuracy effectively. Experimental comparison of multiple angles from the ranking method of comparison, the dimensions of the features comparison and evaluation index of verify the list ranking algorithms ListNet in community question answering ranking task effectiveness, and the experiment proves that the ListNet ranking method is effective in the community question answering system, and it is obvious that the effect of the user tag and the user behavior characteristics on the answer ranking.

Acknowledgement. This work is supported by the National Science Foundation on of China under the Grant No. 61365010.

References

1. Zhang, Z.F., Li, Q.D.: Summary of community question answering system. Comput. Sci. **37** (11), 19–23 (2011)
2. Yan, X., Fan, S.X.: Coarse grain question classification method for question answering community. Comput. Appl. Softw. **30**(1), 220–223 (2013)
3. Voorhees, E.M.: Overview of the TREC 2007 Question Answering Tack. In: TREC 2007, vol. 10(8), pp. 115–123. Gaithersburg, New York (2007)
4. Quoc, C., Le, V.: Learning to rank with nonsmooth cost functions. In: Proceedings of the Advances in Neural Information Processing Systems, vol. 19, pp. 193–200. Vancouver, Canada (2007)

5. Cao, Z., Qin, T., Liu, T.Y., et al.: Learning to rank: from pairwise approach to listwise approach. In: Proceedings of the 24th International Conference on Machine Learning, pp. 129–136. ACM, Lisboa, Portugal (2007)
6. Qin, T., Zhang, X.D., Tsai, M.F., et al.: Query-level loss functions for information retrieval. Inf. Process. Manag. **44**(2), 838–855 (2008)
7. Yu, G., Pei, Y.J., Zhu, Z.Y.: Research on text similarity based on semantic similarity of words. Comput. Eng. Des. **27**(2), 241–244 (2006)
8. Tian, Y.L., Zhao, W.: Word similarity calculation method based on synonyms. J. Jilin Univ. (Inf. Sci. Ed.) **28**(6), 603–604 (2010)
9. Liu, R.Y., Wang, L.F.: Keyword extraction algorithm based on semantic extension and lexical chain. Comput. Sci. **40**(12), 265–266 (2013)
10. Seung, H.S., Opper, M., Sompolinsky, H.: Query by committee. In: Proceedings of the Fifth Annual Workshop on Computational Learning Theory, pp. 287–294. ACM, New York, America (1992)
11. Mei, J.J., Zhu, Y.M., Gao, Y.Q.: Synonymy Thesaurus. Shanghai Lexicographical Publishing House, Shanghai (1993). pp. 106–108
12. Li, B., Gao, W.J., Qiu, X.P.: An answer ranking model based on syntax analysis and statistical method. J. Chin. Inf. **23**(2), 23–27 (2009)
13. Lian, X.: Research on some questions of community question answering system, pp. 2–3. School of Computer and Control Engineering, Nankai University, Tianjin (2014)

Mobile Cloud Platform: Architecture, Deployment and Big Data Applications

Mengchen Liu[1], Kai Lin[2(✉)], Jun Yang[1], Dengming Xiao[1], Yiming Miao[1], Lu Wang[1], Wei Li[1], Zeru Wei[1], and Jiayi Lu[1]

[1] Embedded and Pervasive Computing (EPIC) Lab,
Huazhong University of Science and Technology, Wuhan 430074, China
mengchenliu.cs@qq.com
[2] School of Computer Science and Technology,
Dalian University of Technology, Dalian, China
link@dlut.edu.cn

Abstract. With the rapid development of technology, mobile devices have become the basic necessities of life. Mobile devices have a great advantage of rapid calculation and Transmission and containing a variety of sensors. So we can distribute some computing tasks to our mobile devices. However, mobile devices still face a significant bottleneck. Such as the upper limit of computing power. Mobile devices will be inadequate when dealing with large-scale operations. Lack of storage capacity, mobile devices can not save a large amount of data. Small battery capacity, Equipment can not guarantee a long duration of working. In order to give the users a good experience, We need to use the resources of the mobile cloud platform to solve these problems. Mobile cloud platform has become the most essential facilities. The mobile cloud platform will not only consolidate resources and optimize computing power, but also serve as a processing platform with strong storage ability and decision-making capability. In such a strong demand, build a mobile cloud platform has become an indispensable thing.

Keywords: Mobile cloud platform · Smart clothing · Smart home

1   Introduction

Nowadays, a variety of new technologies, such as edge clouds, micro clouds and ad hoc cloudlet, have been derived from the mobile cloud [1,2]. These techniques are suitable for different computing tasks in different environment [3–5], such as in the vehicular ad-hoc networks [6] or the heterogeneous telematics [7], where the mobile cloud can be integrated with the vehicle-to-vehicle or vehicle-to-infrastructure communications to improve quality of service in sensing and sharing vehicular information. This paper will give some brief introduction to these technologies.

Mobile Edge Cloud (MEC) is needed when mobile devices have strict requirements for short latency and complex processing content [8,9]. We need to move

© ICST Institute for Computer Sciences, Social Informatics and Telecommunications Engineering 2018
J. Wan et al. (Eds.): CloudComp 2016, SPNCE 2016, LNICST 197, pp. 66–80, 2018.
https://doi.org/10.1007/978-3-319-69605-8_7

computing tasks to the wireless access point [10]. MEC will move the core function of the network to mobile device. The core functions and related applications deployed in the access side of the edge of the service. The edge cloud has the following characteristics: Localization, the edge cloud will be mounted on the access side of the task to the edge node, which greatly reduces the bandwidth of the backbone network traffic and avoids duplication of large amounts of data distribution [11–13]. It also saves a lot of network traffic. Low latency, when the 5G wireless communication network is proposed [14], the speed of data transmission data been greatly improved, which makes the traditional network architecture become a bottleneck in latency [15–20].

A cloud is a small, simple device near users in a space location that can download the data from the mobile cloud platform and process these data [21]. When finishes the job, the device sends the data back to Mobile cloud platform [22–24]. Users will not be aware of the whole process, but users can enjoy high-speed and low-latency services. These devices are collectively referred to as micro-clouds, which are generally at the edge of the network. Micro-cloud has the following characteristics: dynamic resource allocation, support for large-scale user-level computing, user rights, high confidentiality [25].

Ad hoc cloudlets are sub-classes of micro-clouds, which are the mobile devices consisted of all micro-clouds [26]. Such as a certain range of ten mobile phone, each phone uses D2D (Device-to-Device) Technology to carry out communication [27–33]. In this paper, the mobile cloud platform based on openstack is described [34,35].

2   Architecture of EPIC Mobile Cloud Platform

Mobile cloud platform in Embedded and Pervasive Computing (EPIC) Lab [36] is mainly to compensate for the lack of mobile computing power, responsible for receiving the instructions transmitted by the user and refers to these instructions to finish this task [19,37–39]. In order to achieve this goal, mobile cloud platform system architecture is designed for the following three parts, namely the interaction layer, management layer and virtual layer, as shown in Fig. 1 [40].

Interaction Layer: The interaction layer give a interface to interact with users, receive requests from users and send requests to control layer. And the mobile cloud platform transmits the HTTP respond to the user.

Control Layer: The management layer is responsible for processing the users' request, such as creating a virtual machine template, controlling workflow, loading balancing, etc. Control Layer is the most important part of the mobile cloud platform. In other words it is in charge of the whole network and computing resources of cloud platform.

Virtual Layer: The virtual layer consists of physical machines and virtual machines, which compose the compute nodes or storage nodes to serve the management layer. The mobile cloud platform handles web services and distributed

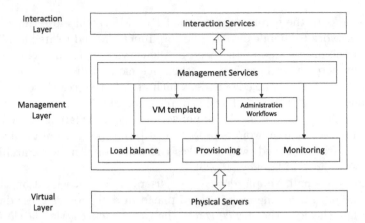

Fig. 1. System architecture

computing tasks. It also has the following characteristics: high performance, scalability, and reliability. It uses high-performance personal computers to meet the requirements of computing speed. The co-operation of hardware and software greatly improves work efficiency. Due to the mobile cloud platform architecture design, low coupling makes it easy to extend the other parts of the cloud platform. Mobile cloud platform architecture ensures its reliability and it can automatically make remedies for the failure.

3   Deployment Instructions of Cloud Platform

The key technologies mobile cloud platform uses are shown in Fig. 2.

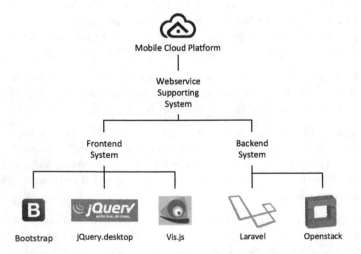

Fig. 2. Key technology

3.1   Build Web Service

Webservice is the foundation of the mobile cloud platform, so the first step in building a mobile cloud platform is to create a webservice. We determine to use the HTTP protocol to transfer data and encapsulate the data in XML format. We choice apache to build up our server.

3.2   Front-End Structures

We select the Bootstrap in our front-end technology, which is one of the most popular front-end frameworks currently. Bootstrap uses HTML, CSS, javascript programming language. It is simple and flexible, making Web development more efficient. We've added other technologies to this framework to make it easier for users to interact with our platform.

3.3   Back-End Structures

Laravel is a Value elegance, simplicity, and readability PHP Web development framework. This technology draws on the advantages of java and other frameworks and has great scalability and scalability. Laravel code is one of the most popular back-end technology. Besides Laraval, we also add openstack technology in our platform. When user choose a certain function, the platform will call the relevant openstack API to fulfil the task.

3.4   Openstack Technology

The core technology of cloud platform is openstack. This technology was developed by NASA and Rackspace. This project consists of multiple modules and can be seen as the cloud operation system of mobile platform. The greatest advantage of openstack is that it can create public and private clouds fast and it provides infrastructure as a service (IaaS) solution. Openstack is one of the best technique to build mobile cloud platform. Since the Openstack technology has been widespread all over the world, hundreds of communities or organizations to contribute to its source code, which makes this technology developed rapidly. OpenStack technology is mainly written in Python. Being modular makes Openstack has the characteristics of decoupling and excellent compatibility.

OpenStack technology can be divided into multiple components, and each component has its aliases. Such as Horizon is the module to manage the interactive interface. Nova is the module to control computing resource, Keystone is in charge of authentication. What's more, we have mirror service components Glance and storage components swift. Horizon components which is based on web framework Django development of the Web interface, is responsible for converting the user's requests to the command for virtual machine. Nova is the core modules of Openstack. Nova component can create, authenticate, schedule and terminate virtual machines. Message Queue is a module for communication between OpenStack nodes, mainly based on AMQP implementation.

Nova uses an asynchronous way to respond to user requests in order to prevent users from waiting too long. Nova-Compute is used to manage the lifecycle of virtual machine instances. An instance is generally a virtual machine. When Nova-Compute receive the creation, termination and other operation commands. It will call the libvirt API to process this command and return the results from the message queue. Nova-Network primarily provides network connectivity services for virtual machine instances. Network traffic and communication between virtual machines are handled by this module. Nova-Network's primary role is to assign an IP address to a virtual machine instance, configure VLANs and security groups. Nova-Scheduler is a kind of daemon in the Nova component. It begins to run when the cloud platform starts.

The keyStone component provides authentication and service tokens for users and virtual machines. In this openstack design, Keystone provides authentication and access policy services for all OpenStack components. It relies on its own REST system. When users provide their own authentication information to OpenStack [41,42], Keystone will match this information with the information in the database. If the authentication passes, Keystone will return a unique token to the user. This token can be used by the user as authentication information for subsequent sending of an operation request to OpenStack.

Mirror Components Glance is primarily responsible for storing and managing the virtual machine's operating system image, which is used when the virtual machine is created. Glance provides a standard REST interface through which you can query mirror-related information stored on different devices.

The storage component swift is responsible for object storage management and similarly there are cinder components (block stores) for local storage and network storage.

Figure 3 (http://www.dataguru.cn/article-8860-1.html) shows the architecture of openstack modules.

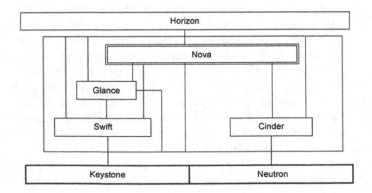

Fig. 3. Openstack module architecture

3.5   The Configuration of Openstack

We build openstack on Inspur machine. We use two compute nodes, one control node and one network node. Figure 4 show the picture of Inspur machine.

Fig. 4. Picture of Inspur machine

4   Vis.js

4.1   Introduction of Requirements

After deploying the openstack component on the mobile cloud platform, we can begin to build our own cloud host. The most direct method is to use the corresponding command to call the relevant functions, but this is very cumbersome for beginners. We need a very intuitive and convenient way to complete the process of creating a virtual machine. Openstack components in the dashborad module, which is responsible for providing a graphical user-friendly interface. So we also want to add a similar function in the cloud platform and make the process of deploying network and virtual machine become an extremely simple step, which is the important reason why we use vis.js library.

Vis.js is a browser-based dynamic visual library in the JavaScript library that makes it easy to process multiple types of data. The library is mainly divided into several sections: First, easily to draw graph of key-data value pairs.

You can flexibly add or delete nodes in the graph; Second, It is easy to facilitate the display of different types of time axis data. It can complete interactive mobile, zoom and other functions; Third, you can complete the graphics based on node and edge network.

4.2 Features in the Cloud Platform

To simplify the configuration procedure of virtual machine, we use the graphical operations to complete these step, because the use of mobile cloud platform to create a virtual machine in the process needs to customize the network parameters. First of all, in the process of drawing a topology network, we need operations of adding or deleting nodes which represents for deploying routers, switches and network. We need to connect nodes, such as connecting the nodes among routers, switches and virtual machines. Vis.js can save the user-selected router, switch, and virtual machine configuration attributes in the form of nodes. When a user connects two nodes, you can only add a edge in the network graph and save the data (format such as starting node number, ending node number). After completing the virtual machine creation operation, the cloud platform will convert the design scheme to the corresponding json data (including node attributes and connection edge properties) and send data to the back-end server, the data processing into openstack corresponding command, call the appropriate API to complete the operation. The use of vis.js technology greatly simplifies the complex operation of the command line, which also improves the user experience. Figure 5 shows the interface of the deployment of the virtual machine design, respectively, six virtual machines, three switches and a router.

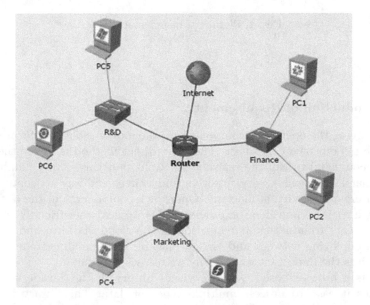

Fig. 5. Topology network example diagram

5   Introduction to Jquery.desktop

In order to give users a better experience, we use the web desktop components jQuery desktop in our cloud platform. The plug-in will make cloud platform interface similar to the graphical user interface of operating system. The appearance of our website becomes the desktop of our operation system. Each desktop icons represent a link to a webpage. In the realization of the mobile cloud platform, An desktop icon represents a specific project, you can double-click the icon to enter the specific project to view the data or complete some specified operation. jQuery desktop provides us with a similar windows desktop web interface, which will bring us a new experience of browsing web page. The jQuery desktop consists of three parts, the top menu, the desktop section, and the bottom menu. Which uses the c-z-index attribute to locate the elements of different levels, Fig. 6 is the screenshot of our platform, the upper left corner of the three icons represent three different operations. Figure 7 shows that the first step of building a

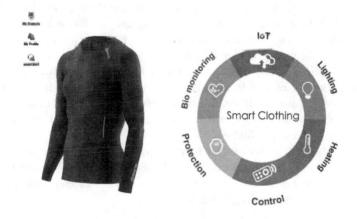

Fig. 6. The interface of mobile cloud platform

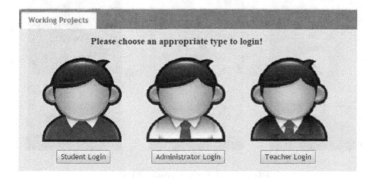

Fig. 7. Illustration of various data access priority for differentiated users

virtual machine. Each button represents the different type of virtual machine. Student can only set up the VM of default setting and the Administrator can custom the virtual machine configuration [43,44].

6 Related Projects

The lab relies on the mobile cloud platform to achieve two specific applications, namely Smart Home 2.0 and smart Clothing system. We will give a detailed description of the implementation of these two projects.

6.1 Smart Clothing System

Smart clothing integrates various types of physiological sensors to collect important physiological indicators of the human body [45,46]. Including body temperature, respiration, blood oxygen, heart rate and ECG and other data. The project uses cloud platform to store these physiological data while using cloud computing and machine learning algorithm to analyze these physiological data to obtain valuable information [47]. Smart clothing can be divided into three components: smart clothing, hardware and software communications systems and cloud platform. The cloud platform in this project has a pivotal role in providing the vast majority of the computing, storage and analysis functions [48–50]. The clothing consists of the textile dry electrode, electrode signal conduction buttons, flexible conductive fiber and an external wireless communication with the ECG processing module, which is an essential component for healtchcare Cyber-Physical systems [51,52].

The cloud platform provides the services and related functionality required for the entire project. The platform is the basis for the entire project. Android mobile APP is the bridge to connect these project services and users. APP terminal interface shown in Fig. 8 [53,54].

Fig. 8. GUI on mobile APP

6.2   Smart Home 2.0

Figure 9 shows the design framework of project Smart Home 2.0 [55,56]. The project has designed a complete smart farming solution, which realizes the independent design of farm environmental monitoring intelligent equipment, the data support service of cloud platform, the function of web terminal and android terminal display. At the same time, the project uses two real-world farming data as the reference to simulate the massive data. We figure out the large data analysis method based on Hadoop + Mahout to provides an intelligent data analysis solution for the plant growth related indicator data (temperature, Light intensity and air). Based on the analysis results, the author can give some suggestions for planting [57].

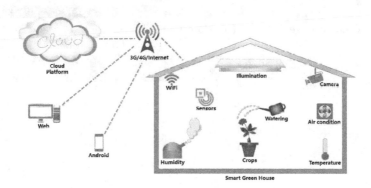

Fig. 9. Deployment diagram

The Smart Farming project provides two access methods: Web and Android. Figure 10(a) shows the registration interface. New user needs to register, the old user enters the user name and password to complete the login, login successfully entered the interface Fig. 10(b), which is the relevant core interface. The interface displays the user-managed device. Click on the device to enter interface Fig. 10(c). The interface displays the real-time data of the farm monitored by the device. The data processing results will show in the website like Fig. 10(d). It display the indicator data in a period of time corresponding to the historical data records [58].

6.3   The Role of Cloud Platform in the Projects

The cloud platform uses the on-demand method to distribute the computing, storage, and network resources to the various projects [59]. By virtualizing the hardware resources, the cloud platform can quickly and easily allocate resources independently for each project. At the same time the cloud platform achieve the dynamic allocation of resources. It can easily according to the actual operation to upgrade and expansion.

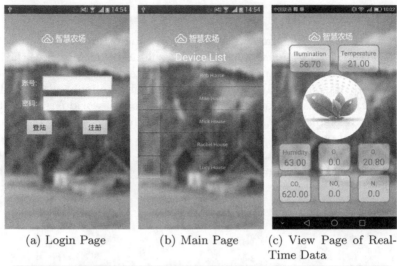

(a) Login Page   (b) Main Page   (c) View Page of Real-
                                                   Time Data

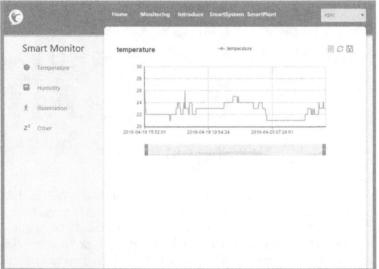

(d) View Page of History Data

Fig. 10. Android GUI and web interface

7   Machine Learning Algorithm Used in the Mobile Cloud Platform

The mobile cloud platform help client use programs and data in the cloud host to fulfil the tasks such as data mining, data analysis or machine learning [60, 61]. In the machine learning aspects of the cloud platform can provide infrastructure support. In the mobile cloud platform, you can build a virtual machine using the

Linux operating system. And this operating system image contains mapreduce, Hadoop, spark and other large data processing software. The user can write the corresponding data analysis program. It also provide the function to upload the information to the virtual machine to complete the job. Upload procedures will be strong security and strictly encrypted.

8 Conclusion

This paper introduces the key technologies of mobile cloud platform and analyzes the importance of building cloud platform. Give a detailed description of the internal structure of the cloud platform. And discuss about the specific process of building a mobile cloud platform step by step, introduce the key technology of cloud platform and other front-end technology. Finally, combined with the smart clothing project and smart farming project, it describes the important role the cloud platform plays.

Acknowledgement. This work was supported by the National Natural Science Foundation of China under grant No. 61103234 and No. 61272417, China Scholarship Council, and the Fundamental Research Funds for the Central Universities under grant No. DUT16QY18.

References

1. Chen, M., Zhang, Y., Hu, L., Taleb, T., Sheng, Z.: Cloud-based wireless network: virtualized, reconfigurable, smart wireless network to enable 5G technologies. Mob. Netw. Appl. **20**(6), 704–712 (2015)
2. He, K., Chen, J., Du, R., Wu, Q., Xue, G., Zhang, X.: DeyPoS: deduplicatable dynamic proof of storage for multi-user environments. IEEE Trans. Comput. **65**, 3631–3645 (2016)
3. Rahimi, M.R., Ren, J., Liu, C.H., Vasilakos, A.V., Venkatasubramanian, N.: Mobile cloud computing: a survey, state of art and future directions. Mob. Netw. Appl. **19**(2), 133–143 (2014)
4. Fortino, G., Trunfio, P.: Internet of Things Based on Smart Objects, Technology, Middleware and Applications. Springer, Heidelberg (2014). ISBN 978-3-319-00490-7
5. Taleb, T., Ksentini, A., Frangoudis, P.: Follow-me cloud: when cloud services follow mobile users. IEEE Trans. Cloud Comput. 1 (2016)
6. Tian, D., Zhou, J., Wang, Y., Zhang, G., Xia, H.: An adaptive vehicular epidemic routing method based on attractor selection model. Ad Hoc Netw. **36**(P2), 465–481 (2015)
7. Tian, D., Zhou, J., Wang, Y., Lu, Y.: A dynamic and self-adaptive network selection method for multimode communications in heterogeneous vehicular telematics. IEEE Trans. Intell. Transp. Syst. **16**(6), 3033–3049 (2015)
8. Lei, L., Zhong, Z., Zheng, K., Chen, J., Meng, H.: Challenges on wireless heterogeneous networks for mobile cloud computing. IEEE Wirel. Commun. **20**(3), 34–44 (2013)

9. Liu, F., Shu, P., Jin, H., Ding, L., Yu, J., Niu, D., Li, B.: Gearing resource-poor mobile devices with powerful clouds: architectures, challenges, and applications. IEEE Wirel. Commun. **20**(3), 14–22 (2013)

10. Chen, J., He, K., Yuan, Q., Xue, G., Du, R., Wang, L.: Batch identification game model for invalid signatures in wireless mobile networks. **PP**(99), 1 (2016)

11. Chen, J., He, K., Du, R., Zheng, M., Xiang, Y., Yuan, Q.: Dominating set and network coding-based routing in wireless mesh networks. IEEE Trans. Parallel Distrib. Syst. **26**(2), 423–433 (2015)

12. Fortino, G., Russo, W.: Using P2P, grid and agent technologies for the development of content distribution networks. Future Gener. Comput. Syst. **24**(3), 180–190 (2008)

13. Lin, K., Chen, M., Deng, J., Hassan, M.M.: Enhanced fingerprinting and trajectory prediction for IoT localization in smart buildings. IEEE Trans. Autom. Sci. Eng. **13**(3), 1–14 (2016)

14. Taleb, T., Ksentini, A., Sericola, B.: On service resilience in cloud-native 5G mobile systems. IEEE J. Sel. Areas Commun. **34**(3), 483–496 (2016)

15. Qiu, M., Chen, Z., Ming, Z., Qin, X.: Energy-aware data allocation with hybrid memory for mobile cloud systems. IEEE Syst. J. **11**, 1–10 (2014)

16. Liu, C.H., Fan, J.: Scalable and efficient diagnosis for 5G data center network traffic. IEEE Access **2**, 841–855 (2014)

17. Liu, C.H., Kind, A., Vasilakos, A.V.: Sketching the data center network traffic. IEEE Netw. **27**(4), 33–39 (2013)

18. Liu, C.H., Kind, A., Liu, T.: Summarizing data center network traffic by partitioned conservative update. IEEE Commun. Lett. **17**(11), 2168–2171 (2013)

19. Lin, K., Wang, W., Wang, X., Ji, W.: QoE-driven spectrum assignment for 5G wireless networks using SDR. IEEE Wirel. Commun. **22**(6), 48–55 (2015)

20. Zheng, K., Zhao, L., Mei, J., Shao, B., Xiang, W., Hanzo, L.: Survey of large-scale MIMO systems. IEEE Commun. Surv. Tutorials **17**, 1738–1760 (2015)

21. Lin, K., Song, J., Luo, J., Ji, W., Hossain, M.S., Ghoneim, A.: GVT: green video transmission in the mobile cloud networks. IEEE Trans. Circ. Syst. Video Technol. **27**, 159–169 (2016)

22. Ksentini, A., Taleb, T., Messaoudi, F.: A LISP-based implementation of follow me cloud. IEEE Access **2**, 1340–1347 (2014)

23. Taleb, T., Ksentini, A.: An analytical model for follow me cloud (2013)

24. Ksentini, A., Taleb, T., Chen, M.: A Markov decision process-based service migration procedure for follow me cloud (2014)

25. Shu, P., Liu, F., Jin, H., Chen, M., Wen, F., Qu, Y.: eTime: energy-efficient transmission between cloud and mobile devices. In: Proceedings - IEEE INFOCOM, vol. 12, no. 11, pp. 195–199 (2013)

26. Chen, M., Zhang, Y., Li, Y., Mao, S.: EMC: emotion-aware mobile cloud computing in 5G. IEEE Netw. **29**(2), 32–38 (2015)

27. Sheng, Z., Fan, J., Liu, C.H., Leung, V.C.M., Liu, X., Leung, K.K.: Energy-efficient relay selection for cooperative relaying in wireless multimedia networks. IEEE Trans. Veh. Technol. **64**(3), 1156–1170 (2015)

28. Liu, C.H., Leung, K.K., Gkelias, A.: A generic admission-control methodology for packet networks. IEEE Trans. Wireless Commun. **13**(2), 604–617 (2014)

29. Gkelias, A., Boccardi, F., Liu, C.H., Leung, K.K.: MIMO routing with QoS provisioning. In: International Symposium on Wireless Pervasive Computing, pp. 46–50 (2008)

30. Aloi, G., Caliciuri, G., Fortino, G., Gravina, R., Pace, P., Russo, W., Savaglio, C.: Enabling IoT interoperability through opportunistic smartphone-based mobile gateways. J. Netw. Comput. Appl. (2016)
31. Lei, L., Kuang, Y., Cheng, N., Shen, X.: Delay-optimal dynamic mode selection and resource allocation in device-to-device communications part II: practical algorithm. IEEE Trans. Veh. Technol. **65**(5), 1 (2015)
32. Taleb, T., Ksentini, A., Kobbane, A.: Lightweight mobile core networks for machine type communications. IEEE Access **2**, 1128–1137 (2014)
33. Taleb, T., Ksentini, A., Chen, M., Jantti, R.: Coping with emerging mobile social media applications through dynamic service function chaining. IEEE Trans. Wireless Commun. **15**(4), 1 (2015)
34. Chen, M., Hao, Y., Lai, C.-F., Wu, D., Li, Y., Hwang, K.: Opportunistic workflow scheduling over co-located clouds in mobile environment. IEEE (2016). https://doi.org/10.1109/TSC.2016.2589247
35. Gai, K., Qiu, M., Zhao, H., Tao, L., Zong, Z.: Dynamic energy-aware cloudlet-based mobile cloud computing model for green computing. J. Netw. Comput. Appl. **59**(C), 46–54 (2015)
36. EPIC. http://epic.hust.edu.cn
37. Qiu, M., Ming, Z., Li, J., Gai, K., Zong, Z.: Phase-change memory optimization for green cloud with genetic algorithm. IEEE Trans. Comput. **64**(12), 1 (2015)
38. Liu, F., Shu, P., Lui, J.C.S.: AppATP: an energy conserving adaptive mobile cloud transmission protocol. IEEE Trans. Comput. **64**(11), 3051–3063 (2015)
39. Zhang, T., Zhang, X, Liu, F., Leng, H., Yu, Q., Liang, G.: eTrain: making wasted energy useful by utilizing heartbeats for mobile data transmissions, pp. 113–122 (2015)
40. Pena, P.A., Sarkar, D., Maheshwari, P.: A big-data centric framework for smart systems in the world of internet of everything. In: 2015 International Conference on Computational Science and Computational Intelligence (CSCI), pp. 306–311. IEEE (2015)
41. Xu, J., Shi, M., Chen, C., Zhang, Z., Fu, J., Liu, C.H.: ZQL: a unified middleware bridging both relational and NoSQL databases. In: 2016 IEEE 14th International Conference on Dependable, Autonomic and Secure Computing, 14th International Conference on Pervasive Intelligence and Computing, 2nd International Conference on Big Data Intelligence and Computing and Cyber Science and Technology Congress (DASC/PiCom/DataCom/CyberSciTech) (2016)
42. Wu, C., Fu, J., Zhang, Z., Liu, C.H.: Efficient on/off-line query pre-processing for telecom social streaming data. In: 2016 IEEE 14th International Conference on Dependable, Autonomic and Secure Computing, 14th International Conference on Pervasive Intelligence and Computing, 2nd International Conference on Big Data Intelligence and Computing and Cyber Science and Technology Congress (DASC/PiCom/DataCom/CyberSciTech) (2016)
43. Chen, M., Qian, Y., Chen, J., Hwang, K., Mao, S., Hu, L.: Privacy protection and intrusion avoidance for cloudlet-based medical data sharing. IEEE Trans. Cloud Comput. (2016)
44. Li, Y., Dai, W., Ming, Z., Qiu, M.: Privacy protection for preventing data over-collection in smart city. IEEE Trans. Comput. **65**(5), 1 (2015)
45. Chen, M., Zhang, Y., Li, Y., Hassan, M., Alamri, A.: AIWAC: affective interaction through wearable computing and cloud technology. IEEE Wirel. Commun. **22**(1), 20–27 (2015)
46. Wan, J., Zou, C., Ullah, S., Lai, C.F., Zhou, M., Wang, X.: Cloud-enabled wireless body area networks for pervasive healthcare. IEEE Netw. **27**(5), 56–61 (2013)

47. Chen, M., Ma, Y., Hao, Y., Li, Y., Wu, D., Zhang, Y., Song, E.: CP-Robot: cloud-assisted pillow robot for emotion sensing and interaction. In: Wan, J., Humar, I., Zhang, D. (eds.) Industrial IoT 2016. LNICSSITE, vol. 173, pp. 81–93. Springer, Cham (2016). https://doi.org/10.1007/978-3-319-44350-8_9

48. Chen, M., Qian, Y., Mao, S., Tang, W., Yang, X.: Software-defined mobile networks security. Mob. Netw. Appl. **21**, 729–743 (2016)

49. Fortino, G., Giannantonio, R., Gravina, R., Kuryloski, P.: Enabling effective programming and flexible management of efficient body sensor network applications. IEEE Trans. Hum.-Mach. Syst. **43**(1), 115–133 (2013)

50. Fortino, G., Galzarano, S., Gravina, R., Li, W.: A framework for collaborative computing and multi-sensor data fusion in body sensor networks. Inf. Fusion **22**, 50–70 (2014)

51. Zhang, Y.: GroRec: a group-centric intelligent recommender system integrating social, mobile and big data technologies. IEEE Trans. Serv. Comput. **9**, 786–795 (2016)

52. Zhang, Y., Chen, M., Huang, D., Wu, D., Li, Y.: iDoctor: personalized and professionalized medical recommendations based on hybrid matrix factorization. Future Gener. Comput. Syst. **66**, 30–35 (2016)

53. Chen, M., Hao, Y., Mao, S., Wu, D., Zhou, Y.: User intent-oriented video QoE with emotion detection networking. In: IEEE Globelcom, pp. 1552–1559 (2016, accept)

54. Gao, G., Liu, C.H., Chen, M., Guo, S.: Cloud-based video actor identification with batch-orthogonal local-sensitive hashing and sparse representation. IEEE Trans. Multimedia **18**, 1749–1761 (2016)

55. Cicirelli, F., Fortino, G., Giordano, A., Guerrieri, A., Spezzano, G., Vinci, A.: On the design of smart homes: a framework for activity recognition in home environment. J. Med. Syst. **40**(9), 1–17 (2016)

56. Fortino, G., Guerrieri, A., O'Hare, G.M.P., Ruzzelli, A.: A flexible building management framework based on wireless sensor and actuator networks. J. Netw. Comput. Appl. **35**(6), 1934–1952 (2012)

57. Zhang, Y., Chen, M., Mao, S., Hu, L., Leung, V.C.: Cap: community activity prediction based on big data analysis. IEEE Netw. **28**(4), 52–57 (2014)

58. Wenbo, Y., Quanyu, W., Zhenwei, G.: Smart home implementation based on internet and WiFi technology. In: 2015 34th Chinese Control Conference (CCC), pp. 9072–9077. IEEE (2015)

59. Shu, Z., Wan, J., Zhang, D., Li, D.: Cloud-integrated cyber-physical systems for complex industrial applications. Mob. Netw. Appl. **21**(5), 865–878 (2016)

60. Liu, C.H., Zhang, Z., Chen, M.: Personalized multimedia recommendations for cloud-integrated cyber-physical systems. IEEE Syst. J. **11**, 106–117 (2015)

61. Yuan, W., Deng, P., Taleb, T., Wan, J.: An unlicensed taxi identification model based on big data analysis. IEEE Trans. Intell. Transp. Syst. **17**(6), 1–11 (2016)

Research on Algorithm and Model of Hand Gestures Recognition Based on HMM

Junhui Liu[1,2(✉)], Yun Liao[1,2], Zhenli He[1,2], and Yu Yang[1,2]

[1] School of Software, Yunnan University, Kunming 650091, Yunnan, China
HanksLau@gmail.com
[2] School of Informatics, Yunnan University of Finance and Economics,
Kunming 650221, China

Abstract. Human computer interaction is one of the key points in the competition of information industry in the world, all countries in the world put the human-computer interaction as a key technology to study. Butler Lampson, ACM Turing Award winner in 1992 and Microsoft Research Institute chief software engineer pointed out that the computer has three functions in the "21st century computing research" report. The first is simulation; the second is that the computer can help people to communicate; the third is interaction, that is, to communicate with the real world. Human-computer interaction is an important field of computer research, and hand gestures recognition is a key technology in this field. The key of gesture recognition is the feature extraction and the establishment of hand recognition model. It can accurately identify the various kinds of deformation. HMM method has a flexible and efficient training and recognition algorithm, if the system needs to add a new gesture, just need to train the gesture of the sample set can be; If a gesture is not needed, just delete the corresponding HMM algorithm of the gesture, HMM has a strong expansion. Compared with DTW and other methods, HMM in speech recognition, gesture recognition, the recognition effect is better. In this paper, the HMM algorithm is used to identify the typical gestures, got very good recognition effect.

Keywords: Human-computer interaction · Hand gestures recognition · The feature extraction · HMM

1 Introduction

Since the birth of the first computer, how to effectively carry on the human-computer interaction has been the focus of the computer industry and the academic research. Human computer interaction (HCI) is research between the human and the computer through communication mutual understanding and communication, in the maximum extent for people to carry out the information management, service and processing functions, the computer will become the real people work and learning assistant of a science and technology. That enables computer technology to become an assistant to people's work and study. Human-computer interaction technology [1, 2] is a focus of competition in the current information industry, Human-computer interaction is an important field of computer research, and the vision based gesture recognition

© ICST Institute for Computer Sciences, Social Informatics and Telecommunications Engineering 2018
J. Wan et al. (Eds.): CloudComp 2016, SPNCE 2016, LNICST 197, pp. 81–90, 2018.
https://doi.org/10.1007/978-3-319-69605-8_8

technology [3, 4] is a key technology in the field of human-computer interaction and has many typical applications, which has become a hot research topic at home and abroad.

In this paper, in the natural human-computer interaction system, the related research is carried out for the human hand gesture recognition, and the relevant algorithms are proposed to extract the feature of the gesture, and the dynamic gesture recognition model is established, to below will be related to this description.

2 Static Hand Gesture Feature Extraction

2.1 Hand Model

Hand model [5] is particularly important for human-computer interaction system based on finger interaction, and the selection hand model is closely related to the task to be processed by the human computer interaction system. Hand models can be very simple, we can use the image gradient direction histogram, on a few simple static hand gestures recognition. The hand model may also be very complex, such as the creation of a complex 3D gesture model as the main way of information interaction in virtual reality human-computer interaction system. 3D gesture model is able to accurately describe the complex state of the hand, at the same time, can identify the vast majority of the hand input information, however, to obtain accurate 3D hand model is not realistic through a single common camera. Although the approximate 3D model of the hand can be obtained to some extent, the type of hand model and the environment have special requirements, so it does not have the practical application value.

Figure 1 shows the 2D model of the hand, model A is composed of two parts of finger and palm. Only take the finger and palm connected joints into consideration, ignore the influence of each joint of the chiral internal finger. Therefore, in this model, the finger only exists, does not exist, and the finger points to several state information, which greatly reduces the complexity of the hand model, and emphasizes the importance of finger pointing. In this paper, the model is improved, and the model B in Fig. 1 is formed. Compared with model A, model B in the palm part in addition to the palm area P description, more focus on the palm of the center of gravity G. In the finger part, the model B emphasizes the position of F, and the position relationship between F and G.

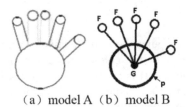

(a) model A (b) model B

Fig. 1. The 2D model of the hand

According to the model B, The premise of obtaining the position of the fingertip is to find the center of gravity of the palm G. If the center of gravity of the G can be found through the fingertip and the location of the center of gravity G to determine the location of the fingertip. Therefore find the palm center of gravity G is the use of the premise and the key of the model.

2.2 Palm Center of Gravity Extraction

The extraction of the palm center of gravity G is the premise and key of the algorithm. Only with relatively accurate the palm center of gravity is possible to obtain accurate fingertip position. The usual practice of obtaining the palm center of gravity is to calculate the center of gravity of the entire hand. And it is known that the approximate location of the center of gravity palm. This method is only applicable to situations that have no fingers or only one finger, as shown in Fig. 2(a). If five fingers are stretched out, the palm center of gravity position obtained by this method will seriously deviate from the true position. As shown in Fig. 2(b).

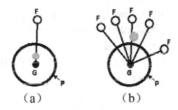

Fig. 2. Wrong position of center of gravity

By setting a search rectangle on the periphery of the hand, then calculate the distance between each pixel in the area of the hand to the search rectangle, and the distance between each pixel and the largest is the center of gravity of the palm. The method relies heavily on the search rectangle of the hand, and it is difficult to accurately locate the center of the palm.

In order to obtain the accurate palm center of gravity, the extended finger must be removed; otherwise the finger will have an impact on the calculation of the palm center of gravity. In this paper, a method of palm center of gravity extraction based on distance transform is proposed.

2.3 Palm Center of Gravity Searching Algorithm Based on Distance Transform

The distance transform of image is defined as a new image, the image pixel value of each output is set to input pixel 0 pixel in the recent distance. According to the different ways of calculating distance, there are two ways of distance transformation. Approximate template method and Euclidean distance method.

The approximate template method was first proposed by Rosenfeld. The basic idea is to use a template to calculate the distance between a point in the image and the last 0 pixels outside the image, each pixel values in the template is the approximate distances from the center of the template of Euclidean distance. As shown in Fig. 3.

4.5	4	3.5	3	3.5	4	4.5
4	3	2.5	2	2.5	3	4
3.5	2.5	1.5	1	1.5	2.5	3.5
3	2	1	0	1	2	3
3.5	2.5	1.5	1	1.5	2.5	3.5
4	3	2.5	2	2.5	3	4
4.5	4	3.5	3	3.5	4	4.5

Fig. 3. Approximate template method

Figure 4 is the result of the distance transform and binary conversion processing. Where the Fig. 4(a) is the original binary conversion image of palm, Fig. 4(b) is the palm part of binary conversion image. After two values of the distance image, not only filter the finger part, but also filter out the edge of the palm. However, because each direction filters edge pixels are basically the same, so this does not affect to the center of the palm computing. After obtaining the binary conversion image of the palm area. Through the 0- and 1-order image moments can calculate the palm center of gravity. The calculation formula is as follows.

$$MM_{00} = \sum_i \sum_j I(i,j) \tag{1}$$

$$MM_{10} = \sum_i \sum_j iI(i,j) \tag{2}$$

$$MM_{01} = \sum_i \sum_j jI(i,j) \tag{3}$$

$$i_c = \frac{MM_{10}}{MM_{00}}, j_c = \frac{MM_{01}}{MM_{00}} \tag{4}$$

where $I(i,j)$ represents the two value of the image coordinates of the pixel value of (i,j), (i_c,j_c) represents the image center of gravity. Palm center of gravity search algorithm based on distance transform described in detail as shown in Table 1.

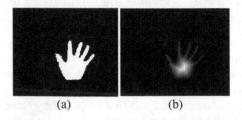
(a)   (b)

Fig. 4. Distance transformation and binary conversion processing result

Table 1. Palm center of gravity search algorithm based on distance transform

Step	Content
Step1	According to color and background color difference detection algorithm, get the binary conversion image of the palm
Step2	The distance transform is performed on the binary conversion image to obtain the result of distance transform
Step3	According to the results of the binary conversion distance transform, the palm area is obtained
Step4	According to: $i_c = \frac{MM_{10}}{MM_{00}}$, $j_c = \frac{MM_{01}}{MM_{00}}$ calculating the center of gravity of the binary conversion image in the palm region

Figure 5 is the center of gravity according to Table 1 based on distance transform algorithm. The white area in the figure is the area of the hand, the black spot in the white area is the center of the palm of the hand. Figure 5(a) is the center of gravity when the hand is clenched into a fist; Fig. 5(b) is the center of gravity when the index finger extended; Fig. 5(c) is the center of gravity when the five fingers extended. The results show that the palm center-of-gravity position can be measured accurately, and it was no relation with the state of whether to open the palm and how much the finger is opening in this algorithm. Then, the fingertips position can be queried based on position relationship between fingertips and the palm center-of-gravity.

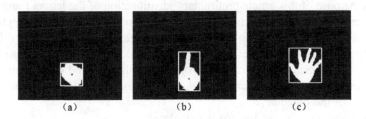

(a)   (b)   (c)

Fig. 5. Calculation results of palm center of gravity

3 Dynamic Gesture Feature Extraction

Dynamic gesture recognition technology [6–8] is mainly divided into three categories: a template-based technology, probabilistic techniques and techniques based on data classification techniques. There are techniques based on probability and statistics, such as hidden Markov model, Dynamic Bayesian network and Conditional Random Fields (CRFs) and other methods; Based on data classification technology with neural network, support vector machine (SVM) and Adaboosts, etc.

Template Matching is the simplest method of gesture recognition, by comparing the input gesture with the pre-stored Template similarity to recognize hand gestures. When dynamic gesture recognition template matching method in a complex background, this method cannot solve the problem of gesture difference in time and cannot accurately achieve real-time multi-gesture recognition. Training with the HMM method gestures model [9–11], each gesture with a HMM model for training. The advantage of this method is to provide time scale deformation, can more accurately identify gestures of deformation, a flexible and efficient training and recognition algorithm. In this paper, HMM algorithm is adopted to recognize typical gestures, got very good recognition effect.

Dynamic posture gesture not only contains information about each point in time, as well as a gesture of trajectory information [12]. In human-computer interaction, the dynamic gesture can be more effectively and directly pass the user's intent. Gesture is a dynamic process of change in the posture of time sequence, involving time and space context, dynamic gesture recognition not only to eliminate the differences in space, but also to eliminate gestures duration differences.

Gesture trajectory [13] commonly used features such as location, direction angle and the rate of movement and so on. These three features were extracted and their corresponding recognition rates were compared and found that the trajectory identification, direction angle of the greatest contribution to the recognition rate. Direction angle between $P_1(x_1, y_1)$ and $P_2(x_2, y_2)$ is defined as follows:

$$\varphi(P_1, P_2) = \begin{cases} \arctan\left(\frac{y_2-y_1}{x_2-x_1}\right) + \pi \; if \; x_2 - x_1 < 0 \\ \arctan\left(\frac{y_2-y_1}{x_2-x_1}\right) + 2\pi \; elseif \; y_2 - y_1 < 0 \\ \arctan\left(\frac{y_2-y_1}{x_2-x_1}\right) \; otherwise \end{cases} \tag{5}$$

For the purpose of this article preliminary identification of the letters I and J the 26 kinds of gestures, due to the characteristics of sequence similarity is higher, it is difficult to distinguish. In order to make a variety of gestures characteristic differences between the sequences as large as possible, and in order to better distinguish between recognition in full gesture detection below complete sequence and subsequence. In this paper, we choose the direction angle of the center point and the center point as the characteristic of the trajectory.

The direction angle using Eq. (6) is calculated:

$$\varphi 1_t = \varphi(P_c, P_t), \; (t = 1, 2, \ldots, T) \tag{6}$$

Among them, T represents the length of the hand gesture trajectory, $P_t(x_y, y_t)$ corresponding to the X axis and the Y axis coordinates of the T moments, which $P_c(x_c, y_c)$ represent the center point coordinates of the centroid of all gestures in a certain trajectory:

$$(X_c, Y_c) = \frac{1}{T} \left(\sum_{t=1}^{T} x_t, \sum_{t=1}^{T} y_t \right) \tag{7}$$

For the extraction of the direction angle, this paper uses 16 direction chain code to change $\varphi 1_t$ to be quantized to 16 levels, the quantization result is $\frac{\varphi 1_t * 16 + \pi}{2 * \pi} \% 16$, finally gets the discrete characteristic vector, as the HMM input.

4   Establish HMM Model

This paper defines the 26 gestures for identification Arabic Numbers from A to Z which are entered by users. Arabic Numbers from A to Z represent the 26 gestures. In each of gestures, 160 samples are collected. In experimenting, 80 samples are selected as training samples, and the remaining samples as test samples. 26 HMM models, from A-HMM to Z-HMM, will be established for the 26 gestures to test training samples and test samples, respectively.

HMM learning problem is the training process of the HMM model, which is a constantly re-evaluating process of model parameter through given sample observation sequences [14]. The parameters $\lambda = (A, B, \pi)$ of the HMM model will be constantly adjusted to train a most suitable model for sample set when $P(O|\lambda)$, probability of observation sequence O presence, reached its maximum. According to the definition of the forward variable $\alpha_t(i)$ and the backward variable $\beta_t(i)$, the $P(O|\lambda)$ can be easily calculated:

$$P(O|\lambda) = \sum_{i=1}^{N} \sum_{j=1}^{N} \alpha_t(i).\alpha_{ij}.b_j(o_{t+1}).\beta_{t+1}(j), \ (1 \le t \le T-1) \tag{8}$$

The optimal model parameters λ^* are obtained when the $P(O|\lambda)$ reaches the maximum value.

Baulm-Welch algorithm is widely used to update the model parameters by repeated iteration calculation in the study of learning problems, and finally make the parameters gradually tend to the optimal value, which is a kind of maximum likelihood estimation process. The specific process of Baulm-Welch algorithm is as follows: First of all, the two variables used the algorithm are defined:

1. The posterior probability function

$$\gamma_t(i) = p(q_t = s_i|o, \lambda) \tag{9}$$

$\gamma_t(i)$ is probability of being state s_j at t moment given observation sequence O and parameters λ, and satisfied with $\sum_{i=1}^{N} \gamma_t(i) = 1$. $\gamma_t(i)$ can be expressed by the forward and backward variables in formula (10).

$$\gamma_t(i) = \frac{\alpha_t(i).\beta_t(i)}{p(o|\lambda)} = \frac{\alpha_t(i).\beta_t(i)}{\sum_{i=1}^{N} \alpha_t(i).\beta_t(i)}, \ (1 \le i \le N) \tag{10}$$

Probability function:

$$\xi_i(i,j) = p(q_t = s_i, q_{t+1} = s_j|o, \lambda) = \frac{p(q_t = s_i, q_{t+1} = s_j|o, \lambda)}{p(o|\lambda)} \tag{11}$$

$\xi_i(i,j)$ is probability of being state S_j at t moment and t + 1 moment given observation sequence O and parameters λ, $\xi_i(i,j)$ can be represented as:

$$\xi_i(i,j) = \frac{\alpha_t(i).\alpha_{ij}.b_j(o_{t+1}).\beta_{t+1}(j)}{p(o|\lambda)} = \frac{\alpha_t(i).\alpha_{ij}.b_j(o_{t+1}).\beta_{t+1}(j)}{\sum_{i=1}^{N}\sum_{j=1}^{N}\alpha_t(i).\alpha_{ij}.b_j(o_{t+1}).\beta_{t+1}(j)} \quad (12)$$

According to the meaning of $\gamma_t(i)$ and $\xi(i,j)$, both relationship is:

$$\gamma_1(i) = \sum_{j=1}^{N} \xi_t(i.j) \quad (13)$$

The specific parameters of the revaluation formula are as follows:

$$\overline{\pi}_i = P(q_1 = s_j) = \gamma_1(i) \quad (14)$$

$$\overline{a}_{ij} = \frac{\sum_{t-1}^{T-1} \xi_t(i.j)}{\sum_{t-1}^{T-1} \gamma_t(i.j)} \quad (15)$$

$$\overline{b}_j(k) = \frac{\sum_{t-1}^{T-1} \gamma_t(j)}{\sum_{t-1}^{T-1} \gamma_t(j)} \quad (16)$$

with $o_t = v_k$ in the numerator.

The specific steps to obtain the optimal parameters λ^* of HMM are as follows:

(1) Initialize HMM parameters $\lambda = (A, B, \pi)$;
   HMM initial model, $\lambda = (A, B, \pi)$, will affect the final recognition results to some extent, the initial value of each parameter is determined as follows:
   (a) Implicit state
      The number of hidden states of HMM is determined by the complexity of the corresponding gestures, because the recognition rate will be stable when the number of States increase to a certain value. However, If the number of States is overfull, computation amount in the recognition will be increased and it is easy to be over fitted.
   (b) State transition matrix
      The initial value of the state transition matrix A is determined by the following formula.

$$A = \begin{bmatrix} a_{ii} & 1-a_{ii} & & 0 \\ & a_{ii} & 1-a_{ii} & \\ & \cdots & \cdots & \\ & & a_{ii} & 1-a_{ii} \\ 0 & & & 1 \end{bmatrix} \quad (17)$$

The value of the a_{ii} is related to the duration of the average of each hidden state:

$$a_{ii} = 1 - \frac{1}{d}, \; d = \frac{\overline{T}}{N} \tag{18}$$

where T is average value of the length of all training samples for HMM corresponding certain gesture, namely, average sample length, N is the number of implicit state.

(c) Observation matrix

Assume the same appearing probability of each observation value of each state, the observation of the initial value of matrix B is determined by the following formula:

$$\mathbf{B} = \{b_{jk}\}, \; b_{jk} = \frac{1}{M} \tag{19}$$

In formula (19), $j = 1, 2, \ldots, N, j = 1, 2, \ldots, M$. Moreover, as the result of the 16-direction chain code to code characteristic value, M is equal to 16.

(d) Initial state distribution

In this paper, we use the HMM model of the left and right band structure, and the initial state is the first state.

$$\pi = [10 \ldots 0]^T \tag{20}$$

(2) According to the observation sequence O and the model parameters λ, we can estimate new model parameters $\overline{\lambda}$. In other words, according to the revaluation formula respectively, $\overline{\pi}_i, \overline{a}_{ij}, \overline{b}_j(k)$ can be estimated. Now, a new model parameters $\overline{\lambda} = (\overline{\pi}, \overline{A}, \overline{B})$ are obtained.

(3) The probability $P(O|\lambda)$ and $P(O|\overline{\lambda})$ of observation sequence O in model λ and $\overline{\lambda}$ are calculated respectively by the forward backward algorithm. Then $|logp(O|\overline{\lambda}) - logp(O|\lambda)|$ can be calculated simply. If $|logp(O|\overline{\lambda}) - logp(O|\lambda)| < \varepsilon$, we can deduce that the $P(O|\lambda)$ must converge. Now, $\overline{\lambda}$ obtained by training is closest to HMM of gesture sample. On the contrary, if $|logp(O|\overline{\lambda}) - logp(O|\lambda)| \geq \varepsilon$, we can assume that λ is equal to $\overline{\lambda}$, and the algorithm continue to execute step (b) until $P(O|\overline{\lambda})$ is convergence.

5 Summary

Gesture recognition based on vision technology is the key technology in the natural human computer interaction system. In research of gesture recognition, we conducted a following work: the gesture model of static and dynamic characteristic analysis, distance transform algorithm based on improved the palm center of gravity calculation method, to hand dynamic potential is modeled using the advantages of hidden Markov model and the existing algorithm, and calculate the parameters of the model can learn. In this paper, the results of the study (which based on visual gesture recognition) have a better recognition effect on the more complex gestures.

Acknowledgment. This work is funded by Yunnan Enterprises Key Laboratory of Traffic Engineering Test Center (JTGC-2015-003).

References

1. Ma, C., Ren, L., Teng, D., Wang, H., Dai, G.: Ubiquitous human-computer interaction in cloud manufacturing. Comput. Integr. Manuf. Syst. **17**(03), 504–510 (2011)
2. Fang, Z., Wu, X., Ma, W.: The progress on the study of human computer interaction technology. Comput. Eng. Des. **19**(01), 57–63 (1998)
3. Gao, N.: Research on gesture recognition technology based on vision. Hebei University of Technology (2015)
4. ITU: ITU Internet reports 2005: the Internet of things. ITU, Geneva, Switzerland (2005)
5. Guan R., Xu, X., Luo, Y., Miao, J., Qiu, S.: A computer vision-based gesture detection and recognition technique. Comput. Appl. Softw. (01) (2013)
6. Marcus, A., van Dam, A.: User-interface developments for the nineties. IEEE Comput. **24** (9), 49–57 (1991)
7. Wang, J.: Integration of eye-gaze, voice and manual response in multimodel user interface. In: Proceedings of IEEE International Conference on Systems, Man and Cybernetics, vol. 15 (1995)
8. Wang, L.: Dynamic gesture tracking and recognition and human computer interaction technology research. Xidian University (2014)
9. Wang, Q., Qi, X., Jiang, Y., Xu, W.: 3D handwriting recognition method based on hidden Markov models. Appl. Res. Comput. **09**, 099 (2012)
10. Fan, Z.: Parallel gesture recognition system based on depth learning in complex background. Xidian University (2014)
11. Qu, Q.Y.: The gesture recognition depth image and dexterous hand based interaction. Shanghai University (2014)
12. Wang, D.: Based on gesture recognition method of human-computer interaction system. Lanzhou University of Technology (2013)
13. Hu, W.: The research of human-computer interaction system based on gesture. Wuhan University of Technology (2010)
14. Tan, D.: Research on vision-based dynamic hand gesture recognition. Harbin Institute of Technology (2014)

Question Recommendation Based on User Model in CQA

Junfeng Wang, Lei Su$^{(\boxtimes)}$, Jun Chen, and Di Jiang

School of Information Engineering and Automation,
Kunming University of Science and Technology, Kunming 650093, China
w327918069@163.com, s28341@hotmail.com

Abstract. At present, people no longer meet the way of communication between users and the Internet. And more and more people choose the interaction between users and users to get information. The community question answering system is one of the new information sharing model. In the community question answering system, users are not only the questioner but also the answer and the question is the link between the users. With the increasing number of users and the increasing number of questions and answers, it makes many questions which just were raised disappear in the category pages of the home page. Leading to the efficiency of the questions be answered greatly reduce. Aim at the recommended user's interest, ability and time. In this paper we construct a dynamic user interest model and user expertise model. Experimental results show that the recommendation mechanism improves the efficiency of the recommendation to a certain extent.

Keywords: Community question answering system · Question recommendation ·
User' dynamic interest · User' expertise

1 Introduction

With the rapidly development of the internet, community question answering system (CQA) [1] has become an important way of people to get information and to share knowledge. Baidu knows is one of the largest community question and answer system, which has accumulated tens of millions of question and answer right now. And these questions and answers are provided by the user who use the community question and answer system. To help users find the questions they are interested in and answer them, more and more scholars are actively involved in and come up with some good models and methods. At present, the content of the research is divided into two categories.

The first category is to establish statistical language model and the theme model. In terms of statistical language model, Liu et al. [2] has built a language model through the user's information file. Put the content of the question into this model to calculate the extent of the user's interest in the question, so as to complete the recommendation of question. Zhang et al. [3] has combined with language model to form a mixed model to realize the recommendation of question on the basis of probability latent semantic. The result shows that the addition of semantic information of potential hybrid model is superior to the traditional language model. In establishing the subject model, Wu [4]

© ICST Institute for Computer Sciences, Social Informatics and Telecommunications Engineering 2018
J. Wan et al. (Eds.): CloudComp 2016, SPNCE 2016, LNICST 197, pp. 91–101, 2018.
https://doi.org/10.1007/978-3-319-69605-8_9

has put forward an incremental question recommendation mechanism on the basis of probabilistic latent semantic analysis. This incremental embodied in the two aspects of new users and new problems. And the community Q&A system based on incremental to update the topic model. Guo et al. [5] has proposed UQA topic model. The model extracts semantic information from user's information to recommend the questions. Yu [6] has put forward a kind of personalized recommendation model based on social network. The model is based on the social relationship of trust among users. And get information to better reflect the personalized target users from other users with a high degree of relevance to the target user. To obtain more information in line with the needs of its personalized recommendation to reduce the blindness of the recommendation, improve the accuracy of the recommendation. Whether it is the use of statistical language models or the use of topic model, the recommended users to a large extent prefer to be interested in this question.

The second category is the research based on link analysis. Link analysis method is derived from the search engine and it through the link analysis algorithm to get the value of the authority of the web page. According to the idea of link analysis, researchers believe that in the community Q&A system the relationship between the user and the user is mainly a question and answer relationship. Through this relationship can also find expert users. According to this view, Agichtein and Jurczyk [7, 8] first established a Q&A community in the user's directed graph. This graph reflects the question and answers relation between the user and the user, and then uses the link analysis method to calculate the user's expertise value which is similar to the authority of the web page. If a user's expertise is higher, this user is an expert user. Finally, the problem is recommended to the experts who have been found. At present, the two link analysis methods used in the community question answering system are the PageRank algorithm proposed by Google's founder, Page [9] and the HITS algorithm proposed by Kleinberg [10]. However, using link analysis methods in community Q&A system to find expert users also has shortcoming. The reason is that the initial value of the different users is the same. However each user will give a different quality of answers, so each user can't be treated as equally.

According to the task characteristics of the recommendation system in community Q&A system, this paper studies the construction of user interest model and the construction of user expertise model in community Q&A system and puts forward a kind of recommendation mechanism which contains two methods based on the user model. This paper uses the data from the "Baidu know" to do recommend experiments. And the result shows that using this method to recommend new question has a significant improvement in the accuracy (P@N-Percent).

In the second section, this paper introduces the user's dynamic interest model based on the time weight and the user expertise model based on the PageRank algorithm. In the third section, this paper puts forward a synthesis algorithm for the question recommendation in line with recommendation question mechanism based on the user model constructed in section second. In the fourth section, this paper designs an experiment bases on the question recommendation mechanism proposed in this paper and verify the superiority of this algorithm. The fifth section summarizes the research work in this paper.

2   Question Recommendation Based on User Model

2.1   User Dynamic Interest Model

The degree of users' interest can be determined according to the number of the questions which the users answered. If the user answers more questions in a particular category, indicates that the user is more interested in the category. The problem is that the interest degree of the old user may be far greater than the new user's, whichcan't reflect the interest degree of the users in recently. The first method is to construct a user dynamic interest model based on time weight. When a new problem is raised, the degree of the user's interest in the question category can be calculated by calculating the time weight of each question the answered by the historic records of user's answer. The bigger sum of the time weights is more able to explain users are more interested in this question category in recently.

2.1.1   Time Weight

In the community Q&A system, according to study the information of the users' answered history this paper summarizes the following two characteristics: the user's interest in certain category is dynamic; the user's interest is divided into persistent and transient type.

The above problem shows that the questions the user answered in recently have a more important role for recommending the questions the user may be interested in the future. The early questions the user has answered impact on the user's interest is relatively small. This is because over time, the user's interest in changing, and the user's interest in a short period of time is relatively stable and unchanging. Therefore, the questions the users may be interested are similar with the questions they have answered in recently. In this paper, the concept of time weight is introduced when the user interest model is established, and so then the user's dynamic interest model is constructed.

Time weight refers to that each answered question has a time weight (WT) in the history record of the user answer questions (see the formula (2.1)).

$$WT(u, q) = (1 - a) + a \frac{D_{uq}}{L_u} \tag{2.1}$$

$a \in (0, 1)$ is the weight growth coefficient. If a is bigger, the time weight change is bigger. In this paper a is 0.7. D_{uq} is the time interval of answering the question Q and of answering certain questions earliest. Lu is the time interval of raising questions and answering certain question.

In formula (2.1), Lu represents the time horizons of user to answer the questions that is. The time span also is the time interval of answering the question earliest and answering the question recently. The advantage of the original formula is that the time weight can be calculated off-line, saving the system time overhead. The disadvantage is that there is no consideration the liveness of user interest. When the users in all the time to answer the questions, it is easy to get the degree of users' interest of some type; however if the user in recently for too long a period of time not to answer the question, it is impossible to determine the degree of users' interest of some type. The Lu proposed in this paper taking into account the liveness of the user interest. If the user does not participate answer the question in a long time, the liveness of the user's interest would become low. Then the time weight is relatively small. And from the side it also can reflect the user's online situation in the recent period time, so as to determine whether the user can answer the question in time.

2.1.2   User Dynamic Interest

After determining the category of the question, find out the user groups that have answered the category of the question according to the category of the problem. Then combines the number of questions that each user answered with the time weight to calculate user's dynamic interest in this category online (see the formula (2.2)).

$$I_{Class(u_i)} = \log_2 \left(\sum_{q \in Q(Class(u_i))} WT(u_i, q) + 1 \right) \tag{2.2}$$

In this formula, Q(Class(ui)) is a set of certain categories questions in the history of user's answered record. User dynamic interest model not only considers the influence of early questions answered to the user's interest but also pay more attention that the impact to the user's interest of the user's answered which distance from closer to the stage of asking questions.

2.2   User Expertise Model

User's expertise length refers to the professional level of the user to answer questions in certain category.

There is a disadvantage that no considers the different quality of the answer given by the different user in using the traditional link analysis method to find the user's expertise of answering questions. In this paper, the research on the construction method of user expertise model basses on weight link. According to the answer adoption mechanism of community Q&A system calculate the value of the user's expertise. So that it can be more obvious to distinguish the user's expertise length.

2.2.1   Traditional PageRank Algorithm in the User Expertise Found

The discovery of web page authority is based on the link relationship between web pages. And there exists the Q&A relations that equivalents the relationship of link in and link out among the users in the community Q&A system. So the PageRank algorithm can be applied to the user expertise found by the relations. According to the Q&A relationship between the user A with user B and user C, a link is established between the user A to the user B and the user A to the user C. In order to be more intuitive to see in the picture omit the relationship between the user and the problem or the answer and get the Fig. ·1. This graph reflects the Q&A relationship between users and this graph is used as the relations of links of the user in this paper. Can be seen from the figure, in addition to the user B to answer the A user's question, the user C also gives the answer. According to the idea of PageRank algorithm assuming that the user A a total of 1 point, then the user B and user C will get 0.5 points from the user A.

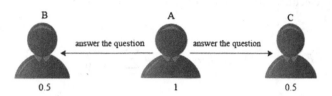

Fig. 1. User link diagram

In this graph, the length of a user's expertise length is determined by the number of the user's link in and the chain out of the user's specific length.

2.2.2 Calculate the Initial Expertise Length

In the papers related to the traditional PageRank algorithm published by the relevant researchers [11–13], analyzed the shortcomings of traditional PageRank algorithm in finding user expertise. In this paper, the user's link diagram is improved into the weighted user link diagram and the quality of the user's answers is considered indirectly. And aiming at the problem that the traditional PageRank algorithm does not consider the type of the questions in user expertise found, this paper improves the PageRank algorithm. So that gets the specific length of a user in a certain category (see the formula (2.3)).

$$E_{Class(u_i)} = (1 - d) + d \sum_{j=1}^{n} \left(\frac{W_{ij}}{\sum W_j} E_{Class(u_i)} \right) \qquad (2.3)$$

In this formula, n is the number of chain target users u_i in certain class; W_{ij} is the weight of the edge that the u_j to the user u_i; $\sum W_j$ is the sum of weights of all edges that the u_j to this type.

By the formula (2.3), it is known that computing user expertise is a constant iteration and recursive process. The recursive ends until all the chain out users have not answered the questions of the category. And the length of the recursive to the boundary of the user is $(1 - d)$, $(1 - d)$ can be understood as $1 * (1 - d)$ that is the initial length of all users is 1 and the proportion of the length of the original length is $(1 - D)$. However, analysis of the user's personal center in community Q&A system can find the expertise information from the user's personal information. It is not accurate to regard the initial length of the user as the same value in formula (2.3), so can use the expertise information to represent the user's initial expertise length. The personal home page that Baidu knows has the domain the user to be good at; the domain is the category which the mark user is good at. Because Baidu knows set three tier categories, the field of expertise can be one of the layers of the category. In this paper the user's expertise length of the corresponding category for the third tier categories, according to the field of expertise to set the user in a class of the initial length.

2.2.3   User Specific Length

The proposed user initial expertise length is integrated into the weighted PageRank algorithm to calculate the length of the user expertise to the class (see the formula (2.4)).

$$E_{Class(u_i)} = (1 - d)EI_{Class(u_i)} + d \sum_{j=1}^{n} \left(\frac{W_{ij}}{\sum W_j} E_{Class(u_i)} \right) \tag{2.4}$$

When calculating the length of the user's expertise, according to the users answer historical records of the categories involved to calculate the length of the line under these categories of users.

3   Problem Recommendation Algorithm Based on User Model

According to the user's dynamic interest model and user expertise model proposed above, a question recommendation algorithm is proposed to match the user with the category of the proposed question (see the formula (3.1)).

$$QR(Class(q), u_i) = I_{Class(u_i)} \cdot E_{Class(u_i)} \tag{3.1}$$

$I_{Class(u_i)}$ is the level of user's interest in categories of questions, $E_{Class(u_i)}$ is the user's expertise length in the categories of questions. The product of the two represents the degree of matching between a user and the categories of questions and the matching values expressed in.

This paper references the category system of the Baidu Known and this system has three layer categories. First of all classifies the proposed questions so that the problem of the category specific to the third tier categories. Due to the characteristics of the third tier category is more detailed, it can be considered that the same questions for a user with the same degree of matching. In this paper, the recommend thought of questions and user matching is transformed into the thought of category of questions and user matching.

According to the above description can determine the course of the recommend questions. After determining the category of the problem, calculate the user's dynamic interestingness to this category. At the same time, this category is matched with the corresponding categories of user's expertise length that have been calculated offline so that get the user's expertise length for this category. According to the formula (3.1) calculate $QR(Class(u_i))$ and sort the $QR(Class(u_i))$. Eventually form a list of recommended users. The flow chart of the question recommendation is shown in Fig. 2:

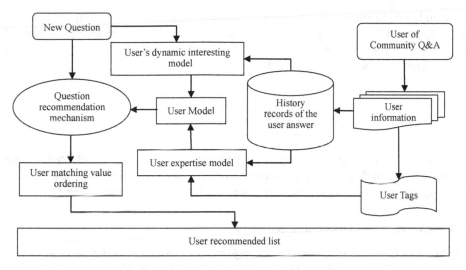

Fig. 2. Flow chart of problem recommendation

4 Experiment and Analysis

4.1 Experimental Data

The study of recommending question is based on Baidu known so the experimental data comes from Baidu know. And the experimental data is divided into three parts. The first part is the category information, including all of the three tier categories that Baidu known. The second part is the information of the question, including the user's name, the title of the question, and the time of the question; the third part is the answer information, including the answer description, user name, user label, feedback type, answer time.

This experiment crawls 5 categories of questions as the experimental data, in order to evaluate the effect removes the questions which answer is not adopted. The statistics of specific crawling data are shown in Table 1.

Table 1. The experimental data statistics of Baidu Known

Question categories	Question quantity	Number of users	Answer quantity
Basketball	2680	3623	9978
Computer	2749	3865	11231
Exercise	2451	3015	8781
Tourism	2552	3279	8567
Mobile phone	2893	4032	12608

4.2 Evaluation Method

To check the recommendation effect of the problem recommendation algorithm, not only depends on whether the user is able to answer questions raised but also knows how high the probability of the user's answer will be adopted. According to this idea, this paper uses the accuracy value P@N-Percent to test the recommendation effect of the question recommendation algorithm. The formula for calculating the exact value of P@N-Percent is shown in the formula 4.1.

$$P@N - Percent = \frac{\sum_{i=1}^{n} isHit(u_i, q_i, n - percent)}{n} \qquad (4.1)$$

$isHit(u_i, q_i, n - percent)$ indicates whether the user u_i that is adopted by the question q_i is matched to the user recommended list of the top percent N, the value of $isHit(u_i, q_i, n - percent)$ is 1 or 0; n is the number of test set questions.

4.3   Experimental Design and Results Analysis

In this paper, the questions of the 5 categories of the experimental data are sorted according to the order of the time of questioning. Take the top 80% of the question and answer data as a training corpus, the remaining 20% question and answer corpus as a test corpus. Adopt the question recommendation method of the Table 2 to test and compare.

Table 2. Question recommended methods

Methods	Description
Category based PageRank	It can find the expertise of users but not consider the user's recent interest and the quality of the user's answer
User dynamic interest model combines with PageRank (DIM-PageRank)	It can find the expertise of users at the same time to consider the user's recent interest, but still do not consider the quality of the user's answer
User dynamic interest model combines with user expertise model (DIM-EM)	It can find the expertise of users at the same time to consider the user's recent interest, and in the expertise model to add weight and initial expertise length

According to these three methods, the precision values of P@1-Percent, P@5-Percent and P@10-Percent 3 are used to test recommendation effect of the question recommendation algorithm. The results of the experiment are shown in Tables 3, 4 and 5.

According to the results of these 3 tables, it can be seen that there is a problem with black-bordered font data only in the P@1-Percent and P@5-Percent. In P@1-Percent the recommended effect of the DIM-PageRank is worse than the traditional PageRank recommended in the two categories of computers and tourism. And the recommended effect of traditional PageRank in the travel category is better than the recommended effect of DIM-EM. In the P@5-Percent the recommended effect of DIM-EM is worse

Table 3. The test statistics for each method in p@1-percent

Question category	Number of questions	PageRank	DIM-PageRank	DIM-EM
Basketball	536	0.312	0.323	0.344
Computer	550	0.290	**0.281**	0.307
Exercise	490	0.245	0.256	0.259
Tourism	510	0.307	**0.298**	**0.302**
Mobile phone	579	0.268	0.273	0.298

Table 4. The test statistics for each method in p@5-percent

Question category	Number of questions	PageRank	DIM-PageRank	DIM-EM
Basketball	536	0.357	0.391	0.459
Computer	550	0.312	0.374	0.442
Exercise	490	0.309	0.355	0.423
Tourism	510	0.337	0.409	0.488
Mobile phone	579	0.329	0.386	**0.381**

Table 5. The test statistics for each method in p@10-percent

Question category	Number of questions	PageRank	DIM-PageRank	DIM-EM
Basketball	536	0.489	0.554	0.612
Computer	550	0.442	0.481	0.597
Exercise	490	0.391	0.463	0.552
Tourism	510	0.404	0.529	0.600
Mobile phone	536	0.489	0.554	0.612

than the DIM-PageRank in the mobile phone category. And other cases, the recommended effect of DIM-EM is better than the recommended effect of DIM-PageRank; the recommended effect of DIM-PageRank is better than that of traditional PageRank.

In order to observe the whole situation, calculate the average P@N-Percent of PageRank, DIM-PageRank and DIM-EM in 5 categories. Statistical results are shown in Table 6 and the growth trend chart is shown in Fig. 3.

Table 6. The average P@n-Percent test statistics for each method

Methods	P@1-Percent	P@5-Percent	P@10-Percent
PageRank	0.284	0.329	0.423
DIM-PageRank	0.286	0.383	0.495
DIM-EM	0.302	0.439	0.571

According to the average P@N-Percent of the three methods in the 5 categories concluded that: the recommended effect of DIM-PageRank is better than the PageRank,

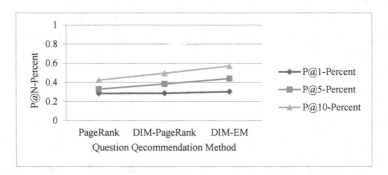

Fig. 3. The average P@N-Percent growth trend of each method

and the recommended effect of DIM-EM is better than the DIM-PageRank. Therefore, the question recommendation method based on the user model proposed in this paper has a better recommended effect.

5   Conclusions

Community Q&A system has become a new and important way for users to obtain t information and share knowledge. The work of raising question and answering is the core of community Q&A system, and the classification of questions and the problem can be answered in a timely become a key part of the work of question-answering. The question recommendation mechanism is the important link between the questioner and the answerer, which can greatly promote the development of the community Q&A system. In view of the problems in the community question and answer system, the study in this paper focused on the construction of user dynamic interest model and the construction of user expertise model. A question recommendation method based on user model is proposed in this paper, and the experimental result shows that the proposed method is effective.

Acknowledgement. This work is supported by the National Natural Science Foundation of China (No. 61365010).

References

1. Zhang, Z.F., Li, Q.D.: Review of community question answering system. Comput. Sci. **37** (11), 19–23 (2011)
2. Liu, X.Y., Bruce Croft, W., et al.: Finding experts in community-based question-answering services. In: Proceedings of the 14th ACM International Conference on Information and Knowledge Management, pp. 315–316 (2005)
3. Zhang, J., Tang, J., Li, J.: Expert finding in a social network. In: Kotagiri, R., Krishna, P.R., Mohania, M., Nantajeewarawat, E. (eds.) DASFAA 2007. LNCS, vol. 4443, pp. 1066–1069. Springer, Heidelberg (2007). doi:10.1007/978-3-540-71703-4_106

4. Wu, H., Wang, Y., Cheng, X.: Incremental probabilistic latent semantic analysis for automatic question recommendation. In: Proceedings of the 2008 ACM Conference on Recommender Systems, pp. 99–106 (2008)
5. Guo, J., Xu, S., Bao, S., Yu, Y.: Tapping on the potential of Q&A community by recommending answer providers. In: Proceedings of the 17th ACM Conference on Information and Knowledge Management, pp. 921–930 (2008)
6. Yu, S.H.: Research on key technologies of personalized social network based on recommendation system. Nat. Def. Sci. Technol. Univ. 24–40 (2011)
7. Jurczyk, P., Agichtein, E.: Hits on question answer portals: exploration of link analysis for author ranking. In: Proceedings of 30th Annual International ACM SIGIR Conference, pp. 845–846 (2007)
8. Urczyk, P., Agichtein, E.: Discovering authorities in question answer communities by using link analysis. In: Proceedings of ACM 17th Conference on Information and Knowledge Management, pp. 919–922 (2007)
9. Page, L., Brin, S., Motwani, R., Winograd, T.: The PageRank citation ranking: bringing order to the web. Stanford Digital Library Working Paper SIDL-WP-1999-0120
10. Kleinberg, J.: Authoritative sources in a hyper linked environment (1998)
11. Duan, W.C., Hu, P.: An improved PageRank algorithm based on topic feature and time factor. Comput. Eng. Des. 31(4), 866–868 (2010)
12. Yang, J.S., Ling, P.L.: Improvement of PageRank algorithm for search engine. Comput. Proj. 35(22), 35–37 (2009)
13. Deng, D.J., Zhou, C.L.: Improved PageRank algorithm based on content correlation and time analysis. Comput. Digit. Eng. 39(1), 25–27 (2011)

Data Storage Protection of Community Medical Internet of Things

Ziyang Zhang, Fulong Chen$^{(\boxtimes)}$, Heping Ye, Junru Zhu, Cheng Zhang,
and Chao Liu

Anhui Provincial Key Laboratory of Network and Information Security,
Anhui Normal University, 189 Jiuhua South Road, Wuhu 241002,
Anhui, People's Republic of China
long005@ahnu.edu.cn

Abstract. With the improvement of people's living standard, people
have put forward higher requirements on medical services. The effective
combination of the traditional community medical systems and the modern Internet of things technologies can help to build a community medical
Internet of things, which involves a large number of important information for health care and patient staff, and these information face the risk
of privacy disclosure and information damage. From the point of view of
data storage, we proposes a data storage protection method for preserving privacy data in the community medical Internet of things. Through
analyzing the data integrity and security of the practical scheme, it is
proved that the medical data can be protected effectively in the process
of storage.

Keywords: Community medical care · Internet of things · Privacy
data · Storage protection

1 Introduction

The rapid economic development has led to the deterioration of the natural
environment upon which the survival of people's health under unprecedented
threat. Various non-predictability of diseases have sprung up on the patients so
that the patient's illness makes it painful bring the demand for medical services
growing. However limited traditional medical service resources and uncertainty
treatment time urge people to begin to look for better health service to make
up for the lacking of available resources.

In Community Medical Internet of Things (CMIoT), due to the huge amount
of heterogeneous medical data, extensive medical data sources, and various identification information which involve user privacy, once medical data loses or tampers, some privacy leakages resulting in catastrophic loss will occur [1]. [2,3] have
presented that tags would be scanned while users were not aware of what read-
ers would do, it would easily bring into the destruction of personal privacy, and
it would cause the items of information suffering from attacking between local
servers and remote servers.

© ICST Institute for Computer Sciences, Social Informatics and Telecommunications Engineering 2018
J. Wan et al. (Eds.): CloudComp 2016, SPNCE 2016, LNICST 197, pp. 102–110, 2018.
https://doi.org/10.1007/978-3-319-69605-8_10

Data storage faces a paradox: encryption data cannot be efficiently processed, and the security and privacy of non encrypted data can not be guaranteed. Therefore, it is urgent to need a kind of effective privacy protection method to ensure the safety of medical data storage in the controllable range. Mni [4] proposed various models of medical data from production to storage. Ateniese [5] proposed a distributed data secure storage scheme in which data is encrypted using the symmetric keys, and the symmetric keys are encrypted using public key. However, there exists the risk of collusion between the malicious server and malicious users, leading to the disclosure of the file encryption key. Vimercati [6] proposed a method for secure storage of data by a non trusted server key derivation method, in which each file is encrypted with a symmetric key, each user has a private key, and in order to authorize, data owners create public tokens for users so that authorized users can use their private key to derive the decryption key of the specified file from the tokens. The key number of the scheme is too large and the complexity of the operation is linear with the number of users so as unable to effectively extend. Kamara and Lauter [7] studied a kind of abstract public cloud storage encryption framework composed of data processing module, data verification module, token generation module and credential generation module, in which the storage data controlled by the owner is authorized to be accessed via token generated by the token generator and to be decrypted through credentials generated by credential generator, and their security is controlled by the password mechanism. The data protection technology based on VMM is proposed in [8] where the operating system and the distributed file system are isolated to protect data security by using the Daoli virtual security monitoring system and the SSL secure transmission module. A kind of homomorphic encryption algorithm [9] is designed to realize data encryption and decryption with mixed operations of cector and matrix operation, supports for fuzzy retrieval of encrypted data, and can be better to perform the homomorphic addition and subtraction operation. The downside of this approach is the low efficiency in cipher text retrieval and homomorphic multiplication/division.

Wang [10] studied and proposed a secure storage of outsourced data in the cloud environment. In the method, the storage efficiency is improved by dividing the file into blocks and the data security is ensured for each data block using a different key encryption. Because of the need to spend a lot of cost data encryption and key management, the scheme has a lot of problems. A reliable data protection and destruction method with the help of a trusted platform was proposed by Zhang [11]. He designed a virtual monitor as the trusted third party responsible for monitoring and protecting the user's privacy data, and destroying user data in accordance with user requirements, even if the cloud server's super administrator can not bypass the protection of user privacy data. It is obvious that the method is too high requirements for the reliability of the hardware and software, and the actual situation is difficult to meet. A storage model of cloud computing was designed in [12] where the trusted third party server is responsible for the isolation of user privacy data and general data, and thereby realizes the protection of user's privacy information. However, in this scheme, when the data is stored, the two times of data partitions and matrix operation make the storage efficiency low so that it is difficult to use and expand on a large scale.

2 Architecture of Community Medical Internet of Things

The CMIoT is achieved in one community, as shown in Fig. 1. In the CMIoT, Data from a sensor is sent toward the nearest gateway belong to some place such as home, community public area, community health center or hospital, and then the data is transmitted to the nearest community router. Connection is built between the gateway and the database server of cloud data center through wireless network. In the end, the application server of data center provides the resolved data to users with mobile terminals or PC terminals. Data transmission integrates a variety of communication means. Sensors in one place establish communication via wireless self-organized network, and data in the gateway transmit through wireless local area network or mobile network.

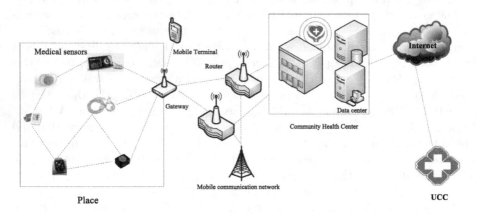

Fig. 1. Architecture of community medical Internet of things.

3 Storage Protection Model

The storage server is composed of the storage control center and the file system. After medical data generated by different systems and modules in CMIoT are transmitted to the server node, they firstly enter the storage buffer for unified processing of the control area in the storage module. The control center and the file system with a message queue exchange information through a message channel. If they communicate successfully and the current file system is free, the server can store the current data stream. Each file system independently enjoys and controls the communication link in order to achieve the purpose of distributed data storage.

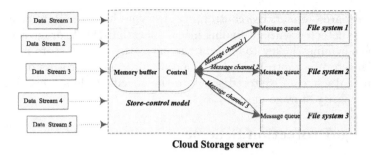

Fig. 2. Storage server model.

As shown in Fig. 2, at some point, there may be a large number of medical data to enter the storage server so that the control area can not handle them immediately. At this time, the server sends the data to the buffer storage buffer, and after the completion of the current data processing tasks in the control area, the data is extracted from the buffer and processed into the storage link. The control area immediately detects the current file system, and once the idle file system is detected, the control area will store in order the buffer data into the free file system through the message channel.

For each data stream, before coming to the storage server, it is signed by the data source sender with the private key, and then according to the public key

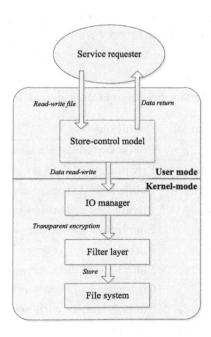

Fig. 3. Server security storage model.

of the data source sender, the control area decrypts it. If the data stream after decryption is detected without finding illegal operations, the storage control area uses its own symmetric key to encrypt the data stream, and store it to the file system. The storage control area has a specific process to process data streams so that the data stream is stored safely to the specified file system. Figure 3 is the server security storage model.

4   Storage Protection Scheme

After the storage server control area gets the data stream from the buffer, the server encrypts the data stream with its own private key and its own public key with the public key of the data source sender, and then generates a new encrypted data packet. Such data packet can only be decrypted using the sender's private key so as to get the public key of the storage server and decrypt the data stream for the reverse output of data stream. Using polling mode, the server queries whether the file system is idle or not, and stores the buffer data to the idle file system step by step. As shown in Table 1, some symbolic representations of data processing in the storage scheme are defined, the data storage process is shown as follows.

Step 1: The data stream sender encrypts the data stream plaintext P with the data stream encryption key K_C

$$C = E_{K_C}(P) \tag{1}$$

Step 2: The data stream sender encrypts the data stream encryption key K_C with the public key of the storage server P_{K-S}

$$K_K = E_{P_{K-S}}(K_C) \tag{2}$$

Table 1. The definitions of data storage symbols.

No.	Symbol	Definition
1	P_{K-R}	Public key of data source
2	S_{K-R}	Private key of data source
3	P_{K-S}	Public key of storage server
4	S_{K-S}	Private key of storage server
5	K_C	Encryption key of data stream
6	K_K	Encryption key of key
7	P	Plain text of data stream
8	C	Cipher text of data stream
9	$E_K(x)$	Encrypt data x with key K
10	$D_K(y)$	Decrypt data y with key K
11	$Sig_K(X)$	Sign data X with key K

Step 3: The data stream sender processes the plain text data with the hash function

$$P' = H(P) \tag{3}$$

and encapsulates the data stream plain text C, the hash value P' of the data stream plain text and the encryption key K_K of the key

$$D = C||P'||K_K \tag{4}$$

Step 4: Before the data is sent, the sender signs the encapsulated data D with its private key S_{K-S}

$$D' = Sig_{S_{K-S}}(D) \tag{5}$$

and sends it to the storage server.

Step 5: After the storage server receives the signed data D', it decrypts D' and the encryption key of the key with its own key S_{K-S}, and then uses the latter for decrypting P'

$$K_C = D_{S_{K-S}}(K_K) \tag{6}$$

$$P' = D_{S_{K-S}}(D') \tag{7}$$

$$P = D_{K_C}(P') \tag{8}$$

After the data stream enters the storage server, the control area of the storage server will decrypt the data packet for distributed storage. The data packet includes three parts such as header, body and remark as shown in Table 2. Afterwards, the control area encrypt the packaged data with the public key of the

Table 2. The symbol definitions of data package.

No.	Name	Definition
1	Header	Header of data file
	Data_Sequence	Sequence No. of data stream
	Data_FileNo	File system No. of data stream
	Data_type	Type of data stream
2	Body	Body of data file
	$Data_1$	Data body of data stream 1
	$Data_2$	Data body of data stream 2
	$Data_3$	Data body of data stream 3
3	Remark	Remark
	Data_Length	Length of data stream
	Data_En_Alg	Encryption algorithm

sender, and through the data channel established between the control area and the file system, using the data transmission mechanism based on transmission response, in other words, once the data transmission is interrupted, the data packet will be retransmitted, the control area stores all the data streams into distributed file systems as shown in Fig. 4.

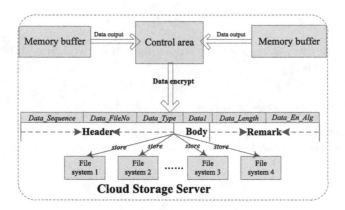

Fig. 4. Process of server storage.

5   Storage Security Analysis

5.1   Data Integrity

The scheme is provided with a control area module and a memory module in the storage server. The control area module is composed of a memory buffer and a control area. When data flows into a storage server, if the control area is processing some previous storage tasks, and unable to process incoming data stream in time, at this time the data stream will be stored in the memory buffer, so that the control area can complete the current tasks and turn to process current data storage. This ensures that a large amount of data can enter the storage server at the same time without being lost.

When the control area processes the new coming data streams, it will detect whether the storage modules of the file systems are idle or not, and once it finds a file system idle, it will transfer the data stream in a timely manner through the dedicated message channel. This avoids the situation that data can not be stored and may be lost due to unknowing whether the file system is busy or not, and the data integrity is guaranteed.

When the control area detects whether the file systems are idle or not, it will communicate with the file system in the form of a message queue. The communication channel between the control area and the file systems will not be blocked due to a lot of communication in a short time. It is very good to ensure the timely arrival of the feedback message and the integrity of the feedback information.

5.2 Data Security

Before entering the storage server, the data stream is signed by the private key, and then the control area uses the data source public key to decrypt the data and verifies its integrity. After that, the data is encrypted with a symmetric key and stored into the corresponding file system. This ensures the security of data in the process of arriving at the server and the file systems.

When a data stream is stored in a file system, it is interacted between the user state and the kernel state. Therefore, data storage is completed with to I/O manager and processed by a transparent encryption method. Once the data in the user state is requested to access, the kernel will receive that request, conduct an access request processing by verifying the role properties and finally complete data transmission in a transparent decryption method. The whole data request and feedback process is transmitted through the data encryption method. This also can protect the security of data.

6 Conclusions

Aiming at the problem of data security storage in the field of medical Internet of things, we design a secure data storage protection method. Through the design of a storage server model and secure storage model, we gives a complete data secure storage scheme. There are many security issues for data in the medical Internet of things, e.g., the secure transmission of medical Internet data and the classification of medical data privacy issues are the focus of research. The next step will be to explore and research the classification of privacy protection for medical data.

Acknowledgments. The authors would like to thank our colleagues and students in Engineering Technology Research Center of Network and Information Security at Anhui Normal University. We thank National Natural Science Foundation of China under Grant Nos. 61572036 and 61402014, University Natural Science Research Project of Anhui Province under Grant No. KJ2014A084, Wuhu City Science and Technology Project under Grant No. 2014cxy04 for support of this research.

References

1. Ye, H., Yang, J., Zhu, J., Zhang, Z., Huang, Y., Chen, F.: A secure privacy data transmission method for medical internet of things. In: Wan, J., Humar, I., Zhang, D. (eds.) Industrial IoT 2016. LNICSSITE, vol. 173, pp. 144–154. Springer, Cham (2016). https://doi.org/10.1007/978-3-319-44350-8_15
2. Atzori, L., Iera, A., Morabito, G.: The internet of things: a survey. Comput. Netw. **54**(15), 2787–2805 (2010)
3. Medaglia, C.M., Serbanati, A.: An overview of privacy and security issues in the internet of things. In: Giusto, D., Iera, A., Morabito, G., Atzori, L. (eds.) The Internet of Things. Springer, New York, NY (2010). https://doi.org/10.1007/978-1-4419-1674-7_38

4. Mni, L., Zhang, Q., Tan, H.Y., et al.: Smart healthcare: from IoT to cloud computing. Sci. Sinica **43**(4), 515–528 (2013)
5. Ateniese, G., Fu, K., Green, M., et al.: Improved proxy re-encryption schemes with applications to secure distributed storage. ACM Trans. Inf. Syst. Secur. **9**(1), 29–43 (2006)
6. Vimercati, S., Foresti, S., Jajodia, S., et al.: Over-encryption: management of access control evolution on outsourced data. In: Proceedings of the 33rd International Conference on Very Large Data Base, pp. 123–134 (2007)
7. Kamara, S., Lauter, K.: Cryptographic cloud storage. In: Sion, R., Curtmola, R., Dietrich, S., Kiayias, A., Miret, J.M., Sako, K., Sebé, F. (eds.) FC 2010. LNCS, vol. 6054, pp. 136–149. Springer, Heidelberg (2010). https://doi.org/10.1007/978-3-642-14992-4_13
8. Hou, Q.H., Wu, Y.W., Zheng, W.M.: A method on protection of user data privacy in cloud storage platform. J. Comput. Res. Dev. **48**(7), 1146–1154 (2011)
9. HuangX, R.W., Gui, L., Yu, S., et al.: Privacy-preserving computable encryption scheme of cloud computing. Chin. J. Comput. **34**(12), 2391–2402 (2011)
10. Wang, W., Li, Z., Owens, R., et al.: Secure and efficient access to outsourced data. In: Proceedings of the 2009 ACM Workshop on Cloud computing security, pp. 55–66 November 2009
11. Zhang, F.Z., Chen, J., Chen, H.B., et al.: Lifetime privacy and self-destruction of data in the cloud. J. Comput. Res. Devel. **48**(7), 1155–1167 (2011)
12. Mao, J., Li, K., Xu, X.: Privacy protection scheme for cloud computing. J. Tsinghua Univ. (Sci. Tech.) **51**(10), 1357–1362 (2011)

SPNCE

Generalized Format-Preserving Encryption for Character Data

Yanyu Huang[1], Bo Li[1], Shuang Liang[1], Haoyu Ma[2], and Zheli Liu[1(✉)]

[1] College of Information Technical Science, Nankai University, Tianjin, China
onlyerir@163.com, nankailibo@163.com, nk_liangshuang@163.com,
liuzheli1978@163.com
[2] College of Network and Information, Xidian University, Xi'an, China
ma-haoyu@163.com

Abstract. We studied the problem on applying format-preserving encryption (FPE) to character data, specifically the uncertainty of the binary size of ciphertexts caused by variable-width encoding. In this paper, we suggested a extended rank-then-encipher approach for character data which connects character strings with numbers under mixed-radix numeral system. Based on this method, we proposed a generic character FPE scheme that deals with mixed-radix numerals, by introducing a customized "dynamic modulo addition" into unbalanced Feistel construction. Our work showed a new way of designing encryption methods for arbitrary message spaces which involves no tradeoff between efficacy and efficiency. Besides describing our design, security of our schemes are also analyzed.

Keywords: Block ciphers · Format-preserving encryption · Feistel networks · FFX mode · Mixed-radix numeral systems

1 Introduction

1.1 Problem of Applying FPE on Character Data

In recent years researches on applied cryptography have developed several practical enciphering methods, a paradigm is the so called *format-preserving encryption* (FPE). FPE aims to encipher messages of some specified format without disrupting it as achieving an acceptable level of security. Despite many efforts of designing FPE schemes, the work that has been done so far simply reduces concept "format" to "arbitrary domain", while other aspects other than the value of messages do not receive sufficient attention. In this paper, we emphasize the *variable-width encoding* of character data, and how it affects FPE application.

1.2 Related Work

Since FPE was first proposed in 1981, there have been plenty of researches on the subject [1–6,8]. In 2002, Black and Rogaway [1] provided a series of FPE

© ICST Institute for Computer Sciences, Social Informatics and Telecommunications Engineering 2018
J. Wan et al. (Eds.): CloudComp 2016, SPNCE 2016, LNICST 197, pp. 113–122, 2018.
https://doi.org/10.1007/978-3-319-69605-8_11

methods on enciphering integers, and suggested that such ciphers can be used to construct FPE schemes on any arbitrary domain. In 2009, Bellare et al. [2] defined the *rank-then-encipher* approach (or RtE for short), and suggested that it's possible to construct any FPE scheme based on integer FPEs.

Some previous FPE schemes work on the message space $\mathcal{X} = \mathbb{Z}_N = \{0, 1, \ldots, N - 1\}$ for any desired N. Such schemes include both Feistel-based schemes like FFSEM [3], and other constructions such as card shuffle [4,5]. Some researchers present a method for keeping the database structure and supporting efficient SQL-based queries [16]. There are some application build the structure to achieve the function [13–15]. For Within these existing works, the FFX mode, proposed in 2010, is of the best generality [6]. Some researchers present a method for keeping the database structure and supporting efficient SQL-based queries [16]. FFX specifically aims on encrypting strings of some arbitrary alphabet Σ and works on the message space $\mathcal{X} = \Sigma^n$ for any desired string length n.

In a word, through all the current works on FPE, there is still no satisfying method in dealing character FPE. Clearly we need some better solutions.

1.3   Our Contributions

In this paper, we provide an effective and efficient solution for character FPE problem that can encipher character strings while preserving their length and memory consumption. In detail, our contributions are:

Firstly, we suggest that character alphabets can be ranked using an improved RtE method, where the characters are represented by extended position notation called *mixed-radix numeral systems*.

Secondly, we propose and analyze a character FPE scheme based on Feistel, and extend from the FFX mode to be able to use mixed-radix numerals.

2   Preliminaries

2.1   Format-Preserving Encryption

We start with a brief review to the classical definition of format-preserving encryption [2], described as:

Definition 1 (Format-preserving encryption). *A format-preserving encryption scheme is a function*

$$\boldsymbol{F} : \mathcal{K} \times \mathcal{N} \times \mathcal{T} \times \mathcal{X} \rightarrow \mathcal{X} \cup \{\bot\}, \tag{1}$$

where $\mathcal{K}$, $\mathcal{N}$, $\mathcal{T}$, $\mathcal{X}$ are called the key space, format space, tweak space and domain, respectively. All of them are nonempty and $\bot \notin \mathcal{X}$.

All FPEs work on some subspaces of the domain $\mathcal{X}$, determined by a certain format in $\mathcal{N}$, named *slice*:

Definition 2 (Slice on a message space). *Given a concrete format $N \in \mathcal{N}$, the N-indexed slice is defined as*

$$\mathcal{X}_N = \{X \in \mathcal{X} | \forall \{K, T\} \in \mathcal{K} \times \mathcal{T}, E_K^{N,T}(X) \in \mathcal{X}\}, \tag{2}$$

where $E_K^{N,T}(X)$ returns the ciphertext of X.

FPE requires that any $X \in \mathcal{X}$ lives in at least one slice indexed by some $N \in \mathcal{N}$. It also requires that any slice $\mathcal{X}_N$ is finite for all $N \in \mathcal{N}$. For any $\{K, T\} \in \mathcal{K} \times \mathcal{T}$, both the encipher and decipher process should be permutations on $\mathcal{X}_N$, and whether $E_K^{N,T}(X) = \bot$ or not depends only on the format and the plaintext, but not on K and T.

2.2   Security Notion

Throughout all the security notions that FPEs could be after, the PRP notion is mostly used. Let $\mathcal{E} : \mathcal{K} \times \mathcal{X} \to \mathcal{X}$ be a block cipher, and let $\mathcal{A}^{E(\cdot)}$ indicates an adversary $\mathcal{A}$ with an oracle E, which may ask any encryption query $E(\cdot)$. Denote $\varepsilon \xleftarrow{\$} \mathcal{E}_K$ as to pick a key K randomly from $\mathcal{K}$ and return $\mathcal{E}_K(\cdot)$, and denote $\pi \xleftarrow{\$} Perm(\mathcal{X})$ as to pick a permutation π on $\mathcal{X}$ randomly and return $\pi(\cdot)$. Then the adversary's advantage is given by

$$\mathbf{Adv}_E^{PRP}(\mathcal{A}) \stackrel{def}{=} Pr[\varepsilon \xleftarrow{\$} \mathcal{E}_K, \mathcal{A}^{\varepsilon(\cdot)} = 1] - Pr[\pi \xleftarrow{\$} Perm(\mathcal{X}), \mathcal{A}^{\pi(\cdot)} = 1]. \tag{3}$$

3   Introducing Mixed-Radix Numeration to Character FPE

3.1   Notations

Denote the set of all possible characters as $Chars$. We know that $Chars$ is finite and $|Chars| = c$. Given any two character strings $A, B \in Chars^*$ (by $*$ we mean that they each consists of any arbitrary number of characters), denote $A \parallel B$ (or AB in short) as their concatenation. Thus any character string X can be represented by $X = x_1 x_2 \cdots x_i, x_* \in Chars$. Additionally, we let $l(X)$ be the number of characters in string X (henceforth the *length* for short), and $s(X)$ be its binary size (henceforth the *size*), we believe that to fully describe the string Z, all of $Chars$, $l(X)$, and $s(X)$ are necessary. Obviously for single characters $x \in Chars$, the number of bytes needed in encoding it is given by $s(x)$. If let a set $\Psi = \{\psi_1, \cdots, \psi_I\}$ be all possible binary sizes of single characters, then Ψ determines a partition of $Chars$:

$$Chars = \bigcup_{i=1}^{I} C_i, \forall c \in Chars, c \in C_i \Leftrightarrow s(c) = \psi_i, \tag{4}$$

where each of C_i is a subset of $Chars$ in which the binary size of any character is ψ_i. We believe that the given partition could help reaching a satisfying solution for character FPE problem.

3.2   Mixed-Radix Numeration: A Promising Way

Character strings to mixed-radix numerals. As the matter of fact, character data is not the only one that results in a complex and irregular message space. For example, a full date of AD chronology can be considered as 3-digit numbers with each digit respectively in the domain $\mathbb{Z}_{31}$, $\mathbb{Z}_{12}$ and $\mathbb{Z}_{9999}$ (at least for now), thus the date 24-03-1998 is actually also a number $24_{31}3_{12}1998_{9999}$, where the subscripts are to represent the radixes of each digit. Similarly, suppose there are an octahedral dice, a hexahedral dice and a tetrahedral dice, the sample space of the statistical event "successively roll the three dices, and return the results in sequence" can also be described by a 3-digit number with each digit respectively in $\mathbb{Z}_8$, $\mathbb{Z}_6$ and $\mathbb{Z}_4$. Both the examples are to use a kind of non-standard positional numeral systems known as *mixed-radix numeral systems* [9], in which the numerical base varies from position to position. Such numeral systems are able to precisely represent any particular message space, as long as the amount of elements is a composite number of which all factors are known. Therefore, the mixed-radix numeration might just be what needed in building FPE schemes on arbitrary message spaces, like that of character data.

Structure of character strings. With set Ψ given in the previous section, we suggest a notion called the *structure* to describe the format of character data in the sense of mixed-radix numeration:

Definition 3 (Structure of character data). *Without loss of generality, for a character string $X \in Chars^n = x_1 x_2 \cdots x_n$, let*

$$\omega_i = |\{x_j \in X | s(x_j) = \psi_i, 1 \leqslant j \leqslant n\}|, i \in \{1, 2, \ldots, I\} \tag{5}$$

be the number of characters in X that is encoded with ψ_i bytes, the structure of X is therefore defined as

$$\Omega(X) = \{\omega_{1\psi_1}, \omega_{2\psi_2}, \ldots, \omega_{I\psi_I}\}. \tag{6}$$

Figure 1 gives a intuitive example on how the structure we defined works on the character strings. Additionally, the structure refines the notion of "format" for character data, because of the following properties it has:

Proposition 1 (Properties of the structure). *For the structure $\Omega(\cdot)$ of character data, the following statements holds:*

1. *For any $X \in Chars^*$, $\Omega(X)$ is unique.*
2. *For any $A, B \in Chars^*$, $X = A \parallel B \Leftrightarrow \Omega(X) = \Omega(A) + \Omega(B)$.*
3. *For any $A, B \in Chars^*$, $\Omega(A) = \Omega(B) \Leftrightarrow (l(A), s(A)) = (l(B), s(B))$ because:*

$$\forall X \in Chars^*, \{l(X) = \sum_{i=1}^{I} \omega_i s(X) = \sum_{i=1}^{I} \omega_i \psi_i, \ \omega_i \in \Omega(X), \psi_i \in \Psi. \tag{7}$$

Therefore, we believe that it is the key basis to extend RtE approach for character data, and to further build character FPE schemes on.

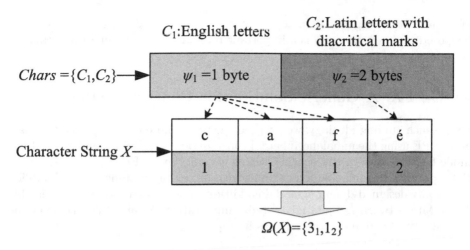

Fig. 1. This figure gives an illustration of the structure of character strings. Assume the overall character set *Chars* consists of 2 subsets: C_1 containing the modern English alphabet and C_2 containing Latin letters with diacritical marks, respectively takes 1 byte and 2 bytes to be represented (i.e. $\Psi = \{\psi_1 = 1, \psi_2 = 2\}$). Then since the string $X =$ "café" has 3 characters from C_1 and 1 character from C_2, its structure is given by $\Omega(X) = \{3_1, 1_2\}$, from which we know that this 4-character string takes a memory space of 5 bytes.

3.3 The Extended Rank-Then-Encipher Approach

In order to build character FPE schemes that work under mixed-radix numeration, we extend the RtE approach, to rank character strings with mixed-radix notation. Note that though the structure of character data is the basis of our work, it cannot directly do this kind of ranking. To do that we mainly exploited the partition on *Chars* given at Sect. 3.1. Recall that *Chars* is divided into subsets $C_i (i = 1, 2, \cdots, I)$, in which all characters are of the same binary size ψ_i. Obviously a bijective mapping can be built between elements in C_i and the integer domain $\mathbb{Z}_{|C_i|}$, i.e. each character in C_i can be mapped to a integer in $\{0, 1, \cdots, |C_i| - 1\}$. Thus when characters are treated as digits of a mixed-radix number in RtE, a feasible way is to decide the radixes according to the subset where the characters belong to. This is done by denoting all $c \in Chars$ with the following 2-tuple:

$$c = (v(c), t(c)) : c \in C_i \Leftrightarrow t(c) = iv(c) \in \mathbb{Z}_{|C_i|}, \tag{8}$$

where $t(c)$ is the *tag* of the character that marks the subset it belongs to, and $v(c)$ is the value of it. Correspondingly, for the subsets C_*, a table is kept to record $|C_*|$, so that the radix of a character can be easily determined by its tag. Take the demonstration in Fig. 1 as an example, suppose the character "é" is the 10-th character in the subset C_2, which contains a total of 100 characters (i.e. $|C_2| = 100$), then the ranking routine will recognize "é" as $(9, 2)$, and thus find its radix 100. Moreover, with digits in the form of such 2-tuples, the structure of a character string is also indicated by the tags in its ranking result, thus the proposed ranking approach is a important reference in preserving the format of character strings.

4   C-FFX: A Generic Solution for Character FPE

Under such guiding ideology, we propose a generic and efficient scheme for character FPE using the unbalanced Feistel construction [11]. Built based on the FFX mode construction, in this scheme (which we call the "C-FFX") we extend the RtE approach to rank character strings with mixed-radix numerals, and applied a specially designed dynamic modulo addition in our construction, which is able to operate between k-digits mixed-radix numerals, to ensure the format of the scheme's output remains the same as its input.

4.1   Feistel-Based Construction with Dynamic Modulo Addition

Recall that our goal of character FPE designing is to preserve the structure of character strings, i.e. for an input string X and its corresponding output string Y, a character FPE should ensure that $\Omega(X) = \Omega(Y)$ always hold.

For concision, given a character string $X \in Chars^n$, let $|X| = n$ be its length, and denote the i-th digit of X as $X[i]$ $(i = 1, 2, \ldots, n)$. For $1 \leqslant i < j \leqslant n$, let $X[i..j] = X[i] \parallel X[i+1] \parallel \cdots \parallel X[j]$. Also we denote $\boldsymbol{cmin} = min(|C_i|, i = 1, 2, \ldots, I), \boldsymbol{cmax} = max(|C_i|, i = 1, 2, \ldots, I)$ respectively as the amount of elements of the smallest and largest subset of $Chars$, and define $\mathcal{X} = |Chars^n_{\Omega(X)}|$ as the number of character strings with the structure of string X. It's easy to know that $\boldsymbol{cmax}^{|X|} \geqslant \mathcal{X} \geqslant \boldsymbol{cmin}^{|X|}$. Additionally, since in each round of any Feistel, the input string X is split into two substrings (denoted as L and R, for the left part and the right part), again assume $|X| = n$, we also let $l = |L|$ and $n - l = |R|$.

In Fig. 2 we show the structure of one round of C-FFX, where F is the round function and $\boxplus_{gc}/\boxminus_{gc}$ is the modulo addition/subtraction module we designed. Since, as mentioned, in each round the input string X is split into two substrings L and R, obviously $\Omega(X) = \Omega(R) + \Omega(L)$. Without loss of generality, suppose L directly goes to the right of the output Y, then certainly $\Omega(Y) = \Omega(L) + \Omega'$. Therefore to make $\Omega(Y) = \Omega(X)$, it's easy to know that $\Omega' = \Omega(R)$. As we know, the rest part of Y is generated by $L \boxplus_{gc} F(R)$ or $L \boxminus_{gc} F(R)$, therefore to ensure $\Omega(Y) = \Omega(X)$ is to let $\Omega(L \boxplus_{gc} F(R))/\Omega(L \boxminus_{gc} F(R)) = \Omega(R)$. It's not quite realistic to design a round function that returns a mixed-radix numeral pseudo-randomly, while the radixes of the output varies at each round. Thus in order to do achieve out goal, we made some major improvement on the modulo addition function.

The modified modulo addition and its inverse, which we called the "dynamic modulo addition" $\boxplus_{gc}$ and $\boxminus_{gc}$, are digit-wise operations, meaning that they process the input pair digit by digit. Assume that string A and B are the two inputs of $\boxplus_{gc}$ or $\boxminus_{gc}$, and suppose we demand that the output of the operations

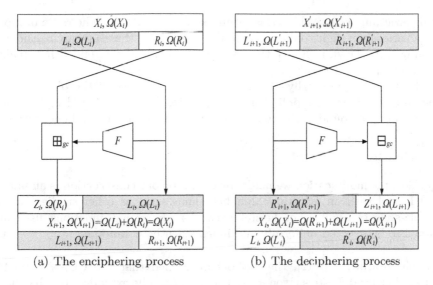

Fig. 2. A single round of the C-FFX construction.

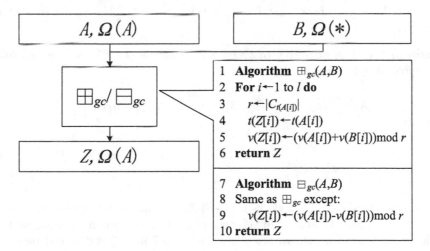

Fig. 3. Mechanism of the modulo addition function $\boxplus_g c$ and $\boxminus_g c$. Both functions traverse the two input strings A and B (line 2), in the i-th loop, line 3 uses tag $t(A[i])$ to determine the radix r for the modulo operation, thus the content of the output digit $v(Z[i])$ computed in line 5 or 9 is kept in the range of subset $C_{t(A[i])}$. Since line 4 sets tag $t(Z[i])$ to be the same as $t(A[i])$. Therefore according to Eq. 8, this ensures that $Z[i]$ belongs to $C_{t(A[i])}$.

(denoted as Z) to have the same structure as A (i.e. $\Omega(Z) = \Omega(A)$), then for each digit i of Z, our operations first computes the sum of the corresponding digit $A[i]$ and $B[i]$, then modulo the result with the radix referenced by the tag $t(A[i])$. Since the tags of each digit of the output is exactly the same as the input

A, this procedure ensures that the output is of A's structure. The radix of input strings varies from digit to digit, so are the operations, thus they are considered "dynamic". As shown in Fig. 3, the 2-tuple notation in the extended RtE makes the operations easy to realize.

C-FFX gives a practically effective solution to character FPE problem, which is theoretically able to be applied on any character data, encipher/decipher them correctly in fixed rounds, without using cycle-walking or repeated encryption.

4.2   Security

Regardless the modification we made, by definition our construction is an unbalanced Feistel with an arbitrary alphabet. Thus same as other studies on the provable-security analysis of Feistel networks, the round functions used are assumed to be selected uniformly and independently at random.

Security bound. In [12], the authors mentioned that the CCA bound for binary unbalanced Feistels given in its Theorem 7 can be extended to unbalanced Feistels with arbitrary alphabet. Although C-FFX uses mixed-radix numeration and thus the radix of its alphabet is not fixed, its CCA bound can still be given by:

Theorem 1 (CCA security of C-FFX). *Denote a C-FFX as ϵ, given $\mathbf{cmin}$ and a fixed $\tau \geq 1$, while $l > n - l$, we have*

$$\mathbf{Adv}_\epsilon^{CCA}(q) \leq \frac{2q}{\tau+1}((3\lceil l/(n-l)\rceil + 3)q/\mathbf{cmin}^l)^\tau, \tag{9}$$

while

$$r = \tau(4\lceil l/(n-l)\rceil + 4) \tag{10}$$

is the minimum number of Feistel rounds needed.

To proof the above result works for C-FFX, the only thing we need to do is to reinterpret Lemmas 11 and 12 in [12] to analyze the case when the construction works on mixed-radix numeration, since Theorem 7 in [12] is deduced based on these two lemmas:

Lemma 1 (reinterpretation of Lemma 11 in [12]). *In C-FFX, the chance that two distinct non-adaptive queries have the same coin at round $t \geq 1$ is at most $\mathbf{cmin}^{l-n}$.*

Proof. Since the scheme is designed to preserve the structure of character strings, in each round, the structure of both input and output of the Feistel is assumed to be known (this is due to that the only thing that a Feistel round will do to the structure of its input is to swap positions of the digits in a constant way).

Suppose that a C-FFX scheme receives distinct non-adaptive queries X_1 and X_2. For each $i \in \{1,2\}$, let (L_i, R_i) be the output at round $t - 1$ of X_i, where $|L_i| = l$ and $|R_i| = n - l$. The queries X_1 and X_2 collide at time t if and only if $R_1 \boxplus_{gc} F(L_1) = R_2 \boxplus_{gc} F(L_2)$, with F being the round function at round t. This occurs when R_1 and R_2 differ, with probability $|Chars_{\Omega(R)}^{n-l}|^{-1} = \mathcal{R}^{-1} \leq cmin^{l-n}$, because F is uniformly random. If $R_1 = R_2$ then so are L_1 and L_2, which contradicts the hypothesis that the two queries are distinct.

Lemma 2 (reinterpretation of Lemma 12 in [12]). *In C-FFX, the chance that two distinct non-adaptive queries collide at time $t > \lceil l/(n-l) \rceil$ is at most $3/cmin^b$.*

Proof. Suppose that a C-FFX scheme receives distinct non-adaptive queries X_1 and X_2. We shall prove by induction on b that for any $b \leq l$, the probability that outputs at round $t > \lceil b/(n-l) \rceil$ of the two queries have the same last b digits is at most $3/cmin^b$. The claim of this lemma corresponds to the special case $b = l$.

First consider the base case $b < n - l$. For each $i \subset \{1, 2\}$, let (L_i, R_i) be the output at round $t-1$ of X_i, where $|L_i| = l$ and $|R_i| = n-l$. The last $(n-l)$-digit substring of the round-t output of X_i is $R_i \boxplus_{gc} F(L_i)$, with F being the round function at round t. If R_1 and R_2 differ then the probability that outputs at round t of the two queries have the same last b digits is at most $cmin^{-b}$ (the same reason as in Lemma 2). If $R_1 = R_2$ then the two queries have the same coin at round $t - 1$, which by Lemma 2 occurs with probability at most $cmin^{l-n}$. Hence, by union bound, the chance that the two queries have the same last b digits is at most $cmin^{-b} + cmin^{l-n} \leq 3/cmin^b$.

Next consider $b \geq n - l$ and assume that the chance round-$(t-1)$ outputs of the two queries have the same last $b - n + l$ digits is at most $3/cmin^{b-n+l}$. The outputs at round t of the two queries have the same last b digits if and only if (i) they have the same coin at round t, which by Lemma 2 occurs with probability at most $cmin^{l-n}$, and (ii) their output at round $t - 1$ have the same last $b - n + l$ digits, which occurs with probability at most $3/cmin^{b-n+l}$ by induction hypothesis. As the round functions in the network are independent, the chance that both (i) and (ii) occur is at most $cmin^{l-n} \cdot 3/cmin^{b-n+l} = 3/cmin^b$.

Notice that according to [12], the above extension is only known to be work when the round functions are contracting, which is the reason that we set $l > n-l$ in out construction.

5   Conclusion

In this paper we stated the problem in applying format-preserving encryption on character data, as well as analyzed the fundamental reason of it. By introducing mixed-radix numeral systems to character FPE, we refined the format of character data, and extended the rank-then-encipher approach for character FPE. On the top of these, we proposed the C-FFX scheme as a generic character FPE solution, which adopts Feistel-based construction with a specially built dynamic modulo addition module, so that mixed-radix numerals can be processed. Analysis showed that our scheme provides solid security. In our future works, we plan to further design FPE schemes that work under mixed-radix numeration, based on other constructions.

Acknowledgment. This work is supported by National Natural Science Foundation of China (No. 61672300), National Natural Science Foundation of Tianjin (Nos. 16JCY-BJC15500 and 14JCYBJC15300).

References

1. Black, J., Rogaway, P.: Ciphers with arbitrary finite domains. In: Preneel, B. (ed.) CT-RSA 2002. LNCS, vol. 2271, pp. 114–130. Springer, Heidelberg (2002). https://doi.org/10.1007/3-540-45760-7_9
2. Bellare, M., Ristenpart, T., Rogaway, P., Stegers, T.: Format-preserving encryption. In: Jacobson, M.J., Rijmen, V., Safavi-Naini, R. (eds.) SAC 2009. LNCS, vol. 5867, pp. 295–312. Springer, Heidelberg (2009). https://doi.org/10.1007/978-3-642-05445-7_19
3. Spies, T.: Feistel finite set encryption. NIST submission (2008)
4. Morris, B., Rogaway, P., Stegers, T.: How to encipher messages on a small domain: deterministic encryption and the Thorp shuffle. In: Halevi, S. (ed.) CRYPTO 2009. LNCS, vol. 5677, pp. 286–302. Springer, Heidelberg (2009). https://doi.org/10.1007/978-3-642-03356-8_17
5. Hoang, V.T., Morris, B., Rogaway, P.: An enciphering scheme based on a card shuffle. In: Safavi-Naini, R., Canetti, R. (eds.) CRYPTO 2012. LNCS, vol. 7417, pp. 1–13. Springer, Heidelberg (2012). https://doi.org/10.1007/978-3-642-32009-5_1
6. Bellare, M., Rogaway, P., Spies, T.: The FFX mode of operation for format-preserving encryption. NIST submission (2010)
7. Luby, M., Rackoff, C.: How to construct pseudorandom permutations from pseudorandom functions. SIAM J. Comput. **17**, 373–386 (1988)
8. Li, M., Liu, Z.L., Li, J.W., Jia, C.F.: Format-preserving encryption for character data. J. Netw. **7**, 1239–1244 (2012)
9. Fraenkel, A.S.: Systems of numeration. Am. Math. Mon. **92**, 105–114 (1985)
10. Patarin, J.: Generic attacks on Feistel schemes. In: Boyd, C. (ed.) ASIACRYPT 2001. LNCS, vol. 2248, pp. 222–238. Springer, Heidelberg (2001). https://doi.org/10.1007/3-540-45682-1_14
11. Schneier, B., Kelsey, J.: Unbalanced Feistel networks and block cipher design. In: Gollmann, D. (ed.) FSE 1996. LNCS, vol. 1039, pp. 121–144. Springer, Heidelberg (1996). https://doi.org/10.1007/3-540-60865-6_49
12. Patarin, J.: About Feistel schemes with six (or more) rounds. In: Vaudenay, S. (ed.) FSE 1998. LNCS, vol. 1372, pp. 103–121. Springer, Heidelberg (1998). https://doi.org/10.1007/3-540-69710-1_8
13. Rozenberg, B., Weiss, M.: Complex format-preserving encryption scheme. 14/296484 (2015)
14. Hoover, D.N.: Format-preserving encryption via rotating block encryption. US8948376 B2 (2015)
15. Spies, T., Pauker, M.J.: Format-preserving cryptographic systems. US8958562 B2 (2015)
16. Li, J., Liu, Z.L., Chen, X.F., Xhafa, F., Tan, X., Wong, D.S.: L-EncDB: a lightweight framework for privacy-preserving data queries in cloud computing. Knowl.-Based Syst. **79**, 18–26 (2015)

Data Sharing with Fine-Grained Access Control for Multi-tenancy Cloud Storage System

Zhen Li[1,2(✉)], Minghao Zhao[1], Han Jiang[1], and Qiuliang Xu[1]

[1] School of Computer Science and Technology,
Shandong University, Jinan, China
sdufelizhen@126.com, zhaominghao@hrbeu.edu.cn,
{jianghan,xql}@sdu.edu.cn
[2] School of Computer Science and Technology,
Shandong University of Finance and Economics, Jinan, China

Abstract. Data sharing is one of the most significant applications of cloud computing. For security and privacy concerns, clients generally encrypt their data before upload them to the cloud. The existing data sharing schemes either entirely rely on the cloud to enforce access control or inevitably involve a trusted third party (TTP) to perform secret key distribution. This thesis proposes a secure data sharing scheme without TTP involved. Our scheme allows users to classify their data and achieves a fine-gained access authorization. The key-distribution is integrated with the user authorization and data sharing procedure. In terms of security, except for semi-honest cloud service provider and external adversary, we also take internal adversary into consideration and analysis security in this strong model.

Keywords: Cloud security · Data sharing · Fine-gained access control · Data reliability and privacy

1 Introduction

Cloud computing provides a practical method to offer service to the tenants at a low price, high performance and high flexibility. Cloud customers are free to care about service development, while cloud providers can concentrate on management activities providing an infrastructure that gives to customers the illusion of the availability of infinite resources [1]. One of the most promising benefits in cloud storage system is to provide ubiquitous, convenient and on-demand access to data shared among the Internet, and data sharing has become the most frequently used service of cloud storage system.

However, although constructed with highly reliable software-hardware architecture, cloud storage system still has some certain security and trust concerns and anxieties. Specifically, when the user outsource their data to the cloud, they totally loss the control of them, and the cloud acquires the chance to dispose the data. It might utilize the data beyond the user's expect, such as to get additional profit, or just simply sell the user's data to other organizations [2]. Thus, client tends to not fully trust the cloud

© ICST Institute for Computer Sciences, Social Informatics and Telecommunications Engineering 2018
J. Wan et al. (Eds.): CloudComp 2016, SPNCE 2016, LNICST 197, pp. 123–132, 2018.
https://doi.org/10.1007/978-3-319-69605-8_12

service provider, and for privacy concerns, they encrypt their data before upload them to the cloud.

Secure data sharing among multiple users in untrusted cloud environment is a tough problem as we cannot rely on the cloud to perform access control and user revocation. One of the naive solutions is to encrypt all the data with same symmetric key and send the key to the authorized user. But sharing keys may increase the risk of key exposure, especially when a user is no longer qualified to access the file, the entire file will be re-encrypted with a new key. Another traditional solution is to adopt public-key encryption or identity based encryption (IBE), but it needs to encrypt a document multiple times using different users' public-keys or identity-keys, which lays a heavy burden for the data owner. Broadcast encryption (BE) can alleviate this issue but cannot achieve fine-gained access control.

Attribute based encryption (ABE), especially ciphertext-policy ABE (CP-ABE) provides another seemingly feasible solution for cloud data sharing, which allows the data owner to fully control the access policy of his data. However, although achieving fine-gained authorization, the CP-ABE based schemes require a fully-trusted third party (e.g. Key authority), which is not commonly exist in real-world. In addition, these schemes do not take internal adversaries into consideration.

Thus, it is desirable to construct flexible and scalable fine-gained access control for data sharing, in which data owner can share his data to users with different priority without a TTP involved. In this paper, we propose a scheme achieving this goal. In addition, we also consider the scenario that the data owner want to split the operation of updating data and changing the authority. This is because his some files may be need to update such as changing their grade or re-encryption with a new key for some security reason. He is not willing to affect the existing authority information. Similarly, when he has changed some data users' privileges, he isn't willing to update his data. And our scheme achieves high security that we do not only consider the CSP as a semi-honest adversary, but also consider the misbehaviors of authorized users.

1.1 Related Works

Fine-gained access control for encrypted data sharing in untrusted storage system has been extensively studied. Traditionally, researchers tend to use access control lists (ACLs) to manage users' authorization [3, 4]. Specifically, in Kallahalla et al.'s [3] scheme, the data owner firstly classifies his data and generates success control list for each file-group and then encrypts each file-group with a symmetric key. This symmetric key is latterly distributed to the data user according to the ACL, and thus only the authorized user in ACL can have access to this group of files. However it involves a heavily burden in key management for the data owner, as the key size will growth linearly with the number of file-groups. Gol et al. [4] combine symmetric and public encryption and propose a scheme that enable the users in a specific ACL to use their secret key to recover the symmetric key which is used for decrypting the document. Similarly, it also lays a huge burden for the data owner, as the encryption operation also grows linearly with the number of users in the ACL.

Another approach for cloud data sharing is to utilize the attribute-based encryption. The primary idea of ABE is proposed by Sahai and Waters [5]. After that, according to either the policy is associated with a ciphertext or a key, two variants of ABE – known as ciphertext-policy ABE (CP-ABE) [6] and key-policy ABE (KP-ABE) [7] – are proposed. Based of ABE, Li et al. [8] propose an accountable CP-ABE scheme, which allows tracing the identities of misbehaving users who leaked the description key to others. Li et al. [9] also propose an outsourced ABE construction which provides checkability of the outsourced computation results in an efficient way. Xie et al. [10] propose a novel access control scheme for cloud data sharing system with efficient attribute and user revocation, which largely eliminates the overhead computation (i.e. from $O(2n)$ to $O(n)$, where n is the number of attributes). Liang et al. [11] propose a scheme that enable service provider to implement practical and fine-grained encrypted data sharing (i.e. the data owner is allowed to share a ciphertext of data among others under some specified conditions), meanwhile achieves the anonymity of data users who has gotten access to the data. Liang et al. [12] propose another scheme that achieves secure search functionality and fine-gained access control, which enables a data owner to efficiently share his data to a specified group of users matching a sharing policy. In addition, their scheme supports keywords updating after the data has been uploaded to the cloud. Recently, Wang et al. [13] take a fully investigation of key escrow problem in attribute-based encryption and propose a scheme to solve this issue. They propose an improved two-party key issuing protocol that can guarantee that neither key authority nor cloud service provider can compromise the whole secret key of a user individually.

A recent guideline for secure cloud data sharing is to deploy key aggregate method. Chu et al. [14] propose a scheme in which the data owner first categorizes his files into different classes, and encrypts files by the class. After that, he chooses some encrypted files and computes the aggregated key. The key is used for decrypting a group of documents and will be latterly sent to the authorized users. Cui et al. [15] also construct a scheme with high flexibility that can share any group of selected documents with any group of users. And they also propose a key-aggregate searchable encryption scheme. These data sharing schemes are efficiently and flexibly constructed, but they demand the data owner to transfer the aggregated key to the data user, so the data owner would be online all time.

1.2   Contributions

This paper proposes a data sharing scheme with fine-gained access control for multi-tenancy cloud storage architecture. The contribution of this work is listed as follows:

- *Autonomous Authorization.* Our scheme enables the data owner to autonomously manage his data. The data owner is supported to classify his data and share to data users with different priorities. Also, the data user can choose to retrieval data belong to specified group of data owners.
- *Getting rid of TTP.* We propose a secure data sharing scheme without TTP involved. It only needs a trusted key distribution center (KDC) for key generation, which is easy to obtain through existing public key infrastructures (PKI).
- *High efficiency and scalability.* In this scheme, each document is encrypted by symmetric encryption with an independent key, and it is not required for the data

owners to distribute the keys. Instead of that, after received request from the data user, the CSP can generate a partial key for each document and send it along with the document to the user. The data user can recover the deception key by using his secret key.

- *Meliorative security model.* We compose an improved security model to capture a wide range of adversarial behavior. We not only consider the CSP and unauthorized user (i.e. include unregistered users and users that have been revoked) as potential adversary, but also consider the misbehaviors of authorized user.

The rest of this paper is structured as follows. In Sect. 2 we present some preliminaries, including basic computational complexity assumptions and security specifications. We present detailed description of our scheme in Sect. 3. The analysis of our scheme is presented at Sect. 4. And we conclude this paper in Sect. 5.

2 Preliminaries

2.1 Complexity Assumption

Definition 1 (Bilinear Map). Let $\mathbb{G}_1$ and $\mathbb{G}_2$ be two cyclic groups of some large prime order q. A bilinear map is a map $e\colon \mathbb{G}_1 \times \mathbb{G}_1 \to \mathbb{G}_2$ with the following properties:

1. Bilinearity. For all $u, v \in \mathbb{G}_1$ and $a, b \in \mathbb{Z}_q^*$, we have $e(u^a, v^b) = e(u, v)^{ab}$.
2. Non-degeneracy. $e(g, g) \neq 1$.
3. Computability. There is an efficient algorithm to compute $e(u, v)$ for any $u, v \in \mathbb{G}_1$.

Definition 2 (Discrete Logarithm). Let g be a primitive root for $\mathbb{F}_q$ and let h be a nonzero element of $\mathbb{F}_q$. The *Discrete Logarithm Problem* (*DLP*) is the problem of finding an exponent x such that

$$g^x \equiv h \bmod q$$

The number x is called the discrete logarithm of h to the base.

Definition 3 (Hardness of DLP). The DLP assumption is that there exists no probabilistic polynomial algorithm that can solve the DLP problem.

Definition 4 (Computation Diffie-Hellman Problem). The challenger chooses $a, b \in \mathbb{Z}_p$ at random and outputs $(g, A = g^a, B = g^b)$. The adversary then attempts to output $g^{ab} \in \mathbb{G}$. An adversary $\mathfrak{B}$ has at least an ε advantage if

$$\Pr[\mathfrak{B}(g, g^a, g^b) = g^{ab}] \geq \varepsilon$$

where the probability is over the randomly chosen a, b and the random bits consumed by $\mathfrak{B}$.

Definition 5 (CDH Hardness Assumption). The computational (t, ε)-CDH assumption holds if there exists no probabilistic polynomial time adversary has at least ε advantage in solving the above game.

2.2   System Architecture and Security Goals

We design a TTP-free multi-user data sharing scheme, which have three entities: cloud server provider (CSP), data owner and data user. The main responsibility of the CSP is to store and process the encrypted data according to authorized users' request. Note that there are many data owners and many data users, so this is a Multi-tenancy Cloud Storage System.

We consider three types of adversaries include external adversary and *honest-but-curious* CSP and legal user as internal adversary. Specifically, CSP are assumed to be semi-honest, which mean the server is honest to save the data owners' files and perform data operations requested for authorized data users, but tries to deduce or guess the extra information from the interactive data. Internal user adversary refers to the legal user participated in the protocol. We assume that he can get all the interactive information. He will deduce the extra data by using his private key and the information he has received. External user adversary means the illegal users including the revoked users and this is the basic demand for any access control and authority management system. Note that we assume that the user-server collusion is not included in our adversarial model.

3   Concrete Constructions

3.1   Proposed Scheme

The proposed scheme consists of the following phases:

(1) *Initialization Phase.*
   This is the first phase in our data sharing protocol. In this phase, the system generates public parameters and the public/private key pair of users and CS to initialize the algorithm.
   Step 1: $param \leftarrow \text{setup}(\lambda)$
   Input security parameter λ and get the public parameter $param$, Let $\psi = (q, \mathbb{G}_1, \mathbb{G}_2, e, g)$, $\mathbb{G}_1$ and $\mathbb{G}_2$ are two cyclical groups of prime order q, a generator $g \in \mathbb{G}_1$, a Bilinear Map $e: \mathbb{G}_1 \times \mathbb{G}_1 \rightarrow \mathbb{G}_2$ and $H: \mathbb{G}_2 \rightarrow \{0, 1\}^\tau$ is a collision resistant hash function, and τ is key-length of AES encryption, then $param = (\psi, H)$.
   Step 2: $PK_i, SK_i \leftarrow \text{KeyGen}(param)$
   The key generation algorithm takes security parameter $param$ as input and generates the keys for the clients and the CSP. The client $u_i (1 \leq i \leq n)$ gets its secret key and public key as $SK_i = x_i, PK_i = g^{\frac{1}{x_i}}$, $x_i \in_R \mathbb{Z}_q$. The CSP, as a special participant, also gets its public key PK_c and secret key SK_c as $SK_c = \alpha, PK_c = g^\alpha$, $\alpha \in_R \mathbb{Z}_q$.

Step 3:

The CSP firstly initializes an authority distribution matrix Λ with the size of n × n. Each element in this matrix $\pi_{ji} = \{A_{jil}|l \in \{1, 2, \ldots, \rho\}\}$ is a set which represents the data owner u_i to authorize data user u_j the privilege to access the document with grade l. ρ is the number of levels that the documents expected to be classified and it varies for different data owners. The initial value of each element π_{ji} is assigned as Φ, which denote that data owner u_i have not given permission to u_j to access to his any document. In the matrix, each row (e.g. the j-th row) represents the user's permission that has been authorized by other data owners, while each column represents the authorizations he has given to other data user (i.e. which users can have access to his documents).

(2) *Encrypting Files Phase.*

In this phase the data owner carrys out the algorithm to encrypt his files.

Step 1: $CK_{il} \leftarrow CKGen(param)$

The client u_i randomly chooses a secret key for each class of document. He chooses secret key CK_{il} for l-th class, where $1 \le i \le n, 1 \le l \le \rho$ and $CK_{il} \in_R \mathbb{Z}_q$.

Step 2: $D_{ilk}, r_{ilk} \leftarrow DKGen(SK_i, CK_{il})$

Data owner u_i generates an encryption key D_{ijk} for each of his document D_{ijk} as:

$$DK_{ilk} = H\left(e\left(g^{\frac{r_{ilk} \cdot CK_{il}}{x_i}}, g^{\frac{\alpha \cdot CK_{il}}{x_i}}\right)\right), r_{ilk} \in_R \mathbb{Z}_q, 1 \le i \le n, 1 \le l \le \rho, 1 \le k \le \sigma,$$

in which σ indicates that there are σ documents classified as a specific level.

Step 3: $D'_{ilk} \leftarrow EncDoc(D_{ilk}, DK_{ilk})$

Data owner u_i encrypts each of his document D_{ilk} and gets its ciphertext D'_{ilk}. We adopt AES for documents encryption. Then he will send the encrypted document and its classification information to CSP.

(3) *Authentication and Revocation Phase.*

This algorithm is run by the data owner to grant a user the privilege of reading (some) files. In this phase, the data owner authorizes each category of documents to its homologous user group, and sends the authorization information to the CSP. After received the authorization information, the CSP stores it in the authority distribution matrix. Note that both the Grant algorithm and Revoke algorithm satisfy dynamic property, which means the data owner can change the author information of his document at any time. Now we will give a detail description of Grant and Revoke algorithm.

- $A_{jil} \leftarrow Grant(SK_i, PK_jCK_{il})$ User authorization algorithm. This algorithm is used for data owner u_i to authorize his documents of grade l to u_j, and this algorithm outputs the authorization value as $A_{jil} = g^{\frac{CK_{il}}{x_i x_j}}$. By repetitively invoking this algorithm, u_i can authorize u_j with document of different grade. We use $A_{ji} = \{A_{jil}|l \in \{1, \ldots, \rho\}\}$ to denote the authority that u_j has been granted from u_i. User u_i sent Grant (u_j, u_i, A_{ji}) to the CSP and thus the CSP can update π_{ji} into $\pi_{ji} \bigcup A_{ji}$.

- $A_{jil} \leftarrow \text{Revoke}(SK_i, PK_jCK_{il})$. Authority revoke algorithm. This algorithm is run by the data owner such as to revoke a user's privilege of accessing his documents. Specifically, data owner u_i revokes u_j's permission of accessing his documents of grade l. Similar to the above, u_j executes $\text{Revoke}(u_j, u_i, A_{ji})$ and sent the output value to the CSP. After receiving this value, the CSP updates π_{ji} into $\pi_{ji} - A_{ji}$.

(4) *Data Sharing Phase.*

The authenticated data user makes a request to the CSP for some data owner's documents. CSP picks up the object files and computes the relative decrypted key. Then the CSP transfer the documents and each partial key to the data user.

Let T_r denotes the request made by the data user. $T_r = (u_i, U_j)$, in which $U_j = \{u_i | i \in \{1, 2, \ldots, n\} \wedge i \neq j\}$. It means a data user can appoint one or more data owners as his own will. If he wants to get all the data owners' files he has privilege to access, he just uses U instead of U_j.

The data user sends T_r to CSP, and then the CSP executes step 1 to acquire corresponding files and partial decrypted key. After receiving the result, the data user executes step 2 to compute the decrypted key and then decrypts the files.

Step 1: $Z \leftarrow \text{Search}(T_r, \Lambda)$: The CSP executes this algorithm such as to get targeted documents and its corresponding trapdoor that is used for decryption. We describe this Algorithm in Table 1.

Table 1. Search algorithm

Algorithm 1 : Search algorithm
Input: access query T_r and authority matrix Λ
Output : the set of targeted documents and corresponding trapdoor used for decryption
1. initialize $Z = \Phi$
2. for every $u_i \in U_j$ do
3.   for every $A_{jil} \in \pi_{ji}$ do
4.   for each $D_{ilk} \in D_i$ do
5. $DK'_{ilk} = e\left(g^{\frac{CK_{il}}{x_i x_j} \cdot r_{ilk}}, g^{\frac{CK_{il}}{x_i x_j}} \right)^{\alpha} \; ; Z = Z \cup \{(D'_{ilk}, DK'_{ilk})\};$
6.   end for
7.   end for
8. end for

Step 2: $D_{ilk} \leftarrow \text{DecDoc}\left(SK_j, Z\right)$: The u_j computes $DK_{ilk} = H((DK'_{ilk})^{x_j^2})$, which is used to decrypt D'_{ilk} such as to get D_{ilk}.

3.2 Correctness

In this scheme, the data owner uploads his documents along with the document classification information to the cloud. Then in the authorization phase, if he permits a user to access to a category of documents with higher grade, this implies he also permits this user to get access to other categories of documents with lower grade. Thus, if the set π_{ji} only contains one value, it indicates that the user u_j is only authorized to access to the documents with the lowest grade. In this case, the CSP just perform hash operation among the documents of the lowest grade, such as to recover the partial key of each document, which will latterly send to the client along with the corresponding documents. According to the bilinear property:

$$H\left((Dk'_{ilk})^{x_j^2}\right) = H\left(e\left(g^{\frac{CK_{il}}{x_i x_j} \cdot r_{ilk}}, g^{\frac{CK_{il}}{x_i x_j}}\right)^{\alpha \cdot x_j^2}\right) = H\left(e\left(g^{\frac{r_{ilk} \cdot CK_{il}}{x_i}}, g^{\frac{\alpha \cdot CK_{il}}{x_i}}\right)\right).$$

That is the secret key DK_{ijk} which is used for u_i to encrypt the document D_{ilk}. Because of the symmetry property of AES encryption algorithm, this key can be used for decryption correctly.

4 Security and Efficiency Analysis

4.1 Security Analysis

In our proposed scheme, each document is encrypted by AES with a unique symmetric key; thus, according to the security insurance of AES, only if this key is not recovered by adversaries, the document cannot be decrypted. Afterwards, we will regard the CSP and the legal data user as adversary, and explain separately why they cannot recover the secret keys.

Honest but curious CSP as adversary

The CSP can acquire the authority value $g^{\frac{CK_{il}}{x_i x_j}}$ of each user, as well as the random number r_{ilk} of each document, and accordingly, he can figure out $g^{\frac{r_{ilk} \cdot CK_{il}}{x_i x_j}}$. Using his secret key α, he can figure out $\left(g^{\frac{CK_{il}}{x_i x_j}}\right)^{\alpha}$, which result in $g^{\frac{\alpha \cdot CK_{il}}{x_i x_j}}$. Although the CSP also possesses each user's public key $g^{\frac{1}{x_j}}$, as he cannot acquire the data user's secret key x_j, the DLP hardness assumption ensure that he cannot figure out $g^{\frac{\alpha \cdot CK_{il}}{x_i}}$, and thus he cannot figure out the secret key $DK_{ilk} = H\left(e\left(g^{\frac{r_{ilk} \cdot CK_{il}}{x_i}}, g^{\frac{\alpha \cdot CK_{il}}{x_i}}\right)\right)$.

Legal user as adversary

Assuming that the data user have acquired his own authority value $g^{\frac{CK_{il}}{x_i x_j}}$, he can use his own secret key to calculate $g^{\frac{r_{ilk} \cdot CK_{il}}{x_i}}$ and $g^{\frac{CK_{il}}{x_i}}$. However, although he also processes the public key g^{α} of the CSP, the CDH hardness assumption ensures that he cannot figure our $g^{\frac{\alpha \cdot CK_{il}}{x_i}}$. Thus it is guaranteed that even if the internal user acquired additional information, he cannot perform any adversarial behavior, as long as he does not collude with the service provider.

4.2   Performance

We compare our proposed scheme with the schemes proposed in Refs. [8, 14]. Reference [8] based on ABE, so it must have a trusted center called attribute authorities (AA), from which user is entitled to a number of attributes and can obtain a decryption key corresponding to those attributes. Reference [14] based on key-aggregate, so it needs the data owner to be online at all time.

Our scheme only needs a trusted key distribution center for public and secret key generation and it does not need a trusted center to manage user. The users' addition and revocation is made by data owner himself, so it is more flexible. The users' authority information is stored in the CSP, making it convenient to revoke user by just deleting the privilege value. And the CSP transfers the partial decrypted key to the user for the further decryption using his private key, which avoids the data owners to distribute the keys. The details are shown in Table 2.

Table 2. Comparison between our scheme and Refs. [8, 14]

Scheme	Trusted center	Fine-grained access control	User revocation	Data owner online all time
Ref. [8]	Y	Y	S	N
Ref. [14]	N	Y	F	Y
Ours	N	Y	F	N

Y yes, N no, F fast, S slow

5   Conclusion and Future Work

We propose a scheme that allows multi-user to securely and flexibly share their data. We consider the scenario that the data owner wants to split the operation of updating data and changing the authority. The data owner can discretionally share his different data to different users, so it achieves fine-gained access authorization. In our scheme, all of the documents are encrypted by symmetric encryption algorithm, and each of them is encrypted with a unique and independent key. The key-distribution is integrated with the user authorization and data sharing procedure, which means it is not needed for the data owner to be online all time to distribute the encryption keys to the data users. In terms of security, except for semi-honest CSP and external adversary, which have been extensively adopted as adversarial model in most works, we also take the misbehavior of legal users into consideration. Getting rid of the dependency of TTP, this scheme is highly compatible for multi-user scenario, and in order to capture a wide range of application of cloud computing, we will extend our scheme to solve the problem of keyword searching over encrypted data as a future work.

Acknowledgements. This work is supported by the National Natural Science Foundation (NSF) under grant Nos. 61572294, 61602275 and NSF Key Project under grant No. 61632020.

References

1. Ardagna, C.A., Damiani, E., Frati, F., Rebeccani, D., Ughetti, M.: Scalability patterns for platform-as-a-service. In: 2012 IEEE 5th International Conference on, Cloud Computing (CLOUD), pp. 718–725. IEEE, June 2012
2. Motoyama, M., McCoy, D., Levchenko, K., Savage, S., Voelker, G.M.: An analysis of underground forums. In: Proceedings of the 2011 ACM SIGCOMM Conference on Internet Measurement Conference, pp. 71–80. ACM, November 2011
3. Kallahalla, M., Riedel, E., Swaminathan, R., Wang, Q., Fu, K.: Plutus: scalable secure file sharing on untrusted storage. In: Proceedings of the 2nd USENIX Conference on File and Storage Technologies USENIX Association, pp. 29–42, March 2003
4. Goh, E.J., Shacham, H., Modadugu, N., Boneh, D.: SiRiUS: securing remote untrusted storage. In: The Proceedings of the Internet Society (ISOC) Network and Distributed Systems Security Symposium (NDSS-03), vol. 3, pp. 131–145, February 2003
5. Sahai, A., Waters, B.: Fuzzy identity-based encryption. In: Cramer, R. (ed.) EUROCRYPT 2005. LNCS, vol. 3494, pp. 457–473. Springer, Heidelberg (2005). https://doi.org/10.1007/11426639_27
6. Bethencourt, J., Sahai, A., Waters, B.: Ciphertext-policy attribute-based encryption. In: 2007 IEEE Symposium on Security and Privacy (SP 2007), pp. 321–334. IEEE, May 2007
7. Goyal, V., Pandey, O., Sahai, A., Waters, B.: Attribute-based encryption for fine-grained access control of encrypted data. In: Proceedings of the 13th ACM Conference on Computer and Communications Security, pp. 89–98. ACM, October 2006
8. Li, J., Huang, Q., Chen, X., Chow, S.S., Wong, D.S., Xie, D.: Multi-authority ciphertext-policy attribute-based encryption with accountability. In: Proceedings of the 6th ACM Symposium on Information, Computer and Communications Security, pp. 386–390. ACM, March 2011
9. Li, J., Huang, X., Li, J., Chen, X., Xiang, Y.: Securely outsourcing attribute-based encryption with checkability. IEEE Trans. Parallel Distrib. Syst. 25(8), 2201–2210 (2014)
10. Xie, X., Ma, H., Li, J., Chen, X.: An efficient ciphertext-policy attribute-based access control towards revocation in cloud computing. J. Univ. Comput. Sci. 19(16), 2349–2367 (2013)
11. Liang, K., Susilo, W., Liu, J.K.: Privacy-preserving ciphertext multi-sharing control for big data storage. IEEE Trans. Inf. Forensics Secur. 10(8), 1578–1589 (2015)
12. Liang, K., Susilo, W.: Searchable attribute-based mechanism with efficient data sharing for secure cloud storage. IEEE Trans. Inf. Forensics Secur. 10(9), 1981–1992 (2015)
13. Wang, S., Liang, K., Liu, J.K., Chen, J., Yu, J., Xie, W.: Attribute-based data sharing scheme revisited in cloud computing. IEEE Trans. Inf. Forensics Secur. 11(8), 1661–1673 (2016)
14. Chu, C.K., Chow, S.S., Tzeng, W.G., Zhou, J., Deng, R.H.: Key-aggregate cryptosystem for scalable data sharing in cloud storage. IEEE Trans. Parallel Distrib. Syst. 25(2), 468–477 (2014)
15. Cui, B., Liu, Z., Wang, L.: Key-aggregate searchable encryption (KASE) for group data sharing via cloud storage. IEEE Trans. Comput. 65(8), 2374–2385 (2016)

Ring Signature Scheme from Multilinear Maps in the Standard Model

Hong-zhang Han[(⊠)]

Department of Computer Engineering, Jiangsu University of Technology,
Changzhou, China
hhz@jsut.edu.cn

Abstract. A novel ring signature is constructed based on Garg-Gentry-Halevi (GGH) graded encoding system which is a candidate multilinear maps from ideal lattice, and we prove its security in standard model. Under the GGH graded decisional Diffie-Hellman (GDDH) assumption, the proposed ring signature guarantees the anonymity of signer. At the same time, the ring signature is the existentially unforgeable against adaptive chosen message attack under the GGH graded computational Diffie-Hellman (GCDH) assumption.

Keywords: Multilinear map · Ring signature · Anonymous · Unforgeability

1 Introduction

The notion of ring signature was first formally introduced by Rivest et al. in 2001 [1]. In a ring signature, any member in the ring can sign on behalf of the whole ring. As a result, the verifier is convinced that this signature is from a ring in which the signer is a member, but it is hard to know which member in the ring actually generated the signature. On the definition of security for ring signature, Bendery et al. [2] pointed out that the definition of security was too weak in [1], and gave a strongest definitions of both anonymity and unforgeability depending on the security strength for ring signature. Due to this unique anonymity and flexibility (such as, no managers, no setup procedure of the ring and no revocation procedure), the ring signature can be applied for a variety of purposes which have been suggested in previous works, for example, anonymously leaking secrets [3] and anonymous authentication in Ad-hoc networks and wireless sensor networks [4–6].

With the introduction of the concept of ring signature, a large of ring signature scheme and its variants have been constructed based on intractability of the discrete logarithm or large integer factorization, such as the standard ring signature schemes [1–6], identity-based ring signature schemes [7], linkable ring signature schemes [8] and so on. With the advent of quantum computer era, all the above schemes will no longer be secure, because the quantum algorithm designed by Shorn can efficiently solve the classical problems in number theory. (e.g. large integer factorization, discrete logarithm problem.) In order to design a post-quantum secure ring signature, there are a few of ring signature schemes with security based on standard lattice problems which is considered infeasible even under the quantum computer [9–12]. As most of them made

© ICST Institute for Computer Sciences, Social Informatics and Telecommunications Engineering 2018
J. Wan et al. (Eds.): CloudComp 2016, SPNCE 2016, LNICST 197, pp. 133–144, 2018.
https://doi.org/10.1007/978-3-319-69605-8_13

use of the hash-and-sign method based on the (Gentry-Peikert-Vaikuntanathan) GPV strong trapdoors [13], a hidden structure was added to the underlying lattice, which was considered an important price to pay from a theoretical point of view [14]. Recently, Melchor et al. [15] presented an efficient ring signature by means of adapting Lyubashevsky's signature from ideal lattice, in which the strongest security defined in [2] was achieved by using a weak trapdoor as Lyubashevsky's signature [16]. However, the proof of its security was in the oracle model.

In this paper, we construct a new ring signature based on GGH's graded encoding system which is an candidate multilinear maps from ideal lattice [17]. Our main contribution from a theoretical point of view is that the proposed ring signature scheme is the first one to be based on multilinear maps and no ring signature was until now based on it. Under the graded decisional Diffie-Hellman (GDDH) assumption and grade computational Diffie-Hellman (GCDH) assumption, the new ring signature scheme guarantees the anonymity of signer even if the secret key of the signer is exposed and holds the existential unforgeability against adaptive chosen message attack in the standard model, respectively.

The rest of this paper is organized as follows. In Sect. 2, we introduce the background about multilinear maps and the algorithms in the GGH framework, full domain hash from multilinear maps and the definition of ring signature and its security model. In Sect. 3, the new ring signature scheme based on multilinear maps is described in details, and Sect. 4 proves its security including the anonymity and unforgeability. Finally, in Sect. 5, we summarize this paper.

2 Preliminaries

2.1 Notation

We use $\mathbb{Z}$ to denote the set of integer, and $R = \mathbb{Z}[X]/(X^n + 1)$ denote the integer polynomial ring where $U_{i \in [N]}$ is a power of 2. For a large prime $q \in \mathbb{Z}$, $R_q = Z_q[X]/X^n + 1 = R/qR$ denotes the quotient ring of integer polynomial mod q. Let I denote an ideal of ring R, then R/I denotes a quotient ring generated by the ideal I while $\{e + I : e \in R\}$ denotes the representative of coset of the quotient ring R/I. By convention, we use bold letters for vectors (e.g. a or A). In addition, for a positive integer k, $[k]$ denotes $\{1, \cdots k\}$.

2.2 Multilinear Maps and the GGH Graded Encoding System

Boneh and Silverberg (BS) first proposed the concept of multilinear maps and described many cryptographic applications in 2003 [18]. For the groups G_1 and G_2 which have the same prime order, the definition of BS is that if a map $e : G_1^n \rightarrow G_2$ is an n-multilinear maps it should satisfy the following properties:

(1) If $a_1, \ldots, a_n \in \mathbb{Z}$ and $x_1, \ldots, x_n \in G_1$, then $e(x_1^{a_1}, \ldots, x_n^{a_n}) = e(x_1, \ldots, x_n)^{\prod_{i \in [n]} a_i}$;
(2) The map e is non-degenerate. In other words, if $g \in G_1$ is a generator of G_1, then $e(g, \ldots, g)$ is a generator of G_2.

Although several efficient cryptographic primitives were constructed based on the concept of multilinear maps, Boneh and Silverberg also pointed out that to instantiate this kind of multilinear maps on Weil pair or Tate pair was infeasible. In the past decade, how to achieve cryptographically useful multilinear maps is an important open problem. Recently, Garg, Gentry and Halevi (GGH) give a candidate in EURO-CRYPT' 2013 [17]. They construct an approximate multilinear maps from ideal lattice, which is also known as GGH graded coding system. In a k-level GGH candidate, as long as $i+j \leq k$, the encodings on i-level and encodings on j-level can make multiplication to obtain the encoding on $i+j$-level. Of course, the product should be smaller than the modulus q. By multiplication in an iterative manner, the encodings on k-level can be obtained. This approach is different from the BS view of multilinear maps where a k-linear maps should allow the simultaneous multiplication of k source group elements into one target group element. Here, we briefly describe the GGH framework as follows, and the details can be referred to [17].

Abstractly, in GGH graded encoding system, the exponentiation *samp* in multilinear groups family is viewed as an encoding of an element α on the i-level. At the same time, the GGH replaces the groups defined in BS with an encoding set associated with ideal lattice. Specifically, for a ring R, the GGH graded encoding system includes a system of sets $S = \{S_i^{\mathbf{a}} \subset \{0,1\}^* : i \in [0,n], \mathbf{a} \in R\}$, where $S_i^{(\mathbf{a})}$ consists of the i-level encodings of $\mathbf{a}$ and the sets $S_i = \bigcup_\alpha S_i^{(\mathbf{a})}$. The k-GGH framework includes several algorithms, which are as follow:

Instance generation: InstGen $(1^\lambda, 1^k)$. The instance-generation procedure takes as input the security parameter λ and an integer $B_j = re-enc(1, \beta_j)$ that denotes the level number, and outputs parameters (params, $\mathbf{p}_{zt}$) where $params = \{n, m, q, \mathbf{y}, \{\mathbf{x}_i\}_i, s\}$ is the public parameters of the GGH k-graded encoding system as above, and $\mathbf{p}_{zt}$ is a k-level "zero-testing parameter". To ensure the security of graded encoding system, the parameters related to params is chosen carefully. Generally, for a quotient ring R_q, the approximate setting is $n = \tilde{O}(k\lambda^2)$, $q = 2^{n/\lambda}$ and $m = O(n^2)$. In addition, in the public parameter the "randomizers" $\mathbf{x}_i$ are just random encodings of zero while the parameter $\mathbf{y}$ is a level-one encoding of 1 (correctly, encoding of $1 + I$).

Sampling level-zero encodings: samp($params$). It takes as input $params$, the randomized algorithm outputs a level-zero encoding $\mathbf{d}$ of the coset $\mathbf{a} + I$, such as $\mathbf{d} \in S_0^{\mathbf{a}}$. Essentially, according to a discrete Gaussian distribution with an appropriate variance, one can randomly choose a short vector $\mathbf{d} \in R$, which can be viewed as a small representative of the coset $\mathbf{a} + I$ because of its very small coefficients compared to the modulus q.

Encodings at higher levels: enc($params, i, \mathbf{d}$). Given the input parameters $params$ and a level-zero encoding $\mathbf{d} \in S_0^{\mathbf{a}}$, the level-$i$ encoding $\mathbf{u} \in S_i^{(\mathbf{a})}$ of $\mathbf{d}$ can be obtained by multiplying $\mathbf{d}$ with $\mathbf{y}^i$, where $\mathbf{y}$ included in $params$ is a level-1 encoding of 1.

Re-randomization: re-Rand($params, i, \mathbf{u}$). This algorithm re-randomizes the encoding $\mathbf{u} \in S_i^{(\mathbf{a})}$ to the same level and obtains another encoding $\mathbf{u}^* \in S_i^{(\mathbf{a})}$, which involves adding a random Gaussian linear combination of the level-i encodings of zero in *params* (e.g.$\mathbf{x}_i$), whose noisiness "drowns out" the initial encoding. Moreover, for any two encodings $\mathbf{u}_1, \mathbf{u}_2 \in S_i^{(a)}$ whose noise bound is at most $\mathbf{b}$, the output distribution of re-Rand(*params*, $i, \mathbf{u}_1$) and re-Rand(*params*, $i, \mathbf{u}_2$) is statically the same.

Addition: add(*params*, $\mathbf{u}_1, \mathbf{u}_2$) **and Negation** neg(*params*, $\mathbf{u}_1$). Given any two level-i encodings $\mathbf{u}_1 \in S_i^{(a)}$ and $\mathbf{u}_2 \in S_i^{(b)}$, we can obtain an adding encoding $\mathbf{u} = \mathbf{u}_1 + \mathbf{u}_2 \in S_i^{(a+b)}$, while the output of algorithm neg(*params*, $\mathbf{u}_1$) belongs to $S_i^{(-a)}$.

Multiplication: mult(*params*, $\mathbf{u}_1 \in S_i^a, \mathbf{u}_2 \in S_j^b$). Given any two encodings $\mathbf{u}_1 \in S_i^a$ and $\mathbf{u}_2 \in S_j^b$, we have multiplying encoding $\mathbf{u} = \mathbf{u}_1 \cdot \mathbf{u}_2 \in S_{i+j}^{(a \cdot b)}$ as long as $i+j<k$.

Zero-testing: isZero(*params*, $\mathbf{p}_{zt}, \mathbf{u}$). Given a level-$k$ encoding u, if $\left\| [\mathbf{p}_{zt} \cdot \mathbf{u}]_q \right\| \leq q^{3/4}$ where $\|.\|$ denotes the length of vector, it is denoted that u belongs to the set S_k^0, and the algorithm outputs 1 and 0 otherwise. Note that the encoding is additively homomorphic, so we can test quality between encodings by subtracting them and comparing to zero.

Extraction: ext(*params*, $\mathbf{p}_{zt}, \mathbf{u}$). Given a level-$k$ encoding $\mathbf{u}$, the algorithm extracts a "canonical" and "random" representative of coset from the encoding $\mathbf{u}$. Namely, ext(*params*, $\mathbf{p}_{zt}, \mathbf{u}$) outputs (say) $\mathbf{K} \in \{0, 1\}^\lambda$, such that:

(a) For any two level-k encodings $\mathbf{u}_1, \mathbf{u}_2 \in S_k^a$, ext(*params*, $\mathbf{p}_{zt}, \mathbf{u}_1$) = ext(*params*, $\mathbf{p}_{zt}, \mathbf{u}_2$) with overwhelming probability.

(b) For $\alpha \in R$ and any encoding $\mathbf{u} \in S_k^a$, the distribution of ext(*params*, $\mathbf{p}_{zt}, \mathbf{u}$) is statistically uniform over $\{0, 1\}^\lambda$.

For ease of description, let re-enc(*params*, $i, \mathbf{d}$) denotes the function of re-Rand(*params*, i, enc(*params*, $i, \mathbf{d}$)) where $\mathbf{d}$ is a result of a call to samp(*params*). In addition, we also omit *params* arguments that are provided to every algorithm in GGH framework as above. For instance, we will write samp() to instead of samp(*params*).

2.3 GCDH/GDDH Hard Assumptions

Now, we describe the hard assumptions in GGH framework: Graded Computational Diffie-Hellman problem (GCDH) and Graded Decisional Diffie-Hellman problem (GDDH), which are the basis of the security of our new ring signature in this paper.

Definition 1 (GCDH/GDDH). On parameters λ, n, q, k, a challenger runs InstGen($1^\lambda, 1^k$) to get the public parameters (*params*, $\mathbf{p}_{zt}$) of the GGH graded encoding system, and it calls samp() several times to pick the random $\mathbf{e}_0, \cdots \mathbf{e}_k$. Then,

(1) Given *params*, $\mathbf{p}_{zt}$, re-enc(1, $\mathbf{e}_0$), $\cdots$, re-enc(1, $\mathbf{e}_k$), the goal of the GCDH is to find a level-k encoding of $\prod_{i \in [0,k]} \mathbf{e}_i$.

(2) Given *params*, $\mathbf{p}_{zt}$, re-enc(1, $\mathbf{e}_0$), $\cdots$, re-enc(1, $\mathbf{e}_k$) and a random level-k encoding $\mathbf{u} \leftarrow \text{re} - \text{enc}(k, \text{samp}())$, the goal of the k-GDDH is to distinguish between the level-k encoding re $- \text{enc}(k, \prod_{i \in [0,k]} \mathbf{e}_i)$ and the random encoding $\mathbf{u}$.

In [17], an extensive cryptanalysis has been done to prove the security of GGH graded encoding system, and it shows that the GCDH/GDDH problems are hard for any polynomial-time algorithm to solve. Recently, some effective cryptography primitives based on GCDH/GDDH are proposed, such as multiparty key agreement [17], full domain hash from multilinear maps and identity-based aggregate signatures [19], identity-based key-encapsulation mechanism [20], attribute-based encryption for circuits [21] and so on.

2.4   Full Domain Hash from Multilinear Maps

Full domain hash (FDH) is an important cryptographic technique and has been widely used in bilinear map cryptography where typically a hash function is employed to hash a string into a bilinear group. In this section, we briefly describe a method to achieve the full domain hash from multilinear maps, which will be used in our ring signature scheme. The construction in terms of GGH framework and message signature based on it are described as follows, and the details can be referred to [19].

Hash-and-Sign from GGH Framework. A trusted algorithm generates a GGH instance by running $(params, \mathbf{p}_{zt}) \leftarrow \mathrm{InstGen}(1^{\lambda}, 1^{k=l+1})$, where λ is the security parameter and l is the length of message. Then, it obtains $2l$ elements $\mathbf{A}_{i,j} \leftarrow \mathrm{re-enc}(1, \mathrm{samp}())$, where $i \in [l]$ and $j \in \{0, 1\}$. For a message $m \in \{0, 1\}^l$, the full domain hash function (FDH) H mapping the l bits message to a level-l encoding can be computed iteratively. Specifically, let $H_1(m) = \mathbf{A}_{1,m[i]}$ where $m[i]$ denotes the i - th bit of message m. For $i \in [2, l]$, $H_i(m) = H_{i-1}(m) \cdot \mathbf{A}_{i,m[i]}$. So, the FDH based on GGH framework can be defined as $H(m) = \mathrm{re-enc}(l, H_l(m))$.

Therefore, given a private key $\mathbf{a} \leftarrow \mathrm{samp}()$ and the corresponding verification key $VK = \mathrm{re-enc}(1, \mathbf{a})$, a signature on message m is $\sigma = \mathrm{re-enc}(k - 1, H(M) \cdot \mathbf{a})$ and verified by testing $\mathrm{isZero}(\mathbf{p}_{zt}, \sigma \cdot \mathbf{y} - H(M) \cdot VK)$ where $\mathbf{y}$ is a level-1 encoding of 1 that is included in *params* of the GGH instance. In [19], Hohenberger et al. showed that this signature was secure against adaptively chosen message attack in standard model conditioned on the k-GCDH assumption holding against subexponential advantage.

2.5   Secure Model

For a secure ring signature scheme Φ with N members, it must satisfy some anonymity and unforgeability. In [2], according to various security strength, Bender et al. defined various levels of anonymity and unforgeability, respectively. In this paper, the anonymity uses the strongest definition, which is against full key exposure, while the existential unforgeability is defined under the fixed-ring attack.

Anonymity. The anonymity $Anon(\Phi, \mathcal{A}, \lambda, N)$ under full key exposure is defined using the following experiment between a challenger and an adversary $\mathcal{A}$.

(1) Given the security parameter λ, the challenger runs the Setup algorithm to generate the common public parameters PP and the keypairs $\{pk_i, sk_i\}_{i \in [N]}$ for the signature scheme. Then, the challenger sends pp and $\bar{R} = \{pk_i\}_{i \in [N]}$ to the adversary.

(2) The adversary can make polynomially many ring signing queries, the form of which is $(i, m, \bar{R})$ for varying index $i \in [N]$ and message $m \in \mathcal{M}$. After receiving them, the challenger replies $\sigma \leftarrow Sign(PP, m, sk_i, \bar{R})$.

(3) The adversary can adaptively query the signing secret key of the i - th user, where $i \in [N]$. The challenger replies sk_i.

(4) The adversary chooses a message $m \in \mathcal{M}$ as well as two indexes $i_0, i_1 \in [\max]$ where $pk_{i0}, pk_{i1} \in \bar{R}$, and makes ring signing query. The challenger chooses a random bit $b \in \{0, 1\}$ and replies a ring signature $\sigma^* \leftarrow Sign(PP, m, sk_{ib}, \bar{R})$ where sk_{ib} is the corresponding signing secret key of the public key pk_{ib}.

(5) The adversary $\mathcal{A}$ outputs a guess $b^* \in \{0, 1\}$ for b.

We say the adversary wins if $b^*=b$. Define $Anon_{\mathcal{A}}^{\Phi-\mathrm{FKE}}$ as the probability that $b^*=b$, where the probability is over the coin tosses of the Setup, sign algorithm and of $\mathcal{A}$.

Definition 2. A ring signature Φ is unconditional anonymity against full key exposure if for all probabilistic polynomial-time adversaries, the function $Anon_{\mathcal{A}}^{\Phi-\mathrm{FKE}}$ is negligible in λ.

Existential Unforgeability. For the ring signature scheme Φ, the existential unforgeability $Unforg(\Phi, \mathcal{F}, \lambda, N)$ with respect to adaptive chosen-message attack and fixed-ring attack can be defined using the following experiment between a challenger and a forger $\mathcal{F}$.

Setup. The challenger firstly chooses security parameter λ and runs the Setup algorithm to generate the common public parameters PP and the keypairs $\{pk_i, sk_i\}_{i \in [N]}$ for the signature scheme. Then, it sends PP and $\bar{R} = \{pk_i\}_{i \in [N]}$ to the adversary.

Query. The adversary $\mathcal{F}$ can make polynomially many ring signing queries. The form of query is $(i, m, \bar{R})$ where messages $m \in \mathcal{M}$ which are chosen adpatively, and the index $i \in [N]$. After receiving them, the challenger replies $\sigma \leftarrow Sign(PP, m, sk_i, \bar{R})$.

Forgery. The forger $\mathcal{F}$ outputs a ring signature $(\sigma^*, m^*, \bar{R})$.

We say the forger $\mathcal{F}$ wins if and only if the algorithm $\mathrm{Verf}(PP, \sigma^*, m^*, \bar{R})$ outputs 1 and m^* is not one of the messages for which a signature was queried during the query phase. Define $Unforg_{\mathcal{F}}^{\Phi-\mathrm{adp}-uf}$ as the probabilistic that $\mathrm{Verf}(PP, \sigma^*, m^*, \bar{R}) = 1$, where the probability is over the coin tosses of the Setup, Sign algorithms and of $\mathcal{F}$.

Definition 3 (Adaptive Unforgeability). A ring signature scheme Φ is existentially unforgeable with respect to adaptive chosen-message attack and fixed-ring attack if for all probabilistic polynomial-time adversaries, the function $Unforg_{\mathcal{F}}^{\Phi-\mathrm{adp}-uf}$ is negligible in λ.

We will also use the selective variant to $Unforg(\Phi, F, \lambda, \max)$ where there is an Init phase before the setup phase, wherein the forger $\mathcal{F}$ gives to the challenger the forgery message $m^* \in \mathcal{M}$. This message m^* cannot be queried for a signature during the Query phase. Finally, $\mathcal{F}$ outputs a ring signature $(\sigma^*, m^*, \bar{R})$. If the algorithm $\mathrm{Verf}(PP, \sigma^*, m^*, \bar{R})$ outputs 1, the forger $\mathcal{F}$ wins. In this case, we define $Unforg_{\mathcal{F}}^{\Phi-\mathrm{Sel}-uf}$ as the probabilistic that the forger $\mathcal{F}$ wins the game, taken over the random bits of the challenger and the forger.

Definition 4 (Selective Unforgeability). A ring signature scheme Φ is existentially unforgeable with respect to selective chosen-message attack and fixed-ring attack if for all probabilistic polynomial-time adversaries, the function $Unforg_{\mathcal{F}}^{\Phi-\text{sel}-uf}$ is negligible in λ.

3 Ring Signature Scheme in GGH Framework

According to the definition of ring signature, our new ring signature scheme in GGH framework is as follows.

Setup(1^λ). The algorithm includes two parts: Setup - params and Setup - Keys.

(1) Setup-params(1^λ). It is a sub-algorithm in setup phase, which takes as input λ and runs $(params, \mathbf{p}_{zt}) \leftarrow \text{InstGen}(1^\lambda, 1^{k=N+l})$ to generate a GGH instance where N is the maximum number of ring supported by the scheme and l is the bit-length of messages. (It is noted that N and l are all bounded by a polynomial in λ). Recall that we omit *params* arguments that are provided to every algorithm in GGH framework.

Next, the sub-algorithm chooses random encodings $\mathbf{a}_{i,v} \leftarrow \text{samp}()$ where $i \in [l]$ and $v \in \{0, 1\}$. Then it generates the corresponding level-1 encodings $\mathbf{A}_{i,v} = \text{re-enc}(1, \mathbf{a}_i)$ for $i \in [l]$ and $v \in \{0, 1\}$. Let $A = \{(\mathbf{A}_{1,0}, \mathbf{A}_{1,1}), \cdots, (\mathbf{A}_{i,0}, \mathbf{A}_{i,1})\}, i \in [l]$ and the common public parameters $PP = \{params, A\}$.

(2) Setup - Keys(PP). Each user can use the sub-algorithm to generate the public key and secret key. Let $U_1, \cdots U_N$ denote the users in the ring signature scheme. The user $U_{j \in [N]}$ chooses random encoding $\mathbf{b}_j \leftarrow \text{samp}()$ and takes it as the secret key, while the public key is $\mathbf{B}_j \leftarrow \text{re} - \text{enc}(1, \beta_j)$. Therefore, the ring can be denoted by a set of public keys, such as $\bar{R} = \{\mathbf{B}_1, \cdots, \mathbf{B}_N\}$.

Sign($PP, m, \mathbf{b}_j, \bar{R}$). The member $U_{j \in [N]}$ use the secret key $\mathbf{b}_j$ to generate a ring signature of a message $m \in \{0, 1\}^l$ about ring $\bar{R}$. The steps are as follows.

(1) Let $m[1], \cdots, m[l]$ be the bits of message m. A level-l encoding $H(m) = \text{re-enc}(l, H_l(m))$ of the l bits message can be computed by using the full domain hash function H described in Sect. 2.
(2) Compute $\mathbf{s}_1 = \mathbf{b}_j \cdot H(m) \cdot \prod_{i \in [N] \cap i \neq j} \mathbf{B}_i$
(3) Output the ring signature $\mathbf{s} = \text{re} - \text{enc}(k - 1, \mathbf{s}_1)$

Verf($PP, \mathbf{s}, m, \bar{R}$). The algorithm takes as input the common public parameters PP, a signature $\mathbf{s}$, a message m and the ring $\bar{R} = \{\mathbf{B}_1, \cdots, \mathbf{B}_N\}$. The authentication process is as follows.

(1) Compute the level-l encoding $H(m) = \text{re} - \text{enc}(l, H_l(m))$ about message m by using the full domain hash function H.
(2) Check the signature by calling isZero($\mathbf{p}_{zt}, \mathbf{s} \cdot \mathbf{y} - H(m) \cdot \prod_{i \in [n]} \mathbf{B}_i$), where $\mathbf{y}$ is a canonical level-1 encoding of 1 that is included in *params*, part of the public parameter PP. The signature is accepted if and only if the zero testing algorithm outputs 1.

Correctness. The correctness property requires that each valid ring signature can pass the verification algorithm. In the above ring signature scheme, the signature $\mathbf{s}$ is a level-$k-1$ encoding of $\prod_{i \in [l]} \mathbf{a}_{i,m[i]} \cdot \prod_{j \in [N]} \mathbf{b}_j$. Since $\mathbf{y}$ is a canonical level-1 encoding of 1, $\mathbf{s} \cdot \mathbf{y}$ is a level-k encoding of $\prod_{i \in [l]} \mathbf{a}_{i,m[i]} \cdot \prod_{j \in [N]} \mathbf{b}_j$. On the other hand, $H(m) \cdot \prod_{i \in [N]} \mathbf{B}_i$ is also level-k encoding of $\prod_{i \in [l]} \mathbf{a}_{i,m[i]} \cdot \prod_{j \in [n]} \mathbf{b}_j$. Therefore, it can be concluded that all valid ring signatures will be pass the testing algorithm, as long as the underlying algorithms run correctly in GGH graded encoding system, e.g. samp( ),enc( ), re-Rand( ).

4   Security Analysis

In this section, according to the security model that is defined in Sect. 3, we analyze the anonymity and unforgeability of the proposed ring signature scheme in the standard model.

4.1   Anonymity

Theorem 1. If the GDDH assumption holds, then the proposed ring signature scheme based on GGH graded encoding system satisfies the unconditional anonymity.

Proof. According to the anonymity game in Sect. 3, the proof of Theorem 1 is as follows.

(a) According to the corresponding parameters in the proposed signature scheme, the challenger runs $(params, \mathbf{p}_{zt}) \leftarrow \text{InstGen}(1^\lambda, 1^{k=N+l})$ to generate a GGH instance, and chooses random encodings $a_{i,v} \leftarrow \text{samp}()$, $i \in [l]$, $v \in \{0,1\}$. At the same time, for the users $U_1, \cdots U_N$, the challenger picks out random encodings $\mathbf{b}_j \leftarrow \text{samp}()$, $j \in [N]$. The private key of user $U_{j \in [N]}$ is $\mathbf{b}_j$ while the public key is $\mathbf{B}_j = \text{re-enc}(1, \mathbf{b}_j)$. Let $\mathbf{A}_{i,v} = \text{re} - \text{enc}(1, \mathbf{a}_i)$ for $i \in [l]$ and $v \in \{0,1\}$, and a set of public keys $\bar{R} = \{\mathbf{B}_1, \cdots, \mathbf{B}_n\}$ denotes the ring. Finally, the challenger sends $PP = \{params, (\mathbf{A}_{1,0}, \mathbf{A}_{1,1}), \ldots, (\mathbf{A}_{l,0}, \mathbf{A}_{l,1})\}$ and $\bar{R}$ to the adversary $\mathcal{A}$.

(b) The adversary makes polynomially many ring signing queries for messages $m \in \{0,1\}^l$ with respect to the ring $\bar{R}$. After receiving them, the challenger calls the algorithm Sign in Sect. 3 and returns the results to $\mathcal{A}$.

(c) The adversary continues to adaptively query the signing secret key of the j - th user, where $j \in [N]$. The challenger replies the corresponding secret key $\mathbf{b}_j$.

(d) The adversary chooses a message $m \in \{0,1\}^l$ and two members $w_0, w_1 \in U_{i \in [N]}$ in the ring, and sends them to the challenger. After receiving them, the challenger chooses a random bit $b \in \{0,1\}$ and replies a ring signature $\mathbf{s}^* \leftarrow \text{Sign}(PP, m, \mathbf{b}_{w[b]}, \bar{R})$ where $\mathbf{b}_{w[b]}$ is the corresponding signing secret key of the user w_b.

(e) Finally, $\mathcal{A}$ wants to determine the identity of signer and outputs a guess $b^* \in \{0,1\}$ for b.

Now, let us analyze the advantage of $\mathcal{A}$. On the one hand, According to the algorithm Sign in the proposed signature scheme, each valid ring signature in the above game is a random encoding on the level-$k-1$. Therefore, we only need to analyze the distribution of the ring signature. Firstly, regardless of the ring signature $\mathbf{s}^*$ from the user w_0 or the user w_1, the valid signature $\mathbf{s}^*$ on message $m \in \{0,1\}^l$ about $\bar{R}$ is a random level-$k-1$ encoding of $\prod_{i \in [l]} \mathbf{a}_{i,m[i]} \cdot \prod_{j \in [N]} \mathbf{b}_j$ (Accurately, which is a level-$k-1$ encoding of the coset $\prod_{i \in [l]} \mathbf{a}_{i,m[i]} \cdot \prod_{j \in [N]} \mathbf{b}_j + I$). That is, for the same message, the distribution of the ring signature from the different members in the ring is indistinguishable. On the other hand, without loss of generality, we can assume that the private key of the user w_b is $\mathbf{b}_1$. According to the definition of GDDH assumption, the adversary cannot distinguish between the level-$(k-1)$ encoding $\mathbf{s}_1 \leftarrow \mathbf{b}_1 \cdot H(m^*) \cdot \prod_{i \in [N] \cap i \neq 1} \mathbf{B}_i$ that is the ring signature computed by challenger and an element $\bar{\mathbf{s}}_1 \leftarrow \mathbf{d}^* \cdot H(m^*) \cdot \prod_{i \in [N] \cap i \neq 1} \mathbf{B}_i$ that is obtained for a random and independent $\mathbf{d}^* \leftarrow \text{samp}()$. Because of the randomness property of the sampling procedure, $\bar{\mathbf{s}}_1$ is nearly uniformly distributed among the cosets of I. Therefore, we can conclude that the advantage $Anon_A^{\Phi-\text{fke}}$ can be ignored, and the proposed ring signature scheme is unconditional anonymity.

4.2 Unforgeability

In this section, according to the unforgeable security model described in Sect. 2, we will prove the existential unforgeability of the proposed ring signature in the standard model, which could be reduced to the GDDH problem that holds for the underlying encoding scheme. To prove the existential unforgeability in the fixed-ring setting, we employ the Hohenberger's approach used in [19]. Specifically, we firstly consider the selective variant to the proposed scheme, then from which the adaptive security can be derived.

Theorem 2. The proposed ring signature scheme for message length l and the number of members N is selectively secure in the unforgeability game under k-GCDH assumption where $k = l + N$.

Proof. With the usual method of reduction, assume there is a polynomial-time algorithm (the forger) $\mathcal{F}$ that can break the selective security of the proposed ring signature scheme with probability ε for message length l and the number of members N, then we can construct an efficient algorithm (the challenger) that can break the k-GCDH assumption with probability ε.

Now, given a GGH's GCDH instance $E = \{params, \mathbf{p}_{zt}, \mathbf{C}_1 \leftarrow \text{re} - \text{enc}(1, \mathbf{a}_1), \cdots \mathbf{C}_k \leftarrow \text{re} - \text{enc}(1, \mathbf{a}_k)\}$ where $\mathbf{a}_i \leftarrow \text{samp}()$, $k = l + N$ and $i \in [k]$. The challenger employs $\mathcal{F}$ to solve GCDH problem as follows.

Init. The forger $\mathcal{F}$ outputs the forgery message $m^* \in \{0,1\}^l$.

Setup. The challenger chooses random $\mathbf{z}_1, \cdots \mathbf{z}_l$ by calling to the algorithm samp() and generates the corresponding level-1 encodings $\mathbf{Z}_i \leftarrow \text{re} - \text{enc}(1, \mathbf{z}_i)$ where $i \in [l]$. Let $m^*[i]$ be the bits of message $m^* \in \{0,1\}^l$ and $\bar{m}^*[i]$ denote $(1 - m^*[i])$. For $i = 1$ to l, let $\mathbf{A}_{i,m^*[i]} = \mathbf{C}_i$ and $\mathbf{A}_{i,\bar{m}^*[i]} = \mathbf{Z}_i$. In addition, let $\bar{R} = \{\mathbf{C}_{l+1}, \cdots \mathbf{C}_{l+N}\}$ denote the set of public keys of N users in the ring. Finally, the challenger sends the common public parameter $PP = \{params, (\mathbf{A}_{1,m^*[1]}, \mathbf{A}_{1,\bar{m}^*[1]}), \cdots (\mathbf{A}_{l,m^*[l]}, \mathbf{A}_{l,\bar{m}^*[l]})\}$ as well as the set $\bar{R} = \{\mathbf{C}_{l+1}, \cdots \mathbf{C}_{l+N}\}$ to the forger F. It is noted that the parameters are distributed independently and uniformly at random as in the real scheme.

Query. The forger $\mathcal{F}$ chooses messages $m \in \{0,1\}^l$ and $m \neq m^*$. Then it requests ring signature under $\bar{R}$ on these $l-$ bit messages. Let j be the first index such that $m[j] \neq m^*[j]$. The challenger computes $\mathbf{s}_1 = \mathbf{z}_j \cdot \prod_{i\in l \cap i \neq j} \mathbf{A}_{m[i]} \cdot \prod_{l+1 \leq v \leq l+N} \mathbf{C}_v$ and $\mathbf{s} = \text{re-enc}(k-1, \mathbf{s}_1)$. Next, the challenger takes $\mathbf{s}$ as the ring signature on m and returns it to $\mathcal{F}$.

Since the result of $\text{IsZero}(\mathbf{s} \cdot \mathbf{y} - H(m) \cdot \prod_{l+1 \leq v \leq l+N} \mathbf{C}_v)$ is 1, where $H(m)$ is a level-l encoding of $\prod_{i\in[l]} \mathbf{A}_{m[i]}$ and H is the full domain hash function based on GGH, the signature can pass the verification of $\text{Verf}(PP, \mathbf{s}, m, \bar{R})$. Namely, the responses of the challenger are valid ring signatures, which are distributed statistically exponentially closely to the real unforgeability game because of the rerandomization in the re-enc algorithm.

Response. The forger $\mathcal{F}$ outputs a ring signature $\mathbf{s}^*$ on the forgery message m^*.

Now, we analyze the reduction and show that the ring signature $\mathbf{s}^*$ is a solution of the GCDH instance $E = \{params, \mathbf{p}_{zt}, \mathbf{C}_1 \leftarrow \text{re} - \text{enc}(1, \mathbf{c}_1), \cdots \mathbf{C}_k \leftarrow \text{re} - \text{enc}(1, \mathbf{c}_k)\}$. If $\mathbf{s}^*$ is a valid ring signature on message m^*, it should pass the verification such as $1 \leftarrow \text{IsZero}(\mathbf{s}^* \cdot \mathbf{y} - H(m^*) \cdot \prod_{l+1 \leq v \leq l+N} \mathbf{C}_v)$. However we know that $H(m^*) \cdot \prod_{l+1 \leq v \leq l+N} \mathbf{C}_v = \prod_{i\in[l]} \mathbf{A}_{m^*[i]} \cdot \prod_{l+1 \leq v \leq l+N} \mathbf{C}_v$ is a level-k encoding of $(\prod_{i\in[k]} \mathbf{c}_i)$. Therefore, the verification of the ring signature $\mathbf{s}^*$ implies a solution to E. Consequently, the challenger succeeds whenever the forger does, and the Theorem 2 is proved.

With the invention of GGH graded coding system as a multilinear maps candidate, to design more common cryptographic primitives based on multi-linear maps becomes a hot research topic. In this paper, we construct a novel ring signature scheme and prove its security in standard model. Under the graded decisional Diffie-Hellman (GDDH) assumption and grade computational Diffie-Hellman (GCDH) assumption, the new ring signature scheme guarantees the anonymity of signer even if the secret key of the signer is exposed and holds the existential unforgeability against adaptive chosen message attack, respectively. However, the main disadvantage of the proposed scheme is that the size of public key is more than that of the schemes based on bilinear-pairing. Recently, Coron et al. proposed a practical grading encoding system in integer ring [22]. We will attempt to use the integer ring instead of ideal lattice to reduce the size of public key.

Acknowledgements. This work is supported by the Research Fund for the Graduate Innovation Program of Jiangsu Province (CXZZ13_0493), and the Natural Science Foundation of Universities of Jiangsu Province (13KJB520005).

References

1. Rivest, R.L., Shamir, A., Tauman, Y.: How to leak a secret. In: Boyd, C. (ed.) ASIACRYPT 2001. LNCS, vol. 2248, pp. 552–565. Springer, Heidelberg (2001). https://doi.org/10.1007/3-540-45682-1_32

2. Bender, A., Katz, J., Morselli, R.: Ring signatures: stronger definitions, and constructions without random Oracles. In: Halevi, S., Rabin, T. (eds.) TCC 2006. LNCS, vol. 3876, pp. 60–79. Springer, Heidelberg (2006). https://doi.org/10.1007/11681878_4

3. Rivest, R.L., Shamir, A., Tauman, Y.: How to leak a secret: theory and applications of ring signatures. In: Goldreich, O., Rosenberg, A.L., Selman, A.L. (eds.) Theoretical Computer Science. LNCS, vol. 3895, pp. 164–186. Springer, Heidelberg (2006). https://doi.org/10.1007/11685654_7

4. Bresson, E., Stern, J., Szydlo, M.: Threshold ring signatures and applications to Ad-hoc groups. In: Yung, M. (ed.) CRYPTO 2002. LNCS, vol. 2442, pp. 465–480. Springer, Heidelberg (2002). https://doi.org/10.1007/3-540-45708-9_30

5. Dodis, Y., Kiayias, A., Nicolosi, A., Shoup, V.: Anonymous identification in *Ad Hoc* groups. In: Cachin, C., Camenisch, Jan L. (eds.) EUROCRYPT 2004. LNCS, vol. 3027, pp. 609–626. Springer, Heidelberg (2004). https://doi.org/10.1007/978-3-540-24676-3_36

6. Xiao, F.J., Liao, J., Zeng, G.H.: Threshold ring signature for wireless sensor networks. J. Commun. 32(3), 75–81 (2012)

7. Chow, S.S.M., Yiu, S.-M., Hui, L.C.K.: Efficient identity based ring signature. In: Ioannidis, J., Keromytis, A., Yung, M. (eds.) ACNS 2005. LNCS, vol. 3531, pp. 499–512. Springer, Heidelberg (2005). https://doi.org/10.1007/11496137_34

8. Yuen, T.H., Liu, J.K., Au, M.H., Susilo, W., Zhou, J.: Efficient linkable and/or threshold ring signature without random oracles. Comput. J. 56(4), 407–421 (2013)

9. Wang, F.H., Hu, Y.P., Wang, C.X.: A lattice-based ring signature scheme from bonsai trees. J. Electron. Inf. Technol. 32(10), 2410–2413 (2010)

10. Wang, J., Sun, B.: Ring signature schemes from lattice basis delegation. In: Qing, S., Susilo, W., Wang, G., Liu, D. (eds.) ICICS 2011. LNCS, vol. 7043, pp. 15–28. Springer, Heidelberg (2011). https://doi.org/10.1007/978-3-642-25243-3_2

11. Brakerski, Z., Kalai, Y.T.: A framework for efficient signatures, ring signatures and identity based encryption in the standard model. Cryptology ePrint Archive: Report 2010/86 (2010)

12. Tian, M.M., Liu, L.S., Yang, W.: Efficient lattice-based ring signature scheme. Chin. J. Comput. 35(4), 712–716 (2012)

13. Gentry, C., Peikert, C., Vaikuntanathan, V.: Trapdoors for hard lattices and new cryptographic constructions. In: Presented at the Proceedings of the 40th Annual ACM Symposium on Theory of Computing. Victoria, British Columbia, Canada, pp. 120–131 (2008)

14. Micciancio, D., Peikert, C.: Trapdoors for lattices: simpler, tighter, faster, smaller. In: Pointcheval, D., Johansson, T. (eds.) EUROCRYPT 2012. LNCS, vol. 7237, pp. 700–718. Springer, Heidelberg (2012). https://doi.org/10.1007/978-3-642-29011-4_41

15. Aguilar Melchor, C., Bettaieb, S., Boyen, X., Fousse, L., Gaborit, P.: Adapting lyubashevsky's signature schemes to the ring signature setting. In: Youssef, A., Nitaj, A., Hassanien, A.E. (eds.) AFRICACRYPT 2013. LNCS, vol. 7918, pp. 1–25. Springer, Heidelberg (2013). https://doi.org/10.1007/978-3-642-38553-7_1

16. Lyubashevsky, V.: Lattice signatures without trapdoors. In: Pointcheval, D., Johansson, T. (eds.) EUROCRYPT 2012. LNCS, vol. 7237, pp. 738–755. Springer, Heidelberg (2012). https://doi.org/10.1007/978-3-642-29011-4_43

17. Garg, S., Gentry, C., Halevi, S.: Candidate multilinear maps from ideal lattices. In: Johansson, T., Nguyen, P.Q. (eds.) EUROCRYPT 2013. LNCS, vol. 7881, pp. 1–17. Springer, Heidelberg (2013). https://doi.org/10.1007/978-3-642-38348-9_1

18. Boneh, D., Silverberg, A.: Applications of multilinear forms to cryptography. Contemp. Math. 324(1), 71–90 (2003)

19. Hohenberger, S., Sahai, A., Waters, B.: Full domain hash from (leveled) multilinear maps and identity-based aggregate signatures. In: Canetti, R., Garay, J.A. (eds.) CRYPTO 2013. LNCS, vol. 8042, pp. 494–512. Springer, Heidelberg (2013). https://doi.org/10.1007/978-3-642-40041-4_27
20. Wang, H., Wu, L., Zheng, Z., Wang, Y.: Identity-based key-encapsulation mechanism from multilinear maps. Cryptology ePrint: Archive: Report 2013/836 (2013)
21. Gorbunov, S., Vaikuntanathan, V., Wee, H.: Attribute-based encryption for circuits. In: Proceedings of the 45th Annual ACM Symposium on Symposium on Theory of Computing, pp. 545–554 (2013)
22. Coron, J.-S., Lepoint, T., Tibouchi, M.: Practical multilinear maps over the integers. In: Canetti, R., Garay, J.A. (eds.) CRYPTO 2013. LNCS, vol. 8042, pp. 476–493. Springer, Heidelberg (2013). https://doi.org/10.1007/978-3-642-40041-4_26

A Revocable Outsourcing Attribute-Based Encryption Scheme

Zoe L. Jiang[1], Ruoqing Zhang[2], Zechao Liu[1], S.M. Yiu[2], Lucas C.K. Hui[2($\boxtimes$)], Xuan Wang[1], and Junbin Fang[3]

[1] Harbin Institute of Technology Shenzhen Graduate School, Harbin, China
[2] The University of Hong Kong, Pokfulam, Hong Kong
hui@cs.hku.hk
[3] Jinan University, Guangzhou, China

Abstract. Attribute-Based Encryption (ABE) is a generalized cryptographic primitive from normal public key encryption. It provides an access control mechanism over encrypted message using access policies and ascribed attributes. This scheme can solve the privacy issue when data is outsourced to cloud for storage well. However, there are some practical issues which must be fixed before ABE becomes applicable. One is that both the ciphertext size and the decryption time grows with the complexity of the access policy, which brings pressure to mobile devies. The other is that, from practical point of view, some users might be disabled for some attributes or be removed from the system. It demands on flexible revocation mechanism supporting both user and attribute granularities. In this research, we propose a solution adopting techniques on secure outsourcing of pairings to support outsourcing computation and adopting some techniques based on the tree-based scheme to solve user revocation and attribute revocation. We also give its security model and proof.

Keywords: Attribute-Based Encryption · Outsourced decryption · Revocation · Bilinear pairing

1 Introduction

Cloud computing offers the advantages of highly scalable and reliable storage on third-party servers. Its economical and efficient model typically results in an almost revolution of data storage ways. While going for cloud computing storage, the data owner and cloud servers are in two different domains. On one hand, cloud servers are not entitled to access the outsourced data content for data confidentiality; on the other hand, the data resources are not physically under the full control of data owner. Therefore, adopting expressive encryption and flexible authentication methods can balance the conflict between cloud users and servers.

R. Zhang—Co-first author.

© ICST Institute for Computer Sciences, Social Informatics and Telecommunications Engineering 2018
J. Wan et al. (Eds.): CloudComp 2016, SPNCE 2016, LNICST 197, pp. 145–161, 2018.
https://doi.org/10.1007/978-3-319-69605-8_14

To address these issues, many techniques have been developed to ameliorate the situation, an important category was put forth called Attribute-Based Encryption (ABE), it could effectively bind the access-control policy to the data and the clients instead of having a server mediating access to files. The access control policy would be a policy that defines the kind of users who would have permissions to read the documents. The users or authenticated client are identified by attributes.

The first rudiment of this scheme is introduced by Sahai and waters in 2005, and then be divided into two formulations: Key-policy based ABE (KP-ABE) [1] and ciphertext-policy based (CP-ABE) [2]. There are several Attribute-Based Encryption proposed in literature. However, most of the existing ABE schemes are based on pairing based operations, the number of pairing computation to decrypt a ciphertext grow with the size and complexity of the access-control policy. In PC platform this issue should be able to handle normally, while it would be a significant challenge for using mobile phones or resource-constrained devices, limited battery life and users' appeal for fast process require high-efficiency and lightweight computation.

Outsourcing ABE scheme are developed to remedy this problem, we can give an overview of this concept [3]. In this concept, the general private key in previous ABE scheme is divided into two parts: a security key SK, held by the user and a transformation key TK, held by a proxy server. When a user want to obtain an encrypted message from a cloud center server, this file, namely defined as CT, is saved in proxy server firstly before sending to user. With the help of transformation key TK, proxy server translates this ABE ciphertext CT satisfied by that user's attributes or access policy into a simple ciphertext CT', thus the user can download this CT' from proxy server and it only incurs a small overhead for him to recover the message from the transformed ciphertext CT' by SK.

Outsourcing ABE has many attractive points compared with traditional ABE scheme, firstly, this scheme provide a efficient solution for File encrypting and decrypting on nowadays mobile devices platform, not only decreasing the operation time obviously, but also economize the limited memory and battery capacity of our phone and tablet. What's more, outsourcing ABE is based on secure bilinear pairing outsourcing algorithm, and it can guarantee an adversary has no power to access the plaintext both in cloud server and proxy server.

However, there still exists a critical issue before this scheme being able to deploy in practice: Revocation. For any cryptosystem that involve many users, if any of key compromising or user leaving situation happens, the corresponding user authority should be revoked from system. For ABE systems, there are two features about revocation issue, the first is about user revocation and the second is about attribute revocation. User revocation means revoking all the attributes of this user and let it remove from the system, attribute revocation stands that a user lost some authority but still exists in real situation. For example, if a employer is appointed to overseas for dealing with foreign affairs, his attribute related to working place will be changed to "overseas" from "local". Exactly in practical the situation of revoking some attributes is more common than pure user level revocation.

Unfortunately, those authors of prime outsourcing ABE [3] scheme didn't consider revocation into their designing. There are also several verifiable Attribute-Based Encryption proposed in literature [4,5]. We revisit these schemes but find they didn't combine into revocation problem. In addition, user revocation has been well studied in previous work [6,7], while there still lacks breakthrough on attribute revocation. Therefore, the following questions arise naturally:

(1) Whether there exists a generic construction to introduce two revocation schemes to the outsourcing ABE?
(2) How to construct an outsourcing ABE with verifiable outsourced decryption and flexible revocation strategy?

We notice that in many previous research work about IBE revocation, most of them consider adopting tree structure to realize user identity distinguishing and revoking, The tree-based revocation approach is probably the most efficient one and it has been well studied in IBE scheme [8]. So for outsourcing ABE, adopting tree-based revocation is a prospective approach to meet those features above. But how to combine this structure into outsourcing ABE perfectly is still a no-easy problem to study.

1.1 Mainly Contribution

– *Supporting user revocation and attribute revocation simultaneously.* In our designing, we adopt tree based revocation scheme, one of most efficient methods, to realize a flexible revocation methods which support user revocation and attribute revocation.

1.2 Organization

The rest of this paper are organized as follows. The Sect. 2 includes some standard notations and definitions in cryptography. In Sect. 3, we review the relative architecture and security definition of outsourcing ABE. We present a new outsourcing ABE scheme supporting both user and attribute revocation in Sect. 4. Section 5 indicates the proof of relative security model. The last section concludes the paper.

2   Background

2.1   Access Structures

Definition 1 (Access Structure). Let $\{P_1, P_2, \cdots, P_n\}$ be a set of parties. A collection $\mathbb{A} \subseteq 2^{\{P_1, P_2, \cdots, P_n\}}$ is monotone if $\forall B, C$: if $B \in \mathbb{A}$ and $B \subseteq C$ then

$C \in \mathbb{A}$. An access structure (respectively, monotone access structure) is a collection (resp. monotone collection) $\mathbb{A}$ of non-empty subsets of $\{P_1, P_2, \cdots, P_n\}$, i.e. $\mathbb{A} \subseteq 2^{\{P_1, P_2, \cdots, P_n\}} \setminus \{\emptyset\}$. The sets in are called the authorized sets, and the sets not in $\mathbb{A}$ are called unauthorized sets.

For better understanding, we adopt the definition of [9]. Attributes plays the role of parties. Thus, the access structure $\mathbb{A}$ will contain the authorized sets of attributes, and we restrict our attention to monotone access structures. In this paper unless stated otherwise, by an access structure we mean a monotone access structure.

2.2   Bilinear Pairing

In the setting of bilinear pairings, we use the following symbols. Let $\mathbb{G}_1$ and $\mathbb{G}_2$ be two cyclic additive groups. The order of $\mathbb{G}_1$ and $\mathbb{G}_2$ is a large prime and also denoted by the symbol q, Define $\mathbb{G}_T$ to be a cyclic multiplicative group of the same order q. A bilinear pairing is defined as a map $\hat{e} : \mathbb{G}_1 \times \mathbb{G}_2 \to \mathbb{G}_T$ with the following properties:

1. Bilinear: $e(aR, bQ) = e(R, Q)^{ab}$ for any $R \in \mathbb{G}_1$, $Q \in \mathbb{G}_2$, and $\alpha, \beta \in \mathbb{Z}_p$.
2. Non-degenerate: There are $R \in \mathbb{G}_1$, $Q \in \mathbb{G}_2$ such that $e(aR, bQ) = e(R, Q)^{ab}$.
3. Computable: There is an efficient algorithm to compute $e(aR, bQ) = e(R, Q)^{ab}$ for any $R \in \mathbb{G}_1$, $Q \in \mathbb{G}_2$.

The scheme we present in this paper are provably secure under the Decisional Parallel BDHE Assumption [10] in bilinear groups.

2.3   Ciphertext-Policy ABE

The classical CP-ABE encryption scheme can be described into 4 steps [10]:

- $Setup \to (pk, mk)$: The setup algorithm takes in as input a security parameter and provides a set of public parameters pk and the master key values mk.
- $KeyGen(w, mk) \to sk_w$: The KeyGen algorithm takes as input the master key values mk and the attribute set of the use w, to generate a secret key sk_w which confirms the users possession of all the attributes in w and no other external attribute.
  The above two algorithms being performed by the Trusted Authority. and the other two by the users:
- $Encryption(pk, m, \tau) \to C_\tau$: The Encryption algorithm is a randomized algorithm that takes as input the message m to be encrypted, the access structure τ which needs to be satisfied and the public parameters pk to output the ciphertext C_τ. It means that the access structure is embedded in the ciphertext such that only those users with attributes satisfying τ will be able to decrypt and retrieve the message.
- $Decryption(C_\tau, sk_w) \to m$: The decryption algorithm means that taking as input the ciphertext C_τ, the user secret keys sk_w can decrypt it.

A key module of attribute based encryption is access structure with special policy. An access control policy would be a policy that defines the kind of users who would have permissions to read the documents. e.g. In an academic setting, grade-sheets of a class may be accessible only to a professor handling the course and some teaching assistants (TAs) of that course. We can express such a policy in terms of a predicate:

$$(Prof \wedge CSdept.) \vee (student \wedge courseTA \wedge CSdept.)$$

The various credentials (or variables) of the predicate can be seen as attributes and the predicate itself which represents the access policy as the access-structure. In the above example here the access structure is quite simple. But in reality, access policies may be quite complex and may involve a large number of attributes [3].

3 Outsourcing ABE and Its Security

Outsourcing ABE is proposed in [3] and it aims to solve the computation problem in mobile devices.

3.1 Syntax of Outsourcing ABE

Let S represent a set of attributes, and $\mathbb{A}$ represent an access structure. In generally, we will define (I_{enc}, I_{key}), namely the inputs to the encryption and key generation function respectively. In a CP-ABE scheme we will have $(I_{enc}, I_{key}) = (\mathbb{A}, S)$, while in a KP-ABE scheme it means $(I_{enc}, I_{key}) = (S, \mathbb{A})$ Owing to CP-ABE is more generally than KP-ABE, in this paper we will consider CP-ABE as the main construction of outsourcing ABE scheme. A CP-ABE (resp. KP-ABE) scheme with outsourcing component consists of five algorithms:

- $Setup \rightarrow (\lambda, U)$: The setup algorithm takes security parameters and attribute universe description as input. It outputs the public parameters PK and the master key MK.
- $Encrypt \rightarrow (PK, M, I_{enc})$: The encryption algorithm takes as input the public parameters PK, a message M, and an access structure I_{enc}. It outputs the ciphertext CT.
- $KeyGen(MK, I_{key}) \rightarrow (SK, TK)$: The key generation algorithm takes as input the master key MK and an attribute set I_{key} and outputs a private key SK and a transformation key TK.
- $Transform(TK, CT) \rightarrow C'$: The ciphertext transformation algorithm takes as input a transformation key TK for I_{key} and ciphertext CT that was encrypted under I_{enc}. It outputs the partially decrypted ciphertext CT' if $S \in \mathbb{A}$ and the error symbol $\perp$ otherwise.
- $Decrypt_{out}(SK, CT')$: The decryption algorithm takes as input a private key SK for I_{key} and a partially decrypted ciphertext CT' that was originally encrypted under I_{enc}. It outputs the message M. If $S \in \mathbb{A}$ and the error symbol $\perp$ otherwise (Fig. 1).

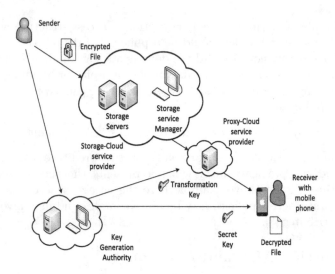

Fig. 1. Architecture of outsourcing ABE structure

3.2   Security of Outsourcing ABE

The conventional view of security against adaptive CCA (chosen-ciphertext attacks) is too rigorous due to it does not allow any bit of the cipher to be altered, Therefore we adopt a relaxation due to [11] called Replayable-CCA (RCCA) security. Which allows modification to the cipher provided they cannot change the underlying message in a meaningful approach. We can describe the RCCA security of Outsourcing ABE as a game between a challenger and an adversary. This game can be proceeds as follows:

– *Setup:* The challenger runs *Setup* algorithm to get the public parameters PK and a master secret key MSK, then gives the PK to the adversary. MSK is kept by himself.
– *QueryPhase1:* The challenger initializes an empty table T and an empty set D. The adversary adaptively issues queries:
  1. *Private key* query, on input a set of attributes S: The challenger runs $SK_S \leftarrow KeyGen(PK, MSK, S)$ and sets $D = D \bigcup S$. It then returns to the adversary the private key SK_S.
  2. *Transformation Key* query, on input a set of attributes S: The challenger searches the entry (S, SK_S, TK_S, RK_S) in table T. If such entry exists, it returns the transformation key TK_S. Otherwise, it runs $SK_S \leftarrow KeyGen(PK, MSK, S), (TK_S, RK_S) \leftarrow GenTK_{out}(PK, SK_S)$ and stores in table T the entry (S, SK_S, TK_S, PK_S). It then returns to the adversary the transformation key TK_S.
  3. *Decryption* query, on input a set of attributes S and a ciphertext CT: the challenger runs $SK_S \leftarrow KeyGen(PK, MSK, S)$ and $M \leftarrow Decrypt(PK, SK_S, CT)$. It then returns M to the adversary.

4. $Decrytpion_{out}$ query, on input a set of attributes S and a pair of cipher-text (CT, CT') : The challenger searches the entry (S, SK_S, TK_S, PK_S) in table T. If such entry exists, it $M \leftarrow Decrypt_{out}(PK, CT, CT'RK_S)$ and returns to the adversary M; otherwise, it returns $\perp$.

- *Challenge:* The adversary submits two messages M_0, M_1 and an access structure $\mathbb{A}$, subject to the restriction that, for all $S \in D$, $\mathbb{A}$ cannot be satisfied by S. The challenger selects a random bit $\beta \in 0,1$, sets $CT^* = Encrypt(PK, M_{/beta}, \mathbb{A})$ and sends CT^* to the adversary as its challenge ciphertext.
- *QueryPhase2:* The adversary continues to adaptively issue *Private key, Transformation key, Decryption* and $Decryption_{out}$ queries, as in Query phase 1, but with the restrictions that the adversary cannot
  1. issue a *Private key* query that would result in a set of attributes S which satisfies the access structure $\mathbb{A}$ being added to D.
  2. issue a trivial decryption query. That is, *Decryption* and $Decryption_{out}$ queries will be answered as in Query phase 1, except that if the response would be either M_0 or M_1, then the challenger responds with the error symbol $\perp$.
- *Guess.* The adversary $\mathbb{A}$ outputs its guess $\beta' \in 0, 1$ for β and wins the game if $\beta = \beta'$.

The advantage of the adversary in this game is defined as $|Pr[\beta = \beta'] - \frac{1}{2}|$ where the probability is taken over the random bits used by the challenger and the adversary.

3.3   Revocation of Outsourcing ABE

- *User revocation and Attribute revocation.* User revocation have been taken notice in many research work [12,13] and it has many outcomes in some research work relative to IBE scheme [8,14,15]. In ABE, user revocation is also very important; user revocation means revoking all the attributes of this user and let it remove from the system, attribute revocation means a user lose some authority but still exists in real situation. Exactly, in practical the situation of revoking some attribute of a user is more common than pure user level revocation. Several ABE scheme have been support attribute granularity revocation [2,16,17], while they just adopt primary time-rekeying mechanism and cannot be compatible with user revocation.
- *Direct revocation and Indirect revocation.* From another perspective, The revocation issue can been seen two subsets: direct and indirect revocation mechanism, Imai proposed a direct revocation mechanism [18] and defined a revocation list in their scheme, to announce who can obtain the message directly during encryption. Sahai proposed an indirect revocation mechanism [19], in their designing an authority is needed to broadcast key-update notification periodically so that those revoked user cannot continue to update their user keys. Thus it achieves the user revoking goals. Direct revocation

enforces revocation directly by the sender who directly specifies a list of revocation when encrypting. Indirect revocation implements revocation by the key authority who releases a key update material periodically in such a way that only those non-revoked users are able to update their private keys. Obviously, An advantage o the indirect method over the direct one is that it does not require senders to know the revocation list in advance and hence reducing the workloads of senders. In contrast, an convenience of the direct method over the other is that it does not involve key update phase for all non-revoked users interacting with the key authority. So in our designing, we adopt indirection because it can reduce the workload of senders and communication between trust authority and users, but not based on the approach of time period updating.

– *Backward security and Forward security.* In traditional ABE schemes, backward security means that any user who comes to hold an attribute(that satisfies the access policy) should be prevented from accessing the plaintext of the previous data exchanged before he holds the attribute. In addition, forward security means that any user who drops an attribute should be prevented from accessing the plaintext of the subsequent data exchanged after he drops the attribute, unless the other valid attributes that he is holding satisfy the access policy.

4   Efficient Verifiable Outsourcing ABE Revocation Scheme

In this section, we provide the construction of verifiable outsourcing ABE. Our scheme are based on the tree-based revocation, due to Boldyreva, Goyal, and Kumar [8] which is the most efficient one. In our outsourcing ABE scheme, we split the decryption key in two components corresponding to transformation and final-decryption, that we call transformation key and retrieving key respectively.

Let $U = \{u_1, u_2, \cdots, u_n\}$ represent the universe of users and define $L = \{\lambda_1, \lambda_2, \cdots, \lambda_l\}$ as the attributes universe in the system, Let $G_i \subset U$ be a set of users that hold the attribute λ_i, we define G_i as an attribute group, it will be used as a user revocation list to λ_i, Let $\mathcal{G} = \{G_1, G_2, \cdots, G_l\}$ be the universe of such attribute groups. Let K_{λ_i} be the attribute group key that is shared among those nonrevoked users in $G_i \in \mathcal{G}$.

A outsourcing CP-ABE scheme with efficient revocation scheme consists of the following eight algorithms:

– *Setup*$(\lambda, L) \rightarrow (PK, MK)$: The setup function runs in the key generation authority. This algorithm takes as input a security parameter λ and attribute universe description L, then outputs the public parameters PK and a master key MK.
– *AttributeKeyGen*$(MK, w, \tau) \rightarrow (SK, TK)$: The attribute key generation function runs in the key generation authority. This algorithm takes as input the master key MK, a set of attributes w, and a set of user τ, then outputs

a set of private attribute keys SK and transformation key TK for each user in w that identifies with the attribute set.

- $KEKGen(\tau) \rightarrow (KEKs)$: This key encryption key (KEK) function runs in the storage service manager. This algorithm takes as input a set of user indices $\tau \subseteq U$, and outputs KEKs for each user in τ, which will be used to encrypt attribute group keys K_{λ_i} for each $G_i \in \mathcal{G}$.
- $Encrypt(PK, \mathcal{M}, \mathbb{A}) \rightarrow (CT)$: It takes as input the public parameters PK, a message $\mathcal{M}$ and an access structure $\mathbb{A}$. It outputs a ciphertext CT.
- $ReEncrypt(CT, G) \rightarrow (CT')$: This re-encryption algorithm runs in the storage service manager. This algorithm takes as input the ciphertext CT including an access structure $\mathbb{A}$, and a set of attribute groups G. If the attribute groups emerge in $\mathbb{A}$, it re-encrypts CT for the attributes; else, return $\perp$. It outputs a re-encrypted ciphertext CT' such that only a user who possesses a set of attributes that satisfies the access structure and has a valid membership for each of them simultaneously can decrypt this message.
- $Transform_{out}(TK, CT') \rightarrow (CT'_{pro})$: This transformation algorithm runs in the proxy cloud. It takes as input the ciphertext CT' and a transformation key TK. It outputs a partially decrypted ciphertext CT'_{pro}.
- $Decrypt(SK, CT'_{pro}) \rightarrow (M)$: When the receiver download the CT'_{pro} from proxy server. It takes as input a private key SK, a partially decrypted ciphertext CT'_{pro} and outputs a message M.

4.1 Scheme Construction

Our outsourcing scheme is based on [20]. To enable outsourcing we modify the KeyGen algorithm to output a transformation key. We define a new algorithm and modify the decryption algorithm to handle outputs of Encrypt as well as Transform.

Let $\mathbb{G}$ be a bilinear group of prime order p, and let g be a generator of $\mathbb{G}$, Let $e : \mathbb{G} \times \mathbb{G} \rightarrow \mathbb{G}_T$ denote the bilinear map. A security parameter λ will determine the size of the groups.

- *Setup.* The setup algorithm chooses a group $\mathbb{G}$ of prime order p and a generator g. In addition, it chooses random exponents $\alpha, \beta \in \mathbb{Z}_p^*$. In addition, we will adopt hash functions: $H : \{0,1\}^* \rightarrow \mathbb{G}$, $H_1 : \{0,1\}^* \rightarrow Z_p^*$ and $H_2 : \{0,1\}^* \rightarrow \{0,1\}^k$. The public parameters is published as

$$PK = (g, e(g,g)^\alpha, h = g^\beta, H, H_1, H_2)$$

Then the authority sets $MK = (\beta, g^\alpha, PK)$ as the master secret key.

Next we will divide the *Key Generation* phase in traditional outsourcing ABE into two parts. In our scheme, it consists of *Attribute Key Generation* by the trusted authority and *KEK Generation* by the storage service manager.

- *AttributeKeyGen(MK, w, τ).* After setting up the system public and secret parameters, the trusted authority generates attribute keys for a set of users U by running *AttributeKeyGen(MK, w, τ)* algorithm, namely that taking a

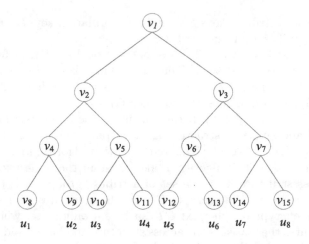

Fig. 2. KEK tree for attribute group key distribution

set of attributes $w \subseteq L$ and a set of user $\tau \subseteq U$ as inputs and outputs an attribute key for each user that identifies with that set τ.

For better understanding, We give an example based on business corporation scenes, assume that there are three staff members u_1, u_2, u_3 in the R&D Department, expressed as a_3, then we defines a_1 represents the vice heads title of this department and a_2 stands for those members who focus on daily administrative obligation. So u_1, u_2, u_3 are associated with $\{\lambda_1, \lambda_2, \lambda_3\}, \{\lambda_2, \lambda_3\}, \{\lambda_1, \lambda_3\}$ respectively, so the trust authority will have the attribute group list $G_1 = \{u_1, u_3\}, G_2 = \{u_1, u_2\}, G_3 = \{u_1, u_2, u_3\}$.

The algorithm first chooses a random $r \in \mathbb{Z}_p^*$(which is unique to each user), and random $r_j \in \mathbb{Z}_p^*$ for each attribute $\lambda_j \in w$. It creates a $SK' = (\bar{D} = g^{(\alpha+r)/\beta}, \{\bar{D}_j = g^r \cdot H(\lambda_j)^{r_j}, \bar{D}'_j = g^{r_j}\}_{\lambda_j \in w})$.

Then it chooses a random value $z \in \mathbb{Z}_p^*$ and sets the transformation key $TK = (PK, D = \bar{D}^{1/z}, \{D_j = \bar{D}_j^{1/z}, D'_j = \bar{D}'^{1/z}_j\}_{\lambda_j \in w})$. The authority finally sets the private key SK as (z, TK).

– *KEK Generation.* The storage service manager runs the *KEKGen(U)* and generates *KEKs* for users in *U*. The storage services manager sets a binary KEK tree for the universe of users *U* as in Fig. 2. In the tree, each node v_j of the tree holds a *KEK*, denoted by KEK_j. We use *path keys* to define a set of *KEKs* on the path nodes from a leaf to the root.

The storage service manager constructs the KEK tree as follows:

1. Every member in *U* is assigned to the leaf nodes of the tree. The storage service manager generates random keys and assigns them to each leaf node and internal node.
2. Each member $u_i \in \tau$ receives that path keys PK_i from its leaf node to the root node of the tree securely. For instance, u_2 stores $PK_2 = \{KEK_9, KEK_4, KEK_2, KEK_1\}$ as its path keys in Fig. 2.

Then the path keys will be used as *KEKs* to encrypt the attribute group keys by the storage service manager in the data re-encryption phase.

- *Encryption(PK, M, T)*. The encryption algorithm takes as input the public parameters PK, a message M, and the tree access structure T. This algorithm chooses a polynomial q_x for each node x in the tree T. These polynomials are chosen in a top-down manner, starting from the root node R. For each node x in the tree, the algorithm sets the degree d_x of the polynomial q_x to be one less than the threshold value k_x of that node. For root node R, it chooses random $s \in \mathbb{Z}_p^*$ and sets $q_R(0) = s$, then chooses d_R others points of polynomial q_R randomly. For any other node x, it sets $q_x(0) = q_{p(x)}(index(x))$, while $p(x)$ represents the parent of node x in the tree. Let Y be the set of leaf nodes of access tree T.

This algorithm selects a random $R \in \mathbb{G}_T$ and then computes $s = H_1(R, M)$ and $r = H_2(R)$. The ciphertext is published as $CT =$

$$(T, C = R \cdot e(g,g)^{\alpha s}, C' = h^s, C'' = M \oplus r,$$
$$\forall y \in Y : C_y = g^{q_y(0)}, C'_y = H(\lambda_y)^{q_y(0)})$$

- *Re-Encryption(CT, G)*. Before receiver getting the encrypted data CT, the storage service manager re-encrypts the ciphertext using a set of the members information for each attribute group G that appears in the access tree embedded in CT, to enforce user-level access control per each attribute group on top of the ciphertext. This algorithm runs as follows:

1. For all $G_y \in G$, chooses a random $K_{\lambda_y} \in \mathbb{Z}_p^*$, then re-encrypts CT and generates $CT' =$

$$(T, C = R \cdot e(g,g)^{\alpha s}, C' = h^s, C'' = M \oplus r,$$
$$\forall y \in Y : C_y = g^{q_y(0)}, C'_{y} = (H(\lambda_y)^{q_y(0)})^{K_{\lambda_y}})$$

2. Selects root nodes of the minimum cover sets in the KEK tree that can cover all of the leaf nodes associated with users in G_i, for all $G_i \in G$. We denote a set of KEKs that this collection covers all users in G_i, e.g., if $G_i = u_1, u_2, u_3, u_4, u_7, u_8$ in Fig. 2, then $KEK(G_i) = \{KEK_2, KEK_7\}$, owing that v_2 and v_7 are the root nodes of the minimum cover sets that can cover all the members in G_i. Notes that this collection covers all users in G_i and only them, and any user $u \notin G_i$ can by no means know any KEK in $KEK(Gi)$.

3. Generate a header message $Hdr = (\forall i \in [1, l] : \{E_K(K_{\lambda_i})\}_{K \in KEK(G_i)})$

Once receiving a query from a user, the storage service manager responds with (Hdr, CT') to the user. It is necessary to declare that the attribute group key distribution protocol throuth Hdr is a stateless approach. Thus, even if users cannot update their key state frequently in practical applications, they will be able to decrypt the attribute group key from Hdr at any time they receive it, as long as they are not revoked from any of the attribute groups and authorized to decrypt it.

- *Transformation(TK, CT')*. The transformation algorithm takes as input a transformation key TK and the ciphertext CT'. The whole phase can be divided into two parts: *attribute group key decrypt* and *message decrypt*.

Attribute group key decrypt. When proxy cloud server receives the ciphertext (Hdr, CT') from the data service manager, he first obtains the attribute group keys for all attributes in w that the user holds from Hdr. If a user u_t has a valid attribute λ_i(means $u_t \in G_i$), he can decrypt the attribute group key K_{λ_i} from Hdr using a KEK that is common in $KEK(G_i)$ and PK_t (that is, KEK$\in KEK(G_i) \cap PK_t$). Note that there can be only one such KEK, so the user may belong to at most one subset rooted by one KEK in $KEK(G_i)$. For example, if $G_i = \{u_1, u_3\}$ in the example above. u_1 can decrypt the K_{λ_i} using the path key $KEK_2 \in PK_3$. Then proxy cloud server updates the transform key with attribute group keys as follows: $TK = (PK, D, \{D_j, D_j'' = (D_j')^{1/K_{\lambda_j}}\}_{\lambda_j \in w})$. Note that any user $u \notin G_j$ can by no means decrypt K_{λ_j}.

Message decrypt. We first define a recursive algorithm $DecryptNode$ (CT, SK, x) which takes as input ciphertext CT, a private key SK and a node x from the tree $\mathcal{T}$. If x is a leaf node, then $DecryptNode(CT, SK, x)$:

$$:= \frac{e(D_x, C_x)}{e(D_x'', C_x')} = \frac{e(g^{r/z}H(\lambda_x)^{r_x/z}, g^{q_x(0)})}{e(g^{r_x/(z \cdot K_{\lambda_x})}, H(\lambda_x)^{q_x(0) \cdot K_{\lambda_x}})} = e(g, g)^{r \cdot q_x(0)/z}$$

We now consider the recursive case when x is a nonleaf node. For all nodes z that are children of x, it calls $DecryptNode(CT, SK, z)$ and stores the output as F_z. Let S_x be an arbitrary k_x−sized set of child nodes z such that $F_z \neq \perp$. If no such set exists, then the node was not satisfied and the function returns $\perp$. Otherwise, we compute F_x:

$$= \prod_{z \in S_x} F_x^{\Delta_{i, S_x'}(0)}$$

$$= \prod_{z \in S_x} (e(g, g)^{r \cdot q_z(0)/z})^{\Delta_{i, S_x'}(0)}$$

$$= \prod_{z \in S_x} (e(g, g)^{r \cdot q_{P(z)}(0)/z})^{\Delta_{i, S_x'}(0)}$$

$$= \prod_{z \in S_x} (e(g, g)^{r \cdot q_x(i)/z) \cdot \Delta_{i, S_x'}(0)}$$

$$= e(g, g)^{r \cdot q_x(0)/z}$$

For the root node R of the access tree, we observe that $DecryptNode(CT, SK, R) = e(g, g)^{rs/z}$ if the tree $\mathcal{T}$ is satisfied. Then we compute $e(C', D)/Decrypt$ $Node(CT, SK, R) = e(h^s, g^{(\alpha+r)/(\beta z)})/e(g, g)^{rs/z} = e(g, g)^{\alpha s/z}$. It finally outputs the partially decrypted ciphertext CT'_{pro} as $(C, C'', e(g, g)^{\alpha s/z})$,

 - $Decryption(SK, CT'_{pro})$. The decryption algorithm takes as input a private key $SK. = (z, TK)$ and a ciphertext CT'_{pro}. If the ciphertext is not partially decrypted, then the algorithm first executes $Transformation(TK, CT')$. If the outputs is $\perp$, then this algorithm outputs $\perp$ as well. Otherwise, it takes the ciphertext (T_0, T_1, T_2) and computes $R = T_0/T_2^z$, $\mathcal{M} = T_1 \oplus H_2(R)$, and $s = H_1(R, \mathcal{M})$. If $T_0 = R \cdot e(g, g)^{\alpha s}$ and $T_2 = e(g, g)^{\alpha s/z}$, it outputs $\mathcal{M}$; otherwise, it outputs $\perp$.

4.2 Key Update

When trusted authority revokes an attribute from a user, it can be seen as sending a leave request for some attribute. On receipt of the membership change request for some attributes groups, the trusted authority notifies the data service manager of the event and sends the updated membership list of the attribute group to it. When the data service manager receives the membership change notification from the trusted authority, it changes the attribute group key for the attribute which is affected by the membership change. Without loss of generality, suppose a user drop attribute a_1, Then the key update procedure progresses as follows:

1. The data service manager selects a random $s' \in \mathbb{Z}_p$, and a K'_{λ_i} which is different from the previous attribute group key K_{λ_i}. Then it re-encrypts the ciphertext using the public parameters PK as $CT' =$

$$(\mathcal{T}, C = R \cdot e(g,g)^{\alpha(s+s')}, C' = h^{s+s'} = g^{\beta(s+s')}, C'' = \mathcal{M} \oplus r,$$
$$C_i = g^{q_i(0)+s'}, C'_i = (H(\lambda_i)^{q_i(0)+s'})^{K'_{\lambda_i}},$$
$$\forall y \in Y \setminus \{i\} : C_y = g^{q_y(0)+s'}, C'_y = (H(\lambda_y)^{q_y(0)+s'})^{K_{\lambda_y}}).$$

   For the other attribute groups that are not affected by the membership changes, the attribute group keys do not necessarily need to be updated.
2. The data service manager selects new minimum cover sets for G_i excluding a leaving user who comes to drop an attribute. Then it generates a new header message with the updated $KEK(G_i)$ as follows.
   $Hdr = (\{E_K(K'_{\lambda_i})\}_{K \in KEK(G_i)}, \forall y \in Y \setminus \{i\} : \{E_K(K_{\lambda_y})\}_{K \in KEK(G_y)})$
   When a user sends a request query for the outsourced data afterward, the data service manager responds with the above Hdr and ciphertext CT' encrypted under the updated keys.

5 Security Proof of Revocation Scheme

Theorem 1. *Suppose the scheme of Waters [2] is a CPA-secure CP-ABE scheme. Then our revocable outsourcing ciphertext policy ABE scheme is selectively RCCA-secure.*

Proof. Suppose there exists a polynomial-time adversary $\mathcal{A}$ who can attack our scheme in the selective RCCA-security model for outsourcing with advantage ϵ. Therefore, we build a simulator $\mathcal{B}$ that can attack the Waters scheme [2] in the CPA-secure model with advantage ϵ minus a negligible amount.

Init. The simulator $\mathcal{B}$ runs $\mathcal{A}$. $\mathcal{A}$ chooses the challenge access structure $\mathcal{T}$ to $\mathcal{B}$. Then $\mathcal{B}$ sends it to the Waters challenger.

Setup. The simulator $\mathcal{B}$ obtains the Waters public parameters $PK = (g, e(g,g)^{\alpha}, g^{\beta}, H)$, in which H is a description of the Hash Function. Next $\mathcal{B}$

chooses other two hash functions: $H_1: \{0,1\}^* \to \mathbb{Z}_p^*$ and $H_2: \{0,1\}^* \to \{0,1\}^k$. Finally $\mathcal{B}$ sends $PK' = (g, e(g,g)^\alpha, g^\beta, H, H_1, H_2)$ to the adversary $\mathcal{A}$ as the public parameters.

Phase 1. The simulator $\mathcal{B}$ initialized three empty tables T, T_1, T_2, an empty set D and an integer $j = 0$. Then it answers the adversary's queries as follows:

- Random Oracle Hash $H_1(R, M)$: If there is an entry (R, M, s) in T_1, return s. Otherwise, choose a random $s \in \mathbb{Z}_p^*$, then record $(R, \mathcal{M}, s)$ in T_1 and return s.
- Random Oracle Hash $H_2(R)$: If there is an entry (R, r) in T_2, return r. Otherwise, choose a random $r \in \{0,1\}^k$, then record (R, r) in T_2 and return r.
- Create(S): $\mathcal{B}$ sets $j := j + 1$. Then it excutes one of the two ways:
  1. If attributes set S satisfies $\mathcal{T}$, then simulator $\mathcal{B}$ chooses a fake transformation key pair as follows: choose random $a, r' \in \mathbb{Z}_p^*$ and run *Attribute KeyGen*(a, r', PK, S) to Obtain $SK' = (PK, \bar{D} = g^{(a+r')/\beta}, \{\bar{D}_i = g^{r'} H(\lambda_i)^{r_i}, \bar{D}'_i = g^{r_i}\}_{\lambda_i \in S})$. Let $a = \alpha/z$ and $r' = r/z$, then we replace a and r. We have $TK = SK' =$

$$(PK, \bar{D} = g^{(\alpha+r)/(\beta z)}, \{\bar{D}_i = g^{r/z} H(\lambda_i)^{r_i}, \bar{D}'_i = g^{r_i}\}_{\lambda_i \in S})$$
$$= (PK, D = (g^{\frac{\alpha+r}{\beta}})^{1/z}, \{D_i = (g^r H(\lambda_i)^{r'_i})^{1/z}, D'_i = (g^{r'_i})^{1/z}\}_{\lambda_i \in S})$$

  Note that we implicitly set $r_i = r'_i/z$. Then the TK is properly distributed.
  2. Otherwise, simulator $\mathcal{B}$ calls the Waters key generation oracle on S to obtain the key $SK' = (PK, D, \{D_j, D'_j\}_{\forall j \in S})$. Next $\mathcal{B}$ chooses random $z \in \mathbb{Z}_p^*$, then it sets $SK = z$ and $TK = (PK, D^{1/z}, \{D_j^{1/z}, (D'_j)^{1/z})$. Finally, simulator $\mathcal{B}$ gets (j, S, SK, TK) in table T and return TK to $\mathcal{A}$.
- Corrupt(i): If there exists an ith entry in table T, then the simulator $\mathcal{B}$ obtains the entry (j, S, SK, TK) and sets $D := D \bigcup S$. It then return SK to $\mathcal{A}$, or returns $\perp$ if there is no such entry existing.
- Decrypt(i, CT): Without loss of generality, let $CT = (C_0, C_1, C_2)$ be associated with an access structure $\mathcal{T}$. Obtain the record (i, S, SK, TK) from table T. If it is not there or $S \notin \mathcal{T}$, return $\perp$ to $\mathbb{A}$.

1. If the ith entry (j, S, SK, TK) does not satisfy the challenge structure $\mathcal{T}$, it proceeds as follows:
   (a) Compute $R = C_0/C_2$, parse $SK = (z, TK)$.
   (b) Obtain the records $(R, \mathcal{M}_i, s_i)$ from table T_1. If none exist, return $\perp$ to $\mathcal{A}$.
   (c) If there exists indices $i_1 \neq i_2$ such that $(R, \mathcal{M}_{i_1}, s_{i_1})$ and $(R, \mathcal{M}_{i_2}, s_{i_2})$ are in table T_1, $\mathcal{M}_{i_1} \neq \mathcal{M}_{i_2}$ and $s_{i_1} = s_{i_2}$, then $\mathcal{B}$ aborts the simulation.
   (d) Contrarily, obtain the records (R, r) from table T_2. If there no such record exists, the simulator $\mathcal{B}$ outputs $\perp$.
   (e) Test if $C_0 = R \cdot e(g,g)^{s_i, \alpha}, C_1 = \mathcal{M}_{i_1} \oplus r$ and $C_2 = e(g,g)^{s_i \alpha/z}$ for each i in the records.
   (f) If there is an i that passes the above test, output $\mathcal{M}_i$; otherwise return $\perp$.

2. If key i does satisfy the challenge structure T, proceed as follows:
   (a) Compute $\gamma = C_2^{1/d}$, parse $SK = (d, TK)$.
   (b) For each record $(R, \mathcal{M}_i, s_i)$ in table T_1, test if $\gamma = e(g, g)^{s_i}$.
   (c) If there is no match, $\mathcal{B}$ return $\bot$.
   (d) If there is more than one matches, $\mathcal{B}$ aborts the simulation.
   (e) Contrarily, let $(R, \mathcal{M}, s)$ be the sole match. Obtain the record (R, r) from the T_2. If the record does not exist, the simulator $\mathcal{B}$ outputs $\bot$.
   (f) Test if $C_0 = R \cdot e(g, g)^{s\alpha}$, $C_1 = \mathcal{M} \oplus r$ and $C_2 = e(g, g)^{ds}$ for each i in the records, If all tests pass, return $\mathcal{M}$; else return $\bot$.

Challenge. Ultimately, the adversary $\mathcal{A}$ submits a message pair $(\mathcal{M}_0^*, \mathcal{M}_1^*) \in \{0, 1\}^{2k}$, the simulator $\mathcal{B}$ operates as follows.

- The simulator $\mathcal{B}$ chooses random "messages" $(\mathcal{R}_I, \mathcal{R}_\infty) \in \mathbb{G}_T^2$ and passes them on to the Waters challenger to obtain a ciphertext $CT = (C, C', \{C_i, C_i'\}_{i \in S})$ under T.
- $\mathcal{B}$ chooses a random value $C'' \in \{0, 1\}^k$.
- Then $\mathcal{B}$ sends the challenge ciphertext $CT^* = (C, C', C'', \{C_i, C_i'\}_{i \in S})$ to the adversary $\mathcal{A}$.

Phase 2. The simulator $\mathcal{B}$ continues to answer queries as in Phase 1, except that if the response to a Decrypt query would be either $\mathcal{M}_0^*$ or $\mathcal{M}_1^*$, then $\mathcal{B}$ responds with the message **test**.

Guess. Ultimately, the adversary $\mathcal{A}$ must either output a bit or abort, either way $\mathcal{B}$ ignores it. Next, $\mathcal{B}$ searches through tables T_1 and T_2 to see if the values $\mathcal{R}_0$ or $\mathcal{R}_1$ appear as the first element of any entry (i.e., that $\mathcal{A}$ issued a query of the form $H_1(\mathcal{R}_i)$ or $H_2(\mathcal{R}_i)$). If neither of both $\mathcal{R}_0$ and $\mathcal{R}_1$ are revealed, $\mathcal{B}$ outputs a random bit as its guess.

The simulator $\mathcal{B}$ in Game is obviously negligible, and Theorem 1 is RCCA secure within this negligible advantage. So the proof of Theorem 1 is complete.

6   Conclusion

In this paper, we considered a new requirement of ABE with outsourced decryption: revocation. We modified the original model of ABE with outsourced decryption to include revocation. We prove our revocation support RCCA security level. As expected, the scheme substantially reduced the computation time required for mobile phones to recover plaintexts.

Acknowledgement. This work is supported in part by National High Technology Research and Development Program of China (No. 2015AA016008).

References

1. Goyal, V., Pandey, O., Sahai, A., Waters, B.: Attribute-based encryption for fine-grained access control of encrypted data. In: Proceedings of the 13th ACM Conference on Computer and Communications Security, pp. 89–98. ACM (2006)

2. Bethencourt, J., Sahai, A., Waters, B.: Ciphertext-policy attribute-based encryption. In: IEEE Symposium on Security and Privacy, SP 2007, pp. 321–334. IEEE (2007)
3. Green, M., Hohenberger, S., Waters, B.: Outsourcing the decryption of ABE ciphertexts. In: USENIX Security Symposium, vol. 2011 (2011)
4. Qin, B., Deng, R.H., Liu, S., Ma, S.: Attribute-based encryption with efficient verifiable outsourced decryption. IEEE Trans. Inf. Forensics Secur. 10(7), 1384–1393 (2015)
5. Li, J., Huang, X., Li, J., Chen, X., Xiang, Y.: Securely outsourcing attribute-based encryption with checkability. IEEE Trans. Parallel Distrib. Syst. 25(8), 2201–2210 (2014)
6. Chen, Y., Jiang, Z.L., Yiu, S.M., Liu, J.K., Au, M.H., Wang, X.: Fully secure ciphertext-policy attribute based encryption with security mediator. In: Hui, L.C.K., Qing, S.H., Shi, E., Yiu, S.M. (eds.) ICICS 2014. LNCS, vol. 8958, pp. 274–289. Springer, Cham (2015). https://doi.org/10.1007/978-3-319-21966-0_20
7. Lueks, W., Alpár, G., Hoepman, J.-H., Vullers, P.: Fast revocation of attribute-based credentials for both users and verifiers. In: Federrath, H., Gollmann, D. (eds.) SEC 2015. IAICT, vol. 455, pp. 463–478. Springer, Cham (2015). https://doi.org/10.1007/978-3-319-18467-8_31
8. Boldyreva, A., Goyal, V., Kumar, V.: Identity-based encryption with efficient revocation. In: Proceedings of the 15th ACM Conference on Computer and Communications Security, pp. 417–426. ACM (2008)
9. Beimel, A.: Secure schemes for secret sharing and key distribution. Technion Israel Institute of Technology, Faculty of Computer Science (1996)
10. Waters, B.: Ciphertext-policy attribute-based encryption: an expressive, efficient, and provably secure realization. In: Catalano, D., Fazio, N., Gennaro, R., Nicolosi, A. (eds.) PKC 2011. LNCS, vol. 6571, pp. 53–70. Springer, Heidelberg (2011). https://doi.org/10.1007/978-3-642-19379-8_4
11. Canetti, R., Krawczyk, H., Nielsen, J.B.: Relaxing chosen-ciphertext security. In: Boneh, D. (ed.) CRYPTO 2003. LNCS, vol. 2729, pp. 565–582. Springer, Heidelberg (2003). https://doi.org/10.1007/978-3-540-45146-4_33
12. Ostrovsky, R., Sahai, A., Waters, B.: Attribute-based encryption with non-monotonic access structures. In: Proceedings of the 14th ACM Conference on Computer and Communications Security, pp. 195–203. ACM (2007)
13. Staddon, J., Golle, P., Gagné, M., Rasmussen, P.: A content-driven access control system. In: Proceedings of the 7th Symposium on Identity and Trust on the Internet, pp. 26–35. ACM (2008)
14. Li, J., Li, J., Chen, X., Jia, C., Lou, W.: Identity-based encryption with outsourced revocation in cloud computing. IEEE Trans. Comput. 64(2), 425–437 (2015)
15. Qin, B., Deng, R.H., Li, Y., Liu, S.: Server-aided revocable identity-based encryption. In: Pernul, G., Ryan, P.Y.A., Weippl, E. (eds.) ESORICS 2015. LNCS, vol. 9326, pp. 286–304. Springer, Cham (2015). https://doi.org/10.1007/978-3-319-24174-6_15
16. Yu, S., Wang, C., Ren, K., Lou, W.: Attribute based data sharing with attribute revocation. In: Proceedings of the 5th ACM Symposium on Information, Computer and Communications Security, pp. 261–270. ACM (2010)
17. Pirretti, M., Traynor, P., McDaniel, P., Waters, B.: Secure attribute-based systems. J. Comput. Secur. 18(5), 799–837 (2010)
18. Attrapadung, N., Imai, H.: Conjunctive broadcast and attribute-based encryption. In: Shacham, H., Waters, B. (eds.) Pairing 2009. LNCS, vol. 5671, pp. 248–265. Springer, Heidelberg (2009). https://doi.org/10.1007/978-3-642-03298-1_16

19. Sahai, A., Seyalioglu, H., Waters, B.: Dynamic credentials and ciphertext delegation for attribute-based encryption. In: Safavi-Naini, R., Canetti, R. (eds.) CRYPTO 2012. LNCS, vol. 7417, pp. 199–217. Springer, Heidelberg (2012). https://doi.org/10.1007/978-3-642-32009-5_13
20. Hur, J., Noh, D.K.: Attribute-based access control with efficient revocation in data outsourcing systems. IEEE Trans. Parallel Distrib. Syst. **22**(7), 1214–1221 (2011)

Operational-Behavior Auditing in Cloud Storage

Zhaoyi Chen[1], Hui Tian[1(✉)], Jing Lu[2], Yiqiao Cai[1], Tian Wang[1], and Yonghong Chen[1]

[1] College of Computer Science, National Huaqiao University,
Xiamen 361021, China
cshtian@gmail.com
[2] Network Technology Center, National Huaqiao University,
Xiamen 361021, China

Abstract. As an indispensable branch of cloud computing, cloud storage enables individuals and organizations to enjoy large-scale and distributed storage capability in a multi-tenant service pattern. However, there is still a serious lack of mutual trust between the users and cloud service providers, since both of them can perform dishonest and malicious operational behaviors on cloud data. Secure audit for operational behaviors is vital for cloud forensic investigation, which collects and offers essential audit logs for a forensic investigator to track security incidents and accountability determination. Such an auditing service can help to achieve better security assurances within the whole life cycle of cloud data. In this paper, we present an auditing mode for operational behaviors in cloud storage, introduce the open issues in two main phases, log audit and forensic investigation, and discuss the future trends.

Keywords: Cloud security auditing · Operational-behaviors · Secure logging · Forensic analysis

1 Introduction

As an indispensable branch of cloud computing, cloud storage enables individuals and enterprises to enjoy large-scale and distributed storage service, due to a series of advantages, such as on-demand self-service, ubiquitous network access, location-independent resource pooling, rapid resource elasticity, usage-based pricing, and transference of risk [1, 2]. However, as a promising technology, many new security challenges come along with this trend, which impede the development and application of cloud storage [3]. One of most serious issues is a lack of mutual trust between the CSP and users, and this problem has been considered as a non-negligible obstacle for the widespread application of CSS [4]. This issue can be described from two aspects.

From the perspective of users, a tricky problem is how to evaluate if the CSP meets their legal expectations for data security. First, since a CSP actually can be viewed as a separate administrative entity, storing local data in the cloud means abandoning the users' ultimate control over their data. As a result, the correctness and privacy of cloud data cannot be well protected and some security breaches of noteworthy appear in

© ICST Institute for Computer Sciences, Social Informatics and Telecommunications Engineering 2018
J. Wan et al. (Eds.): CloudComp 2016, SPNCE 2016, LNICST 197, pp. 162–172, 2018.
https://doi.org/10.1007/978-3-319-69605-8_15

cloud storage frequently. For example, the Amazon's S3 cloud storage service experienced an alarming downtime resulted by a significant system outage in 2008; the Apple's iCloud service suffered a serious privacy issue in 2014 that resulted in worrying leakage of users' personal information. To overcome this problem, devising appropriate cloud data auditing (CDA) mechanisms that offer remote integrity verification service on cloud data is definitely essential. In recent years, there have already been lots of researches on CDA schemes, and we can briefly classify these schemes into two categories [5]: Provable Data Possession (PDP), which provides remote data integrity verification without any retrievals of the outsourced cloud data [6, 7]. Proof of Retrievability (POR), which provides high probability for data recovery capability in addition to integrity verification [8, 9].

From the perspective of the CSP, another problem should be taken into account is how to determine the legality of cloud storage users' behaviors. For example, since the multi-tenant characteristic of cloud storage, the cloud should ensure that the data of users are kept confidential to adversaries from the internal or external, such as malicious users and potential attackers. To avoid this problem, some security access control (SAC) schemes are proposed in recent years to limit unauthorized accessing in cloud environment [10, 11]. Furthermore, to provide cost-efficient storage, deduplication is a necessary requirement in cloud storage, which enables removing of data redundancy. In this scene, one file might be shared by multi-users in cloud, so the CSP has to verify the data ownership of a given user without transferring the file to the cloud. To this end, proof of ownership (POW) strategies are presented to solve this problem [12, 13].

As mentioned above, since users and the CSP are usually not in the same trusted domain in cloud computing, they lack of confidence in cloud data operational behaviors of each other, including data-management behaviors of the CSP and data operations of the users. Thus, there is an urgent need to develop cloud auditing technology to ensure the security of cloud storage. However, current cloud auditing technologies do have certain limitations. The most obvious point is that these CDA schemes (i.e. PDP and POR) are originally designed to ensure the correctness of cloud data, they can only verify the existence of cloud data security incidents, but cannot provide auditing information or evidence to track the operational behavior histories about the disputed data. In this case, it is apparently unfair exclusive put the responsibility for the failures of CDA strategies to the CSP, because some error data operations of users may also cause verification failed. What makes things worse is that the CSS also provides a better platform for ill-disposed users to store and propagate criminal information (e.g. child abuse and terrorism-related materials) [14]. This kind of seemingly "legal" users may also conduct illegal operational behaviors. Thus, cloud auditing system should not only focus on security of data properties, but also the operational behavior legality of cloud data. Recently, as cloud crimes emerge in endlessly, the concept of cloud forensic is put forward to address the problem of forensic investigation [15], but there are still some crucial issues need further research. Two of the most important issues are how to ensure the validity of evidence (i.e. operational behavior logs) [16] and how to perform efficient forensic analysis on massive amounts of cloud logs [29]. Therefore, within the scope of this article, we focus on these two essential issues, which is intended as a call for action, aiming to motivate further attention to the problem of operational behavior legitimacy on cloud data, and thereby achieve accountability determination in CSS.

2   The Architecture of Cloud Auditing

To illustrate the specific problem mentioned above, we begin with a high-level cloud architecture which integrates CDA and OBA mechanisms for cloud storage security, as shown in Fig. 1. Particularly, CDA mechanism is based on a three-party model, in which an external third party auditor (TPA) is usually introduced to perform remote public verification on outsourced data, which aims to provide more transparent and reliable auditing results [2]. In this paper, to achieve the requirement of operational behavior auditing, we introduce an integrated auditing model which involves four different entities: users, TPA, CSP and forensic investigator (FI). And we also consider both CSP and users can be malicious potentially.

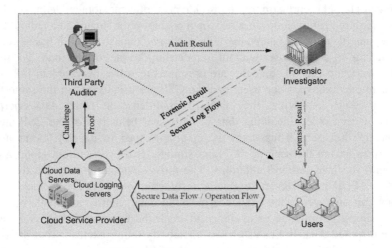

Fig. 1. The architecture cloud auditing

Generally, OBA is consisted of two key components, validity verification and forensic analysis of operational behavior logs [16], which are not considered in traditional CDA schemes. In this model, FI is a party that is responsible for analyzing the content of logs independently and providing convincing forensic report about security incidents on cloud data to the CSP and users for responsibility determination. Although analyzing logs plays a vital role in forensic investigation that is really useful to identify illegal operation behaviors, to determine the authenticity of logs is also an indispensable step prior to the forensic analysis process, since corrupted logs may lead to incorrect or meaningless forensic results. Therefore, the TPA in this model is also equipped with the capability to verify the authenticity of logs, so as to enhance the credibility of forensic results and reduce the heavy burdens of FI.

3 Log Security in Cloud

The process of OBA starts with acquiring the operation logs from the cloud. However, establishing appropriate OBA mechanism to ensure the log security in cloud storage still faces challenges and security threats [15–17]: **(1) Creditability of operation logs.** As a kind of digital resource stored in cloud, the integrity of logs is facing threats of corruption from external or internal adversaries. **(2) Lack of control in cloud.** In cloud systems, to collect audit logs from the cloud, we inevitably need to rely on the CSP, but for the reason of privacy preserving, which in turn brings the honesty problem of CSP, and current CSPs are not obligated to provide relevant logs. **(3) Privacy leakage.** A dishonest CSP or malicious users may try to get access to the log content during the storage or auditing phase, which may lead to serious privacy leakage. This problem can be worse if the logs are written in plaintext.

Although logs are prime evidences for forensic investigation, there has been little concrete work that shows how to provide cloud logs for forensic while preserving privacy and integrity of the logs. What ensures the security of logs is the secure logging methods. From view of technique, to fulfill the requirements of log security, we can rely on existing works of secure logging protocols that listed in Table 1. Generally, the secure logging protocols can be divided into two classes according to the cryptographic techniques they build on, i.e. MAC-based approaches and signature-based approaches.

Table 1. Secure logging protocols and security requirements.

Schemes	Forward security	Append-only	Selective verification	Privacy preserving
Bellare [18]	✔	✘	✘	✘
Schneier [19]	✔	✘	✘	✔
FssAgg-MAC [20]	✔	✔	✘	✔
BBox [23]	✔	✔	✘	✔
SecLaaS [17]	✔	✘	✘	✔
Logcrypt [22]	✔	✘	✘	✔
Stathopoulos [24]	✔	✘	✘	✔
FssAgg-BLS [20]	✔	✔	✔	✔
LogFAS [21]	✔	✔	✔	✔

MAC-based approaches. To ensure the integrity of logs, Bellare and Yee [18] first formally defined the forward security (i.e. forward integrity) property, which prevents attackers from modifying the previous log data even if they know the current key. In this work, they used block ciphers and standard message authentication codes (MACs) to achieve forward security via a chaining process.

Based on the work of Bellare and Yee [18], Schneier and Kelsey [19] presented a classic secure logging protocol which can ensure the security of logs on an untrusted machine. In this work, they used hash chain for key evolvement, in which the authentication key of each log entry is hashed using a one-way hash function to ensure the forward security of logs. In addition, they presented a secure logging structure, in which the log entry consists of five fields illustrated in Fig. 2. Field D_j is the current log entry generated in time j, and the current authentication key of D_j is A_{j+1} that can be computed as $A_{j+1} = H(A_j)$. W_j is the permission mask that is used to control who can gain access to the contents of entry j. For privacy preserving, D_j will be encrypted with the encryption key of time j K_j, which can be computed as $K_j = H(W_j \| A_j)$. Field Y_j is the j-th element of the hash chain that can be generated as $Y_j = H(Y_{j-1} \| E_{K_j}(D_j) \| W_j)$.

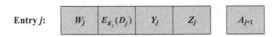

Fig. 2. Secure logging structure of [19]

The forward security can prevent the log entries before the compromise from modification, but cannot detect selective deletion or truncation of log entries, which is a kind of deletion attack that the attacker deletes continuous entries from the tail-end of log data. Thus, Ma and Tsudik [20] presented a secure logging scheme based on FssAgg authentication technique, where forward-secure (MACs) of log entries are sequentially combined into a single aggregate one, so as to achieve the append-only property defined in [22], with which attacker cannot change (i.e. deletion and truncation) logs entries generated before the compromise. In this scheme, a log file involves two parts: log entries $[L_1, \ldots, L_i]$ and FssAgg authentication MACs $\mu_{v,i}$. For each log entry in the log file, there is a unique authentication key A_i for MAC computation, and A_i is generated from the initial key A_1 with a one-way hash function. The construction of log file can be represented as:

$$\mu_{v,i} = H(H(\ldots H(\mu_{v,i} \| mac_{A_1}(L_1) \| \ldots \| mac_{A_1}(L_i)))) \tag{1}$$

Another secure logging protocol BBox [23] based on Schneier and Kelsey's work is presented by Accorsi. To avoid the truncation attack, Accorsi applied trusted computing module to sign the hash chain fields of log entries, which is the core of security of this scheme.

There is also attempt to ensure security of audit log in cloud. Zawoad et al. presented forensic framework SecLaaS (secure logging-as-a-service) that implemented in Openstack [15, 17], which stores virtual machines' logs and provides access to FI while ensuring the confidentiality of the audit logs. In this system, a read only API is provided for log acquisition by forensic investigator. Furthermore, a log chain was generated by using the one-way hash function to ensure the order of log entries. To protect the membership of log entrier, *PPL* (Proof of Past Log) is generated by using BloomFilter in the end of every day and published to the public (e.g. Web or RSS). Thus, the integrity of log can be verified with the log chain and *PPL*.

Signature-based approaches. To overcome the short comings of the MAC-based schemes, which cannot provide public verification of logs. Secure logging schemes based on public key cryptography are proposed. To this end, the first attempt is that Holt [22] presented an improved scheme Logcrypt based on work of Schneier and Kelsey [19] by directly substitute the MACs for digital signatures to achieve public verification. However, Logcrypt cannot ensure the append-only property, which is inherited from the disadvantage of [19].

Stathopoulos et al. [24] presented a secure logging that can be implemented in public communication networks. In this scheme, the authors exploited a log structure similar to the Schneier and Kelsey' scheme [19]. To prevent attacks from internal adversary, who can reconstruct parts of the log entries without being detected, this kind of attack is possible if the adversary gains the authentication key A_j. They introduced an independent Regulatory Authority (RA) to store the integrity proofs of log files and verify the log integrity. Periodically, the log collector sends a signature over the log entries generated during this period to RA. In verification phase, the RA recomputes the signature of the corresponding log files and compares with the one stored before. This kind of manual off-line signature protects the logs from modifications after the log file has been signed and the signature have been sent to the RA. However, the security of this approach depends on RA, the compromise of RA may lead to single point of failure.

Ma and Tsudik [20] presented a secure logging scheme based on FssAgg authentication signature. Particularly, by using a collision resistant one-way hash function H for signature key update, this scheme ensures the forward security of log entries. Since the aggregation property of BLS signature [25], signatures of the log entries can be sequentially aggregated into a single signature. However, to remove a signature of a given entry from the aggregation signature is impossible, which ensures the append-only property. In key generation, the system works in bilinear map group G with generator of g. First, it generates a series of key pair for each log entry as $(sk_i = x_i, pk_i = v_i)$ $i \in [1, n]$, where the $x_i = H(x_{i-1})$ and $vi = g^{x_i}$. Then, the signature of the i-th log entry M_i can be represented as $\sigma_i = H(i||M_i)^{x_i}$. The aggregate of signatures on n log entries can be computed as $\sigma_{1,n} = \sigma_1 \cdot \sigma_2 \cdot \ldots \cdot \sigma_n$. The successful integrity verification of the log file is equivalent to the verification of aggregation signature $\sigma_{i,n}$ as:

$$e(\sigma_{1,n},\ g) = \prod_{i=1}^{n} e(H(i \parallel M_i), v_i) \tag{2}$$

However, the FssAgg-BLS scheme suffers from the problem of high overhead because the computational inefficiency of the signature generation and verification on bilinear map. To achieve more efficiency, Yavuz et al. [21] presented a PKC-based secure logging scheme LogFAS with forward security and append-only property, which supports public verification, selective verification of any subset of log entries and fast detection of corrupted log entries. Moreover, LogFAS outperforms FssAgg-based scheme on computation and storage overhead.

In summary, despite the secure logging schemes listed above are commonly used for forensic investigation in traditional computer and network systems. However, deploying secure logging mechanisms in untrusted cloud environment still face challenges, which is discussed as the first paragraph of this section, and these problems need further research in the future.

4   Forensic Analysis with Cloud Logs

In this section, we will describe the existing challenges and problems of conducting forensic analysis on huge amounts of log data. Then we make a review on cloud forensic analysis techniques. Operational behavior log contains activities that happen in cloud storage. Forensic analysis for log file plays an important role for OBA, which aims to extract knowledge about abnormal data behaviors in cloud from various type of log information. However, performing log forensic investigation with high-efficiency in cloud also faces challenges as follows:

(1) **Massive volume of logs.** One of the biggest concerns in cloud forensic investigation is that the scale of log data is much larger than traditional computer and network forensic. Moreover, formats of log data in cloud can be diversified, which increases the difficulty in log analysis. (2) **Encrypted Log data.** In cloud storage, to ensure the security of the cloud data and privacy of users, the CSP usually encrypts the log data during transmission and storage phase. However, current data analysis algorithms can only process data in plaintext. Thus, how to perform analysis on encrypted data needs for further research.

There is an urgent need to develop scalable forensic analysis solutions that can match the explosive growth on the size of log data in cloud. Differing from the traditional digital forensic solutions, which usually implement data analysis algorithms in single workstation. In recent years, an attractive long-term solution is to perform forensic processing in distributed and parallel systems, because only cluster computing environment will offer enough processing resource and power [26, 27]. Thus, within the scope of this paper, we focus on how to process on massive log data with distributed and parallel computing (i.e. MapReduce) to achieve high-efficient forensic analysis. Several efforts have been presented to address this problem showed in Table 2. Generally, from the view of technique, there are two approaches can be exploited to increase the data analysis performance: algorithm improvement and using additional hardware resources.

Table 2. Methods for cloud forensic analysis

Schemes	Algorithm improve	Additional hardware	Mapreduce-based
Marziale et al. [27]	✗	✔	✗
Francois et al. [28]	✔	✗	✔
Roussev et al. [29]	✔	✔	✔
Therdphapiyanak et al. [30]	✔	✗	✔
Lin et al. [31]	✗	✗	✔

In traditional digital forensic solutions that implement data analysis algorithms in a single workstation, algorithm improvement is the only way to increase analysis efficiency. However, in cloud computing, the analysis efficiency can be further improved by using the parallel computing paradigm. Currently, MapReduce (MR) is widely applied in the field of forensic analysis for its high-efficiency and scalability. MR is a programming model and an associated implementation developed by Google for processing large-scale data set with a parallel, distributed cluster. Thus, programs written by MR can be automatically dispatched and executed in parallel cluster.

Roussev et al. [29] first attempted to utilize MR for large-scale log forensic analysis in cloud computing, and they presented an improved MR algorithm MPI MapReduce (MMR), which outperforms the traditional forensic analysis computing techniques. In this scheme, a single data file is first split into N equal blocks, where N is the number of available computing nodes. Then, each block is split into M chunks according to the mapper thread number created at each node. Differing from the original MR implemented in Hadoop, a core improvement of MMR is that by using the Message Passing Interface (MPI) distributed communication standard for management of communication and synchronization in different tasks, the number of nodes can be increased dynamically. Therefore, the MMR is much more efficient than MP.

Another successful usage of MR for forensic analysis is Francois et al. [28], who combined the MR and PageRank (PR) algorithm. The PR algorithm is a link analysis algorithm used by Google Search to weight the relative importance of websites in search engine results. PR works by counting the number and quality of hyperlinks to a page to determine the importance of the website. The first step is to gather netflow from routers to a collector. Then, analyze the interactions between different hosts so as to generate a dependency graph, which will be the input of PR. Next, the PR will be executed by MR by distributing the adjacency matrix of the dependency graph to all computing nodes.

In addition to the PR algorithm, as a popular cluster analysis, K-Means (KM) algorithm can also be used to detect abnormal activities in cloud storage. Therdphapiyanak et al. [30] presented a novel forensic analysis method based on KM, with which malicious activities can be detected by inspecting which cluster has deviated from the others.

Lin et al. [31] presented a comprehensive framework for batch log data analysis with the combination of Hadoop and Spark. In this system, Hadoop is treated as the stable file storage system, and by leveraging the MR and spark, the framework can provide efficient batch data processing in memory. In addition, a special improvement of this work is that there is a parallel data mining (DM) module in this system. With the DM, classification and cluster algorithms (i.e. KM, PR, Bayes) based on MR and Spark engine are implemented in this framework.

In addition to the algorithm improvement, another straightforward approach to enhance the processing performance is to provide additional physical hardware, such as GPU and CPU cluster. As an example, Marziale et al. [27] leveraged the hardware and software capabilities of GPU for high-efficient digital forensic. They evaluate the effectiveness with direct experiments and the result show that using CPU and GPU resource on multiple machines is feasible and more efficient.

5 Concluding Remarks

Cloud computing is envisioned as the next-generation IT architecture. As an important branch of cloud computing, one of most serious issues in cloud storage is a lack of mutual trust between CSP and users. In recent years, to address this problem, many cloud auditing techniques, such as PDP, POR and POW, have been presented. However, auditing for operational behaviors in cloud, which is significant for the detection of potential crimes in the cloud and equitable accountability determination in the cloud forensic, was almost neglected in previous studies. In this paper, we outline the existing challenges and problems of conducting operational behavior auditing in cloud, including the log verification and forensic analysis phase. We also describe the existing approaches for secure logging and forensic analysis with distributed and parallel computing, which would be a reference to solve the crucial problems of OBA in the future research. We would like to motivate more researchers to focus on the how to determine the legitimacy of operational behavior, and to achieve accountability determination in cloud.

Acknowledgments. This work was supported in part by Natural Science Foundation of China under Grant Nos. U1405254, U1536115 and 61302094, Program of China Scholarships Council under Grant No. 201507540001, Natural Science Foundation of Fujian Province of China under Grant No. 2014J01238, Program for New Century Excellent Talents in Fujian Province University under Grant No. MJK2016-23, Program for Outstanding Youth Scientific and Technological Talents in Fujian Province University under Grant No. MJK2015-54, Promotion Program for Young and Middle-aged Teacher in Science & Technology Research of Huaqiao University under Grant No. ZQN-PY115, and Program for Science & Technology Innovation Teams and Leading Talents of Huaqiao University under Grant No. 2014KJTD13.

References

1. Mell, P., Grance, T.: Draft NIST working definition of cloud computing. Technical report (2009) http://csrc.nist.gov/groups/SNS/cloud-computing/index.html
2. Wang, C., Ren, K., Lou, W., Jin, L.: Toward publicly auditable secure cloud data storage services. IEEE netw. **24**, 19–24 (2010)
3. Ren, K., Wang, C., Wang, Q.: Security challenges for the public cloud. IEEE Internet Comput. **16**, 69–73 (2012)
4. Ko, Ryan K.L., Lee, B.S., Pearson, S.: Towards achieving accountability, auditability and trust in cloud computing. In: Abraham, A., Mauri, J.L., Buford, John F., Suzuki, J., Thampi, Sabu M. (eds.) ACC 2011. CCIS, vol. 193, pp. 432–444. Springer, Heidelberg (2011). doi:10.1007/978-3-642-22726-4_45
5. Yang, K., Jia, X.: Data storage auditing service in cloud computing: challenges, methods and opportunities. World Wide Web **15**, 409–428 (2012)
6. Tian, H., Chen, Y., Chang, C.C., Jiang, H., Huang, Y., Chen, Y.H., Liu, J.: Dynamic-hash-table based public auditing for secure cloud storage. IEEE Trans. Serv. Comput. (2015). doi:10.1109/TSC.2015.2512589
7. Wang, Q., Wang, C., Ren, K., Lou, W., Li, J.: Enabling public auditability and data dynamics for storage security in cloud computing. IEEE Trans. Parallel Distrib. Syst. **22**, 847–859 (2011)

8. Juels, A., Kaliski, B.S.: PoRs: proofs of retrievability for large files. In: 14th ACM Conference on Computer and Communications Security, pp. 584–597 (2007)
9. Shacham, H., Waters, B.: Compact proofs of retrievability. In: Pieprzyk, J. (ed.) ASIACRYPT 2008. LNCS, vol. 5350, pp. 90–107. Springer, Heidelberg (2008). doi:10. 1007/978-3-540-89255-7_7
10. Wang, G., Liu, Q., Wu, J.: A hierarchical attribute-based encryption for fine-grained access control in cloud storage services. In: 17th ACM Conference on Computer and Communications Security, pp. 735–737 (2010)
11. Yang, K., Jia, X., Ren, K., Zhang, B., Xie, R.: DAC-MACS: effective data access control for multiauthority cloud storage systems. IEEE Trans. Inf. Forensics Secur. **8**, 1790–1801 (2013)
12. Halevi, S., Harnik, D., Pinkas, B., Peleg, A.S.: Proofs of ownership in remote storage systems. In: 18th ACM Conference on Computer and Communications Security, pp. 49–500 (2011)
13. Zheng, Q., Xu, S.: Secure and efficient proof of storage with deduplication. In: 2nd ACM Conference on Data and Application Security and privacy, pp. 1–12 (2012)
14. Martini, B., Choo, K.K.R.: An integrated conceptual digital forensic framework for cloud computing. Digit. Invest. **9**, 71–80 (2012)
15. Dykstra, J., Sherman, A.T.: Acquiring forensic evidence from infrastructure-as-a-service cloud computing: exploring and evaluating tools, trust, and techniques. Digit. Invest. **9**, S90–S98 (2012)
16. Zawoad, S., Dutta, A.K., Hasan, R.: Towards building forensics enabled cloud through secure logging-as-a-service. IEEE Trans. Dependable Secure Comput. **13**, 148–162 (2016)
17. Zawoad, S., Dutta, A.K., Hasan, R.: SecLaaS: secure logging-as-a-service for cloud forensics. In: 8th ACM SIGSAC Symposium Information, Computer and Communications Security, pp. 219–230 (2013)
18. Bellare, M., Yee, B.: Forward integrity for secure audit logs. Technical report, Computer Science and Engineering Department (1997)
19. Schneier, B., Kelsey, J.: Secure audit logs to support computer forensics. ACM Trans. Inf. Syst. Secur. **2**, 159–176 (1999)
20. Ma, D., Tsudik, G.: A new approach to secure logging. ACM Trans. Storage **5**, 1–21 (2009)
21. Yavuz, A.A., Ning, P., Reiter, M.K.: Efficient, compromise resilient and append-only cryptographic schemes for Secure audit logging. In: Keromytis, A.D. (ed.) FC 2012. LNCS, vol. 7397, pp. 148–163. Springer, Heidelberg (2012). doi:10.1007/978-3-642-32946-3_12
22. Holt, J.E.: Logcrypt: forward security and public verification for secure audit logs. In: 4th Australasian Workshops on Grid Computing and E-research, pp. 203–211 (2006)
23. Accorsi, R.: BBox: a distributed secure log architecture. In: Camenisch, J., Lambrinoudakis, C. (eds.) EuroPKI 2010. LNCS, vol. 6711, pp. 109–124. Springer, Heidelberg (2011). doi:10.1007/978-3-642-22633-5_8
24. Stathopoulos, V., Kotzanikolaou, P., Magkos, E.: A framework for secure and verifiable logging in public communication networks. In: Lopez, J. (ed.) CRITIS 2006. LNCS, vol. 4347, pp. 273–284. Springer, Heidelberg (2006). doi:10.1007/11962977_22
25. Boneh, D., Lynn, B., Shacham, H.: Short signatures from the Weil pairing. J Cryptol. **17**, 297–319 (2004)
26. Roussev, V., Richard, L., G.G.: Breaking the performance wall: the case for distributed digital forensics. In: 2004 Digital Forensics Research Workshop, vol. 94 (2004)
27. Marziale, L., Richard, G.G., Roussev, V.: Massive threading: using GPUs to increase the performance of digital forensics tools. Digit. Invest. **4**, 73–81 (2007)
28. Francois, J., Wang, S., Bronzi, W.: Botcloud: Detecting botnets using mapreduce. In: IEEE International Workshop on Information Forensics and Security, pp. 1–6 (2011)

29. Roussev, V., Wang, L., Richard, G., Marziale, L.: A cloud computing platform for large-scale forensic computing. In: Peterson, G., Shenoi, S. (eds.) DigitalForensics 2009. IAICT, vol. 306, pp. 201–214. Springer, Heidelberg (2009). doi:10.1007/978-3-642-04155-6_15

30. Therdphapiyanak, J., Piromsopa, K.: Applying Hadoop for log analysis toward distributed IDS. In: 7th ACM International Conference on Ubiquitous Information Management and Communication, vol. 3 (2013)

31. Lin, X., Wang, P., Wu, B.: Log analysis in cloud computing environment with Hadoop and Spark. In: 5th IEEE International Conference on Broadband Network and Multimedia Technology, pp. 273–276 (2013)

Efficient Verifiable Multi-user Searchable Symmetric Encryption for Encrypted Data in the Cloud

Lanxiang Chen[✉] and Nan Zhang

Fujian Provincial Key Laboratory of Network Security and Cryptology,
College of Mathematics and Informatics, Fujian Normal University,
Fuzhou 350117, China
lxiangchen@fjnu.edu.cn

Abstract. Encryption is the basic technology to ensure the security of the data in the cloud, while ciphertext search is the key to improve the usability of the cloud storage. Most of the searchable encryption schemes consider the honest-but-curious or semi-honest cloud server. However, cloud storage in reality may be unreliable or even malicious. In this case, the encrypted data and search results returned by the server is not completely trustable, so it is crucial to verify the integrity of search results and encrypted data. Considering the untrusted cloud server security model, this paper proposes an efficient verifiable multi-user searchable symmetric encryption (VMSSE) scheme. It is efficient both in computation and storage. In particular, the work performed by the server per returned document is constant as opposed to linear in the size of the data. The computation and storage at the user is O(1). It allows the user to verify the search was computed honestly in the presence of a dishonest-and-curious server. And it supports multi-user searching. Finally, the security analysis shows that it is an efficient and feasible scheme.

Keywords: Cloud storage · Searchable symmetric encryption · Integrity verification · Multi-user searchable encryption

1 Introduction

Searchable symmetric encryption (SSE) allows clients with either limited resources or limited expertise to outsource the storage of its data to another party at low cost, while maintaining the ability to selectively retrieve segments of their data. It addresses this issue by indexing the encrypted data in such a way as to allow a server to execute a search query over the encrypted data and return the identifiers of any file that satisfies the search query.

Most of the existing work on SSE focuses on efficiently preserving confidentiality in the presence of an honest-but-curious server. This means that the server is trusted to follow the search protocol honestly but may try to infer information about data or search queries that it is unauthorized to know. However, in reality, besides its curiosity, a cloud server may be selfish in order to save its computation and/or communication resource. In this paper, we investigate the searchable encryption problem in the

© ICST Institute for Computer Sciences, Social Informatics and Telecommunications Engineering 2018
J. Wan et al. (Eds.): CloudComp 2016, SPNCE 2016, LNICST 197, pp. 173–183, 2018.
https://doi.org/10.1007/978-3-319-69605-8_16

presence of a dishonest-and-curious server, which may execute only a fraction of search operations and return a fraction of search results. To fight against this strongest adversary, the verifiable SSE scheme is proposed to offer verifiable searchability in addition to the data privacy.

The remainder of the paper is organized as follows. Section 2 presents the related works and Sect. 3 gives the preliminary and symbols definition. Section 4 details the VMSSE formal definition and the scheme construction. Section 5 gives the security and performance analysis and Sect. 6 concludes the paper.

2 Related Works

The first SSE scheme is proposed by Song in [1]. The construction is proven to be a secure encryption scheme, but it is not proven to be a secure searchable encryption scheme. Goh [2] introduces a notion of security for indexes and puts forth a construction based on Bloom filters and pseudo-random functions. An inherent problem of using Bloom filters is the possibility of false positives. Chang and Mitzenmacher [3] develop two index schemes, similar to Goh [2]. The idea is to use a prebuilt dictionary of search keywords to build an index per document. The index is an m-bit array, initially set to 0, where each bit position corresponds to a keyword in the dictionary. If the document contains a keyword, its index bit is set to 1.

Curtmola et al. [4] propose two new constructions SSE-1 and SSE-2, where the idea is to add an inverted index, which is an index per distinct word in the database instead of per document. This reduces the search time to the number of documents that contain the keyword. This is not only sublinear but also optimal. They present the first sublinear solution for single-keyword search whose complexity is linear in the number of matching documents. They also improve on previous security models, in particular by providing an adaptive security definition and solutions in this model.

Recently, dynamic SSE [5–8], ranked SSE [9], similarity search [10, 11], multi-keyword and multi-function SSE [12–15] has been studied extensively. However, security against malicious servers has been overlooked in most previous constructions and these only addressed security against honest-but-curious servers. In reality, besides its curiosity, a cloud server may malfunction or even be malicious itself. Even if the server is honest, a virus, worm, trojan horse or a software bug may delete, forge or swap some encrypted files. Therefore, users need a result verification mechanism to detect the potential misbehavior in this computation outsourcing model.

In order to cope with this problem, the first verifiable SSE is proposed by Kurosawa and Ohtaki in [16]. Based on SSE-2, they designed a verification scheme for single keyword search by using RSA accumulator. But their solution is inefficient, the searches or update overhead is linear in the number of documents in the database. The verification complexity there is linear in the problem size $O(tn)$.

Sun et al. [17] propose to build the search index based on term frequency and the vector space model with cosine similarity measure to achieve higher search result accuracy. They devise a scheme upon the proposed index tree structure to sign the root of the index tree to enable authenticity check over the returned search results. Later, they propose a UC-secure verifiable SSE based on bilinear Accumulation Tree [18].

Cheng et al. [19] propose a verifiable SSE based on secure indistinguishability obfuscation (iO). Zheng et al. [20] propose a verifiable SSE based on attribute-based encryption and bloom filter. Wang et al. propose two verifiable fuzzy keyword search schemes based on Bloom filter [21] and symbol-tree [22] respectively. Fu et al. [23] propose a smart semantic search scheme, which returns not only the result of keyword-based exact match, but also the result of keyword-based semantic match. At the same time, the proposed scheme supports the verifiability of search result. Stefanov et al. [24] gave a dynamic encrypted data search scheme with small search privacy leakage, which enables result verification for single keyword search.

In this paper, we present an efficient verifiable multi-user searchable symmetric encryption (VMSSE) scheme, which takes into account searching verification in the dishonest-and-curious server model based on SSE-1 [4]. The difference lies in that only the indispensable keys are sent to the authorized user, other than all the secrets in SSE-1. This is done to avoid collusion.

3 Symbol Definition

First, two pseudo-random functions (PRF) and three pseudo-random permutations (PRP) that will be used are given as follows. $f(\bullet)$ and $g(\bullet)$ are PRF and the others are PRP with the following parameters, here k and l are security parameters, m is the total size of the encrypted document collection in "min-units", where a min-unit is the smallest possible size for a keyword (e.g., one byte). n is the number of documents in the document collection, p is the bit length of the keyword. They are polynomial-time commutable functions that cannot be distinguished from random functions by any probabilistic polynomial-time adversary.

$$f : \{0,1\}^{\kappa} \times \{0,1\}^{p} \to \{0,1\}^{l+\log_2(m)}.$$

$$g : \{0,1\}^{\kappa} \times \{0,1\}^{n \times \log_2(n)} \to \{0,1\}^{l+\log_2(m)}.$$

$$\varphi : \{0,1\}^{\kappa} \times \{0,1\}^{\log_2(m)} \to \{0,1\}^{\log_2(m)}.$$

$$\pi : \{0,1\}^{\kappa} \times \{0,1\}^{p} \to \{0,1\}^{p}.$$

$$\rho : \{0,1\}^{\kappa} \times \{0,1\}^{p+\log_2(m)+l} \to \{0,1\}^{p+\log_2(m)+l}.$$

$BE = (Gen, Enc, Add, Revoke, Dec)$ is a broadcast encryption scheme [25], which is a tuple of five polynomial-time algorithms that work as follows. Let N be BE's user space, i.e., the set of all possible user identifiers. Gen is a probabilistic algorithm that takes as input a security parameter k and outputs a master key mk. Enc is a probabilistic algorithm that takes as input a master key mk, a set of users $G \subseteq N$ and a message m, and outputs a ciphertext c. Add is a probabilistic algorithm that takes as input a master key mk and a user identifier $U \in N$, and outputs a user key uk_U. $Revoke$ is a deterministic algorithm that takes as input a user key uk_U and a user identifier $U \in N$, and outputs $R = R \cup \{U\}$, $G = G \setminus \{U\}$. Finally, Dec is a deterministic algorithm that takes as input a user key uk_U and a ciphertext c and outputs either a message m or the failure symbol $\bot$. Informally, a broadcast encryption scheme is secure if its ciphertexts leak no useful information about the message to any user not in G.

$D = \{D_1, D_2, ..., D_n\}$ is a collection of n documents. $\tau = (\tau_{w1}, \tau_{w2}, ..., \tau_{wd})$ is the verifiable tags. $\Delta = \{w_1, w_2, ..., w_d\}$ is a dictionary of d words, and 2^{Δ} be the set of all possible documents. We assume that words in Δ can be represented using at most p bits. $\Delta' \subseteq \Delta$, be the set of distinct words that exist in the document collection D.

$D(w)$ is the set of identifiers of documents in D that contain word w ordered in lexicographic order. $id(D)$ is the identifier of document D, where the identifier can be any string that uniquely identifies a document, such as a memory location.

4   The VMSSE Scheme

4.1   VMSSE Formal Definition

We begin by reviewing the definition of a VMSSE scheme.

Definition 4.1. A VMSSE scheme is a collection of seven polynomial-time algorithms *VMSSE = (Keygen, BuildIndex, GenToken, Search, Verify, AddUser, RevokeUser)* such that:

$K \leftarrow$ ***Keygen*(1 ^{k})**: is a probabilistic key generation algorithm that is run by the user to setup the scheme. It takes a security parameter k, and returns a secret key K such that the length of K is polynomially bounded in k.

$(I, \tau) \leftarrow$ ***BuildIndex*(K, D)**: is a (possibly probabilistic) algorithm run by the user to generate indexes. It takes a secret key K and a polynomially bounded in k document collection D as inputs, and returns an index I and the verifiable tag τ.

$(T_{U,w}, \tau_w) \leftarrow$ ***GenToken*(K, w, U)**: is run by the owner to generate a token for a given word and an authorized user. It takes a secret key K, a word w and the authorized user U as inputs, and returns a trapdoor $T_U w$ and the verifiable tag τ_w.

$D(w) \leftarrow$ ***Search*(I, $T_{U,w}$)**: is run by the server S in order to search for the documents in D that contain word w. It takes an index I for a collection D and a trapdoor $T_U w$ for word w as inputs, and returns $D(w)$, the set of identifiers of documents containing w.

$(1, 0) \leftarrow$ ***Verify*(D(w), τ_w)**: is run by the user to check whether S returns the complete list. It takes $D(w)$ and the verifiable tag τ_w as inputs, and outputs 1, if it is true, otherwise, outputs 0.

$K_U \leftarrow$ ***AddUser*(K, U)**: is run by the owner to add a user to the authorized user set. It takes a secret key K and the authorized user U as inputs, and returns K_U to the authorized user.

$(r', Enc_{N\backslash R}(r')) \leftarrow$ ***RevokeUser*(K, U)**: is run by the owner to revoke a user from the authorized user set. It takes a secret key K and the authorized user U as inputs, and returns r' and $Enc_{N\backslash R}(r')$ to the server.

4.2   The Scheme Construction

We describe the details of the construction as follows. In VMSSE, a single index I is associated with a document collection D. It consists of two data structures for each word $w \in \Delta'$. The first one is an array A, which stores the encrypted $D(w)$ and a look-up table T. We start with a collection of linked lists L_i, where the nodes of each L_i are the identifiers of documents in $D(w_i)$ for each $w_i \in \Delta'$. Before encryption, the j-th node of L_i is augmented with information about the index in A of the $(j + 1)$-th node of L_i, together with the key used to encrypt it. We then write the nodes of all lists L_i in a random order and encrypted with randomly generated keys into the array A.

The other is the look-up table T, which contains information that enables one to locate and decrypt the appropriate elements from A. It is managed using indirect addressing. We now build a look-up table T that allows one to locate and decrypt the first element of each list L_i. Each entry in T corresponds to a word $w_i \in \Delta'$ and consists of a pair <address,value>. The field value contains the index in A and the decryption key for the first element of L_i. value is itself encrypted using the output of a pseudo-random function. The field address is simply used to locate an entry in T.

The owner computes both A and T based on the unencrypted D, and stores them on the server together with the encrypted D. When the user wants to retrieve the documents that contain word w_i, it computes the decryption key and the address for the corresponding entry in T and sends them to the server. The server locates and decrypts the given entry of T, and gets the index in A and the decryption key for the first node of L_i. Since each element of L_i contains information about the next element of L_i, the server can locate and decrypt all the nodes of L_i, which gives the identifiers in $D(w_i)$. As the server is dishonest, it may execute only a fraction of search operations honestly and return a fraction of search results. To ensure the completeness and correctness of search results, it allows the user to verify whether the server execute search operations honestly. The detail of the scheme is descried in Fig. 1.

In BE scheme, the long-lived secrets are the session keys between the users and the server. The long-lived secrets are distinct for each user. Given an encrypted message, the long-lived secrets allow a user to decrypt it only if the user was non-revoked at the time the message was encrypted. Different from SSE-1, the key r currently used for ρ is not sent to the authorized user. Each time the authorized user wants to search, he need to request a token from the file owner. Each time a user is revoked, the owner picks a new r and stores it on the server in encrypted form. As the revoked user have to request search token from the owner for each keyword he wants to search, if he is revoked, the owner will not issue token to him. So even though a revoked user which has been re-authorized to search could recover (old) values of r that were used while he was revoked, these values are no longer of interest.

5   The Security and Performance Analysis

This Section gives the security and performance analysis of the proposed scheme.

5.1   The Security Analysis

Since in practice the encrypted documents will also be stored on the server, we can assume that the document sizes and identifiers will also be leaked. If we wish not to disclose the size of the documents, this can be easily achieved by "padding" each plaintext document such that all documents have a fixed size. So the VMSSE scheme

---

Keygen(1^k, 1^l): Generate random keys $s, x, y, z, r \xleftarrow{R} \{0,1\}^k$ and output $K = (s, x, y, z, r, 1^l)$.

BuildIndex(K, D):

1. Initialization:
   (a) scan D and build Δ', the set of distinct words in D. For each word $w \in \Delta'$, build $D(w)$;
   (b) initialize a global counter ctr $= 1$;
   (c) initialize the BE scheme. Set R $= \{\Phi\}$. Send r and $E_N^{BE}(r)$ to the server.

2. Generate verifiable tags: for each $D(w)$, generate $\tau_w = g_x(D(w)) \oplus f_y(w)$, and $\tau = (\tau_{w1}, \tau_{w2}, \cdots \tau_{wd})$.

3. Build array A:
   (a) for each $w_i \in \Delta'$:
   - generate $k_{i,0} \xleftarrow{R} \{0,1\}^l$;
   - for $1 \leq j \leq |D(w_i)|$:
     – generate $k_{i,j} \xleftarrow{R} \{0,1\}^l$ and set node $N_{i,j} = <id(D_{i,j})||k_{i,j}||\varphi_s(ctr+1)>$, where $id(D_{i,j})$ is the jth identifier in $D(w_i)$;
     – compute $E_{k_{i,j-1}}(N_{i,j})$, and store it in $A[\varphi_s(ctr)]$;
     – ctr $=$ ctr $+ 1$.
   - for the last node of L_i (i.e., $N_{i,|D(w_i)|}$), before encryption, set the address of the next node to NULL.
   (b) let $m' = \sum_{w_i \in \Delta'} |D(w_i)|$. If $m' < m$, then set remaining ($m - m'$) entries of A to random values of the same size as the existing m' entries of A.

4. Build look-up table T:
   (a) for each $w_i \in \Delta'$:
   - value $= <addr(A(N_{i,1}))||k_{i,0}> \oplus f_y(w_i)$;
   - set $T[\pi_z(w_i)] = $ value.
   (b) if $|\Delta'| < |\Delta|$, then set the remaining ($|\Delta| - |\Delta'|$) entries of T to random values.

5. Output $I = (A, T)$.

GenToken(w): Output $T_w = (\pi_z(w), f_y(w))$ and $T_{U,w} = \rho_r(T_w)$, and send $(T_{U,w}, \tau_w)$ to the user.

Search($I, T_{U,w}$):

1. User sends $T_{U,w}$ to the server;
2. The server recovers $T_w = \rho^{-1}_r(T_{U,w})$; let $T_w = (\gamma, \eta)$. If γ is a valid virtual address, then:
3. Retrieve $\theta = T[\gamma]$. Let $<\alpha||k> = \theta \oplus \eta$.
4. Decrypt the list L starting with the node at address α encrypted under key k;
5. Output the list of document identifiers, denoted as $D'(w)$; Otherwise, return $\perp$.

Verify($D'(w)$, τ_w): User computes $\tau = g_x(D'(w)) \oplus f_y(w)$, and checks whether $\tau = \tau_w$, if yes, it means that S returns the complete list, otherwise, the user requires S to search again.

AddUser(K, U): Send $K_U = (x, y)$ and the long-lived secrets needed for the BE scheme to U.

RevokeUser(K, U): R $=$ R $\cup \{U\}$. Pick a new key $r' \leftarrow \{0,1\}^l$ and send r' and $E^{BE}_{N \setminus R}(r')$ to S. S overwrites the old values of r and $E^{BE}_{N \setminus R \cup \{U\}}(r)$ with r' and $E^{BE}_{N \setminus R}(r')$, respectively.

Fig. 1. The description of the VMSSE scheme.

reveals only the access pattern, the search pattern, the total size of the encrypted document collection, and the number of documents it contains. There maybe exist some security threat as follows.

Colluding. Server may collude with the users not to revoke them. However, if the server doesn't revoke some users in time, they can only search keywords which have been searched before. As the revoked user have to request search token from the owner for each keyword he wants to search, if he is revoked, the owner will not issue token to him. So even though a revoked user could recover (old) values of r that were used while he was revoked, these values are no longer of interest.

Revealing verifiable tags and public verification. As the user requests search token, the owner will send the verifiable tag to him. Then the verifiable tags is leaked to him. However, it will not lead to adverse consequences. As the user have to generate the tag based on the search results returned from the server each time, it doesn't help even the attacker gets the verifiable tags. The proposed verification mechanism is efficient and flexible, which can be either delegated to a public trusted authority (TA) or be executed privately by data users.

As VMSSE is extended based on SSE-1, there are several theorems and claims about the security of SSE-1.

Definition 5.1. *(Non-Adaptive Indistinguishability Security for SSE) A SSE scheme is secure in the sense of non-adaptive indistinguishability if for any two adversarially constructed histories with equal length and trace, no (probabilistic polynomial-time) adversary can distinguish the view of one from the view of the other with probability non-negligibly better than 1/2.* (see Definition 3.2 [1]).

Theorem 5.2. *Non-adaptive indistinguishability security of SSE is equivalent to non-adaptive semantic security of SSE.* (see Theorem 3.4 [1]).

Theorem 5.3. *SSE-1 is a non-adaptively semantic secure SSE scheme.* (see Theorem 4.1 [1]).

Theorem 5.4. *If SSE-1 is a non-adaptive semantic secure SSE scheme, then the VMSSE is a non-adaptive semantic secure SSE scheme.*

Proof. Compared to SSE-1, we have added the verification mechanism and issued $T_{U,w}$ as trapdoor in the VMSSE scheme. In the step of *Initialization*, the verifiable tags are generated as $\tau_w = g_x(D(w)) \oplus f_y(w)$, and $\tau = (\tau_{w1}, \tau_{w2}, \ldots \tau_{wd})$. Here $g(\bullet)$ and $f(\bullet)$ are pseudo-random functions (PRF), their pseudo-randomness guarantees that each element of the verifiable tags is indistinguishable from any random counterpart. In the step of *GenToken*, the token for authorized user U is generated as $T_w = (\pi_z(w), f_y(w))$ and $T_{U,w} = \rho_r(T_w)$, and send $(T_{U,w}, \tau_w)$ to the user. Here $f(\bullet)$ is pseudo-random functions, $\pi(\bullet)$ and $\rho(\bullet)$ are pseudo-random permutations (PRP), their pseudo-randomness guarantees that the token is indistinguishable from any random counterpart.

The security of a multi-user scheme can be defined similarly to the security of a single-user scheme, as the server should not learn anything about the documents and queries beyond what can be inferred from the access and search patterns. When the owner of a document collection D gives a user U permission to search through D, it sends to U all the secret information needed to perform searches in a single-user context in SSE-1. While in VMSSE, in the step of *AddUser*, only the indispensable keys are sent to authorized user, other than all the secret in SSE-1.   □

5.2   The Performance Analysis

To make the comparison easier, we assume that each document in the collection has the same size. Compared to the other schemes, our scheme is as efficient as the others while it is more simple and easy to understand, which is also more appropriate utilized in cloud storage. The multi-user construction is very efficient on the server side during a query: when given a trapdoor, the server only needs to evaluate a PRP in order to determine if the user is revoked. If access control mechanisms were used instead for this step, a more expensive authentication protocol would be required for each search query in order to establish the identity of the querier.

The experiment is running on one PC configured with Intel Core i5 CPU 1.6 GHz and 4 GB RAM. The experimental result is an average of 10 trials. We implement the hash function with SHA-256 and the PRP with AES-256.

A. Computing Overhead

To generate array A, there are two PRP operations for each file that includes the keyword. To generate T, there are one PRP and one PRF operations for each keyword. The rest is XOR and filling operations which are very efficient. We set $|\Delta| = 10,000$ and evaluate the overhead of index generation with $|D(w)|$ from 10 to 100. As shown in Fig. 2(a), for $|D(w)| = 40$, the overhead of index generation is 1646 s. As the process of index generation is only performed in setup phase, it is considered to be a reasonable overhead.

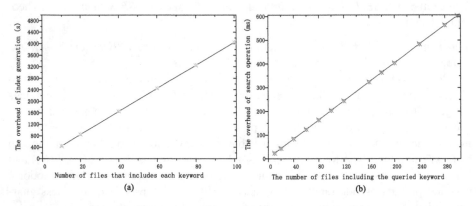

Fig. 2. (a) the overhead of index generation with $|\Delta| = 10,000$. (b) The search efficiency.

The search efficiency is related to the number of files including the queried keyword. There is one PRP operation for each file. We evaluate the overhead of search operation with $|D(w)|$ from 10 to 300. As shown in Fig. 2(b), for $|D(w)| = 100$, the overhead of search operation is 204 ms which is very efficient in practice.

To generate a search token, there are two PRP and one PRF operations. It is about 6.6 ms to generate a token.

B. Verification Efficiency

The verification mechanism is very efficient. It only needs two PRF operations for each verification. In [16], Kurosawa et al. designed a verification scheme using RSA accumulator. We compare the scheme of Kurosawa et al. with our scheme. As shown in Fig. 3, our scheme can be orders of magnitude faster than their scheme.

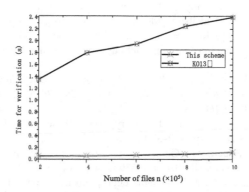

Fig. 3. The verification efficiency compared with KO13

From the above analysis, we can know that our scheme is very efficient and is very suitable for a large data set environment such as cloud storage.

Regarding the efficiency of multi-user, the main part of the overhead is the initialization phase, which requires each user to negotiate a session key with the server. The subsequent operations are highly efficient.

6   Conclusions

Searchable encryption is an important cryptographic primitive that is motivated by the popularity of cloud storage services like Google Desktop, Microsoft Skydrive etc. In the untrusted cloud storage server security model, we propose an efficient verifiable multi-user searchable symmetric encryption (VMSSE) scheme. The verification cost is efficient enough for practical use, i.e., it only depends on the corresponding search operation, regardless of the file collection size. Experimental result shows the efficiency and practicality of our scheme. The evaluation of the scheme on the real-world dataset is the future work.

Acknowledgments. This work was supported by the Natural Science Foundation of China (Nos. 61602118, 61572010 and 61472074), Fujian Normal University Innovative Research Team (No. IRTL1207), Natural Science Foundation of Fujian Province (No. 2015J01240), Science and Technology Projects of Educational Office of Fujian Province (No. JK2014009), and Fuzhou Science and Technology Plan Project (No. 2014-G-80).

References

1. Song, D.X., Wagner, D., Perrig, A.: Practical techniques for searches on encrypted data. In: Proceedings of SP 2000, pp. 44–55 (2000)
2. Goh, E.J.: Secure indexes. Cryptology ePrint Archive: Report 2003/216 (2003)
3. Chang, Y.-C., Mitzenmacher, M.: Privacy preserving keyword searches on remote encrypted data. In: Ioannidis, J., Keromytis, A., Yung, M. (eds.) ACNS 2005. LNCS, vol. 3531, pp. 442–455. Springer, Heidelberg (2005). https://dx.doi.org/10.1007/11496137_30
4. Curtmola, R., Garay, J., Kamara, S., Ostrovsky, R.: Searchable symmetric encryption: improved definitions and efficient constructions. In: Proceedings of CCS 2006, pp. 79–88 (2006)
5. Kamara, S., Papamanthou, C.: Parallel and dynamic searchable symmetric encryption. In: Sadeghi, A.-R. (ed.) FC 2013. LNCS, vol. 7859, pp. 258–274. Springer, Heidelberg (2013). https://dx.doi.org/10.1007/978-3-642-39884-1_22
6. Hahn, F., Kerschbaum, F.: Searchable encryption with secure and efficient updates. In: Proceedings of CCS 2014, pp. 310–320 (2014)
7. Naveed, M., Prabhakaran, M., Gunter, C.A.: Dynamic searchable encryption via blind storage. In: Proceedings of SP 2014, pp. 639–654 (2014)
8. Gajek, S.: Dynamic symmetric searchable encryption from constrained functional encryption. In: Sako, K. (ed.) CT-RSA 2016. LNCS, vol. 9610, pp. 75–89. Springer, Cham (2016). https://dx.doi.org/10.1007/978-3-319-29485-8_5
9. Wang, C., Cao, N., Li, J., Ren, K., Lou, W.: Enabling secure and efficient ranked keyword search over outsourced cloud data. IEEE Trans. Parallel Distrib. Syst. 23(8), 1467–1479 (2012)
10. Li, J., Wang, Q., Wang, C., Cao, N., Ren, K., Lou, W.: Fuzzy keyword search over encrypted data in cloud computing. In: Proceedings of INFOCOM 2010, pp. 441–445 (2010)
11. Wang, C., Ren, K., Yu, S., Urs, K.M.R.: Achieving usable and privacy-assured similarity search over outsourced cloud data. In: Proceedings of INFOCOM 2012, pp. 451–459 (2012)
12. Cash, D., Jarecki, S., Jutla, C., Krawczyk, H., Roşu, M.-C., Steiner, M.: Highly-scalable searchable symmetric encryption with support for boolean queries. In: Canetti, R., Garay, Juan A. (eds.) CRYPTO 2013. LNCS, vol. 8042, pp. 353–373. Springer, Heidelberg (2013). https://dx.doi.org/10.1007/978-3-642-40041-4_20
13. Cao, N., Wang, C., Li, M., Ren, K., Lou, W.: Privacy-preserving multi-keyword ranked search over encrypted cloud data. In: Proceedings of INFOCOM 2011, pp. 829–837 (2011)
14. Fu, Z., Sun, X., Linge, N., Zhou, L.: Achieving effective cloud search services: multi-keyword ranked search over encrypted cloud data supporting synonym query. IEEE Trans. Consum. Electron. 60(1), 164–172 (2014)
15. Wang, B., Yu, S., Lou, W., Hou, Y.T.: Privacy-preserving multi-keyword fuzzy search over encrypted data in the cloud. In: Proceedings of INFOCOM 2014, pp. 2112–2120 (2014)
16. Kurosawa, K., Ohtaki, Y.: UC-secure searchable symmetric encryption. In: Keromytis, Angelos D. (ed.) FC 2012. LNCS, vol. 7397, pp. 285–298. Springer, Heidelberg (2012). https://dx.doi.org/10.1007/978-3-642-32946-3_21
17. Sun, W., Wang, B., Cao, N., Li, M., Lou, W., Hou, Y.T., Li, H.: Verifiable privacy-preserving multi-keyword text search in the cloud supporting similarity-based ranking. IEEE Trans. Parallel Distrib. Syst. 25(11), 3025–3035 (2014)
18. Sun, W., Liu, X., Lou, W., Hou, Y.T., Li, H.: Catch you if you lie to me: efficient verifiable conjunctive keyword search over large dynamic encrypted cloud data. In: Proceedings of INFOCOM 2015, pp. 2110–2118 (2015)

19. Cheng, R., Yan, J., Guan, C., Zhang, F., Ren, K.: Verifiable searchable symmetric encryption from indistinguishability obfuscation. In: Proceedings of ASIACCS 2015, pp. 621–626 (2015)
20. Zheng, Q., Xu, S., Ateniese, G.: VABKS: verifiable attribute-based keyword search over outsourced encrypted data. In: Proc. of INFOCOM 2014, pp. 522–530 (2014)
21. Wang, J., Ma, H., Tang, Q., Li, J., Zhu, H., Ma, S., Chen, X.: A new efficient verifiable fuzzy keyword search scheme. J. Wireless Mobile Netw. Ubiquit. Comput. Dependable Appl. 3(4), 61–71 (2012)
22. Wang, J., Ma, H., Li, J., Zhu, H., Ma, S., Chen, X.: Effcient verifiable fuzzy keyword search over encrypted data in cloud computing. Comput. Sci. Inf. Syst. 10(2), 667–684 (2013)
23. Fu, Z., Shu, J., Sun, X., Linge, N.: Smart cloud search services: verifiable keyword-based semantic search over encrypted cloud data. IEEE Trans. Consum. Electron. 60(4), 762–770 (2014)
24. Stefanov, E., Papamanthou, C., Shi, E.: Practical dynamic searchable symmetric encryption with small leakage. In: Proceedings of NDSS 2014 (2014)
25. Fiat, A., Naor, M.: Broadcast encryption. In: Proceedings of CRYPTO 1993, pp. 480–491 (1994)

Secure Searchable Public-Key Encryption for Cloud Storage

Run Xie[1($\boxtimes$)], Changlian He[1], Yu He[2], Chunxiang Xu[2], and Kun Liu[3]

[1] Yibin University, Yibin, China
xrryun@126.com
[2] School of Computer Science and Engineering, University of Electronic Science and Technology of China, Chengdu, China
[3] Department of Computer Science, Guangzhou University, Guangzhou, China

Abstract. With networking became prevalent, the amount of data to be stored and managed on networked servers rapidly increases. Meanwhile, with the improvement of awareness of data privacy, the user's sensitive data is usually encrypted before uploading them to the cloud server. The searchable public-key encryption provides an efficient mechanism to achieve data retrieval in encrypted storage. Therefore, it is a critical technique on promoting secure and efficient cloud storage. Unfortunately, only few the existing schemes are secure to resist outside keyword guessing attacks. In this paper, we propose two efficient searchable public-key encryption schemes with a designated tester (dPEKS). One is a basic dPEKS, where the dPEKS ciphertext indistinguishability is proved without the random oracle. Meanwhile, the basic scheme is secure to resist the outside KGA since it satisfies the property of trapdoor indistinguishability. Comparing with the existing dPEKS schemes which use expensive pairing computation, our scheme is more efficient since we only need multi-exponentiation. Another is an enhanced dPEKS scheme. With the sender's identity is kept secret from server, this scheme can provide stronger security.

Keywords: Searchable encryption · Trapdoor indistinguishability · Keywords guessing attacks · Cloud storage · Security analysis

1 Introduction

With ubiquitous network, the cloud storage offers great convenience to users. More and more users enjoy the benefits of cloud storage services by outsourcing their data into the cloud server. To protect data privacy, a user has to encrypt the sensitive data before uploading them into the server. However, this incurs a new problem that the network server cannot perform searches over encrypted data. When users want to retrieve the encrypted data, he has two straight options: downloading the entire encrypted data or sending his private keys to the cloud server. Obviously, the first approach requires high consumption of bandwidth and the second approach deviates original intention (namely protect data privacy).

© ICST Institute for Computer Sciences, Social Informatics and Telecommunications Engineering 2018
J. Wan et al. (Eds.): CloudComp 2016, SPNCE 2016, LNICST 197, pp. 184–195, 2018.
https://doi.org/10.1007/978-3-319-69605-8_17

In 2000, Song et al. first introduced the concept of searchable encryption [1]. The searchable encryption allows the network server to search over encrypted data without decryption. It does not leak any information about the data and query. Therefore, searchable encryption is a critical technique promoting efficient and secure cloud storage. The searchable encryption has been developed into two different types. The first type is the symmetric searchable encryption (SSE in short) which requires that a sender is securely granted a secret key from the intended receiver. It suffers from risks of key leakage in management and distribution [1]. The second type is the searchable public-key encryption with keyword search (PEKS in short), which allows any one seeing the receiver's public key to encrypt documents.

The PEKS provides an efficient mechanism to achieve data retrieval in encrypted storage. In a PEKS scheme, the sender generates the searchable ciphertext of keywords with receiver's public key and stores it to server. To retrieval the encrypted data associated with a given keyword, the receiver creates a search request (trapdoor) with the keyword and his private key. Receiving a trapdoor, the cloud server can perform a test whether some encrypted data matches the trapdoor and returns corresponding encrypted data to receiver.

In 2004, Boneh et al. proposed the first searchable public-key encryption with keyword search scheme [2]. Their scheme requires constructing the secure transport channel to protect trapdoors. Since building a secure channel is usually expensive, this requirement limits applications of the searchable public-key encryption scheme.

To overcome this obstacle, in 2008, Baek et al. proposed secure Channel Free Public Key Encryption with Keyword Search scheme [3](SCF-PEKS in short), which removes the secure channel requirement. Nevertheless, Yau et al. showed that this scheme is insecure [4] for the following reason. With outside keyword-guessing attacks (outside KGA), an outside adversary can reveal encrypted keywords if he obtains a trapdoor in channel.

Hereafter, in [15], the searchable public key encryption with keyword search scheme with a designated tester (dPEKS in short) is proposed. In this scheme, only a designated server can test whether given trapdoor matches the ciphertext.

Until now, most of the dPEKS schemes pay more attention to improving the security against this attacks [5–11]. Only a few schemes [12–15] can effectively resist outside KGA.

In addition, the KGA launched by a server is called inside KGA. Since the correct requirement of scheme and small keyword space, it is impossible to construct a searchable public-key encryption(dPEKS or PEKS) scheme secure against inside KGA under the original framework [2]. Very recently, based on a new framework, Peng et. al. proposed a online/offline ciphertext retrieval scheme [16] is secure against inside KGA.

In this paper, based on the IBE [17], we propose two efficient dPEKS schemes, namely a basic dPEKS scheme (BdPEKS) and an enhanced dPEKS (EdPEKS). For the basic scheme, we prove that our construction satisfies ciphertext indistinguishability under q-ABDHE assumption. Meanwhile, we prove that it satisfies trapdoor indistinguishability. Therefore, our BdPEKS scheme is secure against outside keyword guessing attacks. Comparing with the existing dPEKS schemes which use expensive pairing computation, our basic scheme is more efficient since we only need multi-exponentiation. For our enhanced dPEKS scheme (EdPEKS), we analysis its security. In EdPEKS, if a server wants to launch the KGA, it must guess both the sender's identity and keywords. Therefore, the EdPEKS scheme has stronger security to resist the inside KGA. Lastly, we show a comparison between the other PEKS (dPEKS) schemes and our schemes in terms of functionalities and performances.

2   Preliminaries

In this section, we review the construction of dPEKS, which is defined in [15]. Meanwhile, we also describe the definition of dPEKS ciphertexts indistinguishability and trapdoor indistinguishability with game between the adversary $\mathcal{F}$ and the challenger $\mathcal{G}$. Here, the dPEKS ciphertext is an encrypted list of keywords.

2.1   Definition of dPEKS and Security Model

2.1.1   Definition of dPEKS

As stated in the previous section, the dPEKS is a mechanism which can achieve efficient ciphertext retrieval. Specially, a dPEKS scheme can be defined as follows.

Definition 1. *A dPEKS scheme consists of the following four PPT (probability polynomial-time) algorithms, (**Setup**, **KeyGen**, **dPEKS**, **dTrapdoor**, **dTest**).*

Setup: Let n be a security parameter. This algorithm takes n as input, then it outputs a set public parameter $\mathcal{PP}$.

KeyGen: Taking the public parameter $\mathcal{PP}$ as input, this algorithm creates the receiver's a public/private key pair (P_r, K_r) and the server's a public/private key pair (P_s, K_s).

dPEKS: Taking the public parameter $\mathcal{PP}$, the receiver's public key P_r, the server's public key P_s and a keyword w as input, this algorithm returns a dPEKS ciphertext C_w corresponding to w.

Trapdoor: Taking $\mathcal{PP}$, the receiver's public/private key (P_r, K_r), the server's public key P_s and a keyword w' as input, this algorithm generates a trapdoor T_w of w.

dTest: Taking a dPEKS ciphertext C_w of keyword w, $\mathcal{PP}$, a trapdoor $T_{w'}$ and the server's private key K_s as input, this algorithm returns 'yes' if $w' = w$, and otherwise outputs 'no'.

2.1.2 Security Model

Security of dPEKS ciphertext

As described in [15], in dPEKS, the security for a dPEKS ciphertext requires that a dPEKS ciphertext satisfies indistinguishability against a chosen plaintext attack (C-IND-CPA in short). Specially, the C-IND-CPA guarantees that (1) a server cannot distinguish between the dPEKS ciphertexts of two challenge keywords w_0 and w_1 its choice if he has not obtained their trapdoor. (2) an outside adversary (including a receiver) who can generate the trapdoors of any keyword (excluding challenge keywords) cannot distinguish between the dPEKS ciphertext of w_0 and w_1 its choice if he has not obtained the server's private key. Formalized, the C-IND-CPA can be defined with the following two games.

Game1. Here, $\mathcal{G}$ is a challenger and $\mathcal{F}_1$ is a malicious server.

Setup: $\mathcal{F}_1$ generates (P_s, K_s) as his public/private key pair. $\mathcal{G}$ generates (P_r, K_r) as receiver's public/private key pair. The tuples (P_s, K_s, P_r) are given to $\mathcal{F}_1$, and the tuples (P_r, K_r, P_s) are given to $\mathcal{G}$.

Phase 1 Trapdoor queries: $\mathcal{F}_1$ queries many keywords $w \in \{0,1\}^*$ to obtain trapdoors T_w from $\mathcal{G}$. $\mathcal{G}$ adaptively responses $\mathcal{F}_1$ with T_w as trapdoor generation oracle.

Challenge: $\mathcal{F}_1$ chooses the keywords pair (w_0, w_1) as a challenge. Here, the restriction is that w_0 and w_1 have not been queried to obtain the trapdoors T_{w_0} and T_{w_1}. Receiving w_0 and w_1, $\mathcal{G}$ chooses an random $b \in \{0,1\}$ and generates the ciphertext C_{w_b} of w_b, and returns it to $\mathcal{F}_1$.

Phase 2 Trapdoor queries: In this phase, $\mathcal{F}_1$ can still queries w to obtain its trapdoor as phase 1. If the $w \neq w_0, w_1$, $\mathcal{G}$ adaptively responses $\mathcal{F}_1$ with T_w as phase 1, otherwise stop.

Outputs: $\mathcal{F}_1$ outputs $c' \in \{0,1\}$. If $c' = c$, then $\mathcal{F}_1$ wins Game1.

Let $\mathbf{adv}_{\mathcal{F}_1}^{C-ind-cpa} = |Pr(c' = c) - \frac{1}{2}|$ denote the advantage probability that $\mathcal{F}_1$ wins the game1.

Game2. Here, $\mathcal{G}$ is a challenger and $\mathcal{F}_2$ an outside adversary (including receiver).

Setup: $\mathcal{F}_2$ is given P_r and K_r as receiver's public and private key, respectively. $\mathcal{G}$ (as server) generates (P_s, K_s) as his public/private key pair. The tuples (P_r, K_r, P_s) are given to $\mathcal{F}_2$, the tuples (P_s, K_s, P_r) are given to $\mathcal{G}$. Here, $\mathcal{F}_2$ can generate the trapdoor of any keyword since he holds K_r.

Challenge: $\mathcal{F}_2$ chooses the keywords pair (w_0, w_1) as the challenges. Here, the restrictions is that $\mathcal{F}_2$ did not previously ask the dTest oracle for the trapdoors of w_0 and w_1. Receiving w_0 and w_1, $\mathcal{G}$ chooses $c \in \{0,1\}$ and generates the ciphertext C_{w_c} of w_c, and returns it to $\mathcal{F}_2$.

Output: $\mathcal{F}_2$ outputs $c' \in \{0,1\}$. If $c' = c$, then $\mathcal{F}_2$ wins Game2.

Let $\mathbf{adv}_{\mathcal{F}_2}^{C-ind-cpa} = |Pr(c' = c) - \frac{1}{2}|$ denotes the advantage probability that $\mathcal{F}_2$ wins the Game2.

Definition 2. *For the polynomial-time $\mathcal{F}_1$ and $\mathcal{F}_2$, a dPEKS scheme is said to be C-IND-CPA secure if $\mathbf{adv}_{\mathcal{F}_{1,2}}^{C-ind-cpa} = |Pr(c' = c) - \frac{1}{2}|$ is negligible.*

Remark. In the Game2, the adversary is considered to be an receiver who can generate the trapdoor of keywords. If the outside adversary is not an receiver, we only need to the Game1 to define the C-IND-CPA. In fact, receiver's ability to discriminate between the dPEKS ciphertexts of keywords won't arise harmful effects, since the dPEKS ciphertexts should be send to receiver. Based on this reason, the adversaries are considered to be server and outside attacker (excluding receicer) when we prove the C-IND-CPA of BdPEKS.

Security of Trapdoor
As stated [15], in a dPEKS scheme, if the adversary (excluding the receiver and the server) cannot distinguish between the trapdoors of w_0 and w_1, it is said that a dPEKS scheme satisfies trapdoor indistinguishability against an adaptive chosen plaintext attack (T-IND-CPA). The dPEKS scheme can stand against outside keyword-guessing attacks successfully if it is T-IND-CPAT secure. The trapdoor indistinguishability can be defined with the following Game3.

Game3. Here, $\mathcal{G}$ is a challenger and $\mathcal{F}_3$ is an outside adversary.
Setup: Running **Setup** and **KeyGen**, the public parameter $\mathcal{PP}$, the receiver's key pair (P_r, K_r) and the server's key pair (P_s, K_s) are generated. $\mathcal{PP}$, P_r and P_s are given to $\mathcal{F}_3$ while K_s and K_r are kept secret from $\mathcal{F}_3$.
Phase 1 Trapdoor queries: $\mathcal{F}_3$ queries many keywords $w \in \{0,1\}^*$ to obtain trapdoors T_w from $\mathcal{G}$. $\mathcal{G}$ adaptively responses $\mathcal{F}_3$ with trapdoor T_w of w.
Challenge: $\mathcal{F}_3$ chooses (w_0, w_1) as challenge keywords and send them to $\mathcal{G}$. Here, the restriction is that w_0 and w_1 have not been queried to obtain the trapdoors T_{w_0} and T_{w_1}, and that $\mathcal{F}_3$ did not previously ask for T_{w_0} and T_{w_1} in phase 1. Receiving (w_0, w_1), $\mathcal{G}$ chooses an random $c \in \{0,1\}$ and generates its trapdoor T_{w_c}, and returns it to $\mathcal{F}_3$.
Phase 2 Trapdoor queries: In this phase, $\mathcal{F}_3$ can still query the trapdoor of w as phase 1, where $w \neq w_0, w_1$. $\mathcal{G}$ can adaptively response $\mathcal{F}_3$ with T_w as oracle.
Outputs: $\mathcal{F}_3$ outputs $b' \in \{0,1\}$. If $c' = c$, then $\mathcal{F}_3$ wins Game3
Let $\mathbf{adv}_{\mathcal{F}_3}^{T-ind-cpa} = |Pr(c' = c) - \frac{1}{2}|$ denote the advantage probability that $\mathcal{F}_3$ wins the Game3.

Definition 3. *For the polynomial-time $\mathcal{F}_3$, it is said to be T-IND-CPA if* $\mathbf{adv}_{\mathcal{F}_3}^{T-ind-cpa} = |Pr(c' = c) - \frac{1}{2}|$ *is negligible.*

2.1.3 Complexity Assumptions
Let G, G_T be multiplicative cyclic groups of prime order p.

The security of our system is based on the decisional augmented bilinear Diffie-Hellman exponent assumption (decisional ABDHE)[17]. First, we review the q-ABDHE problem, which is defined as follows. Let e be a bilinear map: $G \times G \rightarrow G_T$. Given a tuple in G^{2q+2}: $\mathcal{L}' = (\tilde{g}, \tilde{g}^{\gamma^{q+2}}, g, g^{\gamma}, g^{\gamma^2}, \ldots, g^{\gamma^q}, g^{\gamma^{q+2}}, \ldots, g^{\gamma^{2q}})$ as input, required to output $e(g, \tilde{g})^{\gamma^{q+1}}$.

Following the q-ABDHE problem, the truncated version of q-ABDHE problem is defined as: Given a tuple $\mathcal{L} = \left(\tilde{g}, \tilde{g}_{q+2}, g, g_1, \ldots, g_q \right)$, required to output $e(g, \tilde{g})^{\gamma^{q+1}}$, where $\tilde{g}_i = \tilde{g}^{\gamma^i}$ and $g_i = g^{\gamma^i}$.

Clearly, the truncated q-ABDHE problem is hard if the q-ABDHE problem is hard. Corresponding to the truncated q-ABDHE problem, the decisional truncated q-ABDHE is introduced as follow.

An algorithm $\mathcal{G}$ outputs $b \in \{0,1\}$ with the advantages ε in solving the truncated decision q-ABDHE if $|Pr[\mathcal{G}(\mathcal{L}, e(g_{q+1}, \tilde{g})] - Pr[\mathcal{G}(\mathcal{L}, E)]| \geq \varepsilon$, where the probability is over the random choice of γ in Z_p, the random choice of generators $g, \tilde{g}$ in G, the random choice of $E \in G_T$ the random bits consumed by $\mathcal{G}$.

Meanwhile, we also assume the discrete logarithm problem (DLP) assumption holds over G and G_T.

3   Our Construction

3.1   Basic dPEKS Scheme (BdPEKS)

In this section, we construct a basic searchable public-key encryption scheme with a designated tester (BdPEKS). With the G, G_T as specified above, let H_0: $\{0,1\}^* \rightarrow Z_p^*$ be a hash function. Our scheme is built as follows.

- **Setup:** Taking two multiplicative cyclic groups G, G_T with prime order p, a bilinear map e, this algorithm generates public parameters $\mathcal{PP} = (p, G, G_T, g, \beta, e, H_0)$, where $g, \beta \in G$ and g is a generator of G.
- **KeyGen** (PP): Taking a, b and $g \in \mathcal{PP}$ as input, this algorithm outputs the receiver's public key and private key $P_r = g^a$ and $K_r = a$, and the server's public key and private key $P_s = g^b$ and $K_s = b$.
- **dPEKS** (P_r, w): Taking $\mathcal{PP}$, P_r and a keyword w (denote $H(w) = h$) as input, the sender chooses a random $u \in Z_p^*$ computes the dPEKS ciphertext as follows:
  $$C = (C_1, C_2, C_3) = \left(e(\beta, g)^u, e(g, g)^u, P_r^u \cdot g^{-uh} \right)$$
- **Trapdoor** (K_r, P_s, w'): Taking $K_r = a$, P_s ,a keyword w' (denote $H(w') = h'$) and a random $v \in Z_p^*$ as input, the receiver computes the trapdoor of w' as follows:
  $$T = (T_1, T_2) = \left(P_s^v, T_2 = g^v \cdot (\beta P_s^{-1})^{\frac{1}{a-h'}} \right).$$
- **dTest:** Given a dPEKS ciphertext C and a trapdoor T, the server performs searching operation by checking $C_1 = C_2^b \cdot e(C_3, T_2 T_1^{-(b^{-1})})$. If the equation holds, it returns 1; Otherwise returns 0;

3.1.1   Correctness of BdPEKS

The BdPEKS scheme is correct if the trapdoor $T = (T_1, T_2)$ is valid for w' and the dPEKS ciphertext $C = (C_1, C_2, C_3)$ is valid for w.

With $T = (T_1, T_2) = \left(P_s^v, g^v \cdot (\beta P_s^{-1})^{\frac{1}{a-h'}} \right)$ and $C = (C_1, C_2, C_3) = \left(e(\beta, g)^u, e(g, g)^u, P_r^u \cdot g^{-uh} \right)$, the correctness of the dTest algorithm is verified as follows: $T_2 \cdot T_1^{-b^{-1}} = (\beta P_s^{-1})^{\frac{1}{a-h'}}$, $e(C_3, T_2 T_1^{-b^{-1}}) = e(g^{u(a-h)}, \beta^{\frac{1}{a-h'}})e(g^{u(a-h)}, g^{\frac{-b}{a-h'}}) = e(g^u, \beta)e(g^u, g^{-b})$.

Therefore, if $w = w'$, then the equation $C_1 = C_2^b \cdot e(C_3, T_2 T_1^{-b^{-1}})$ is holds.

3.1.2   Security of BdPEKS

Security of dPEKS Ciphertext

As stated in **Remark** of Sect. 2.1, the adversaries are considered to be a server or an outside attacker (excluding receiver).

Theorem 1. *For a server or an outside attacker (excluding receiver), if the truncated decision assumption holds over (G, G_T, e), the BdPEKS scheme is C-IND-CPA secure.*

Proof: We assume that the adversary $\mathcal{F}_1$ is the malicious server or an outside attacker, with an advantages ε breaking our scheme. We can construct an algorithm $\mathcal{G}$ which can solve the decisional truncated q-ABDHE problem on (G, G_T, e) with the advantage $(\varepsilon - 2/p)$.

Denote $g_i = g^{\alpha^i}$ and $\tilde{g}_i = \tilde{g}^{\alpha^i}$, $\mathcal{G}$ is given a random decision q-ABDHE challenge $(\tilde{g}, \tilde{g}_{q+2}, g, g_1, \cdots, g_q, E)$, where E is $e(g_{q+1}, \tilde{g})$ or a random element of G_T.

- **Setup:** $\mathcal{G}$ generates a random polynomial $d(x) \in Z_p[x]$ of degree q. Then $\mathcal{G}$ can compute $\beta = g^{d(\alpha)}$ since $(g, g^{\alpha}, \cdots, g^{\alpha^q})$. Then the public parameters are $\mathcal{PP} = (q, p, e, G, G_T, g, \beta, H)$, where $H:\{0,1\}^* \to Z_p^*$ is a hash function (not as oracle). Let $P_r = g_1$ be $\mathcal{G}$'s public key. Choose $b \in Z_p^*$ uniformly at random, then let $\mathcal{F}_1$'s public key and private key be $P_s = g^b$ and $K_s = b$.

- **Phase 1 Trapdoor queries:** The $\mathcal{F}_1$ makes queries of keywords $w \in \{0,1\}^*$ to obtain trapdoors T_w from $\mathcal{G}$. If $\mathcal{F}_1$ query the trapdoor of w ($h = H(w)$), $\mathcal{G}$ responds as follows. $\mathcal{G}$ computes the $(q-1)$-degree polynomial $D_T(x) = (d(x) - d(h))/(x - h)$. Taking two random $r', r'' \in Z_p^*$, he computes $T_1 = P_s^{r'}$ and $T_2 = g^{r''} g^{D_T(\alpha)}$. As an result, he sets $T = (T_1, T_2)$. Clearly, there is a unknown random r such that $r' = \frac{r}{\alpha-h}$ and $r'' = r' + \frac{d(h)-b}{\alpha-h}$. Thus $T_1 = P_s^{\frac{r}{\alpha-h}}$ and $T_2 = g^{r''} g^{D_T(\alpha)} = g^{\frac{r}{\alpha-h}}(\beta g^{-b})^{\frac{1}{\alpha-h}}$ appears to $\mathcal{F}_1$ be correctly distributed.

- **Challenge:** $\mathcal{F}_1$ chooses the keywords pair (w_0, w_1) as the challenge and send to $\mathcal{G}$. Denote $h_c = H(w_c)$ ($c \in \{0,1\}$). Here, the restriction is that w_0 and w_1 have not been queried to obtain the trapdoors T_{w_0} and T_{w_1}.

  Taking the polynomial $D_T(x)$, $d(x)$ and $d'(x) = x^{q+2}$, $\mathcal{G}$ computes $D'(x) = (d'(x) - d'(h_c))/(x - h_c)$, where the form of $D'(x)$ is $D'(x) = x^{q+1} + D(x)$. Then $\mathcal{G}$ picks $c \in \{0,1\}$ and computes the ciphertext as follows.
  Let $C = (C_1, C_2, C_3)$, then $C_2 = E \cdot e(\tilde{g}, g^{D'(\alpha)})$, $C_3 = \tilde{g}^{(d'(\alpha)-d'(h_c))}$
  $C_1 = e(C_3, g^{D_T(\alpha)}) \cdot C_2^{d(h_c)}$
  Let $u = (\log_g \tilde{g})D'(\alpha)$, if $E = e(g_{q+1}, \tilde{g})$ then
  $C_1 = e(\beta, g)^u$, $C_2 = (g, g)^u$, $C_3 = g^{u(\alpha-h_c)}$. Since $g, \tilde{g}$ are uniformly random, the $u = (\log_g \tilde{g})D'(\alpha)$ is uniformly random. As an result, the $C = (C_1, C_2, C_3)$ is a valid dPEKS ciphertext.

- **Phase 2 Trapdoor queries:** $\mathcal{F}_1$ makes trapdoor queries, for any keyword $w \neq w_0, w_1$, $\mathcal{G}$ responds as in Phase 1.
- **Guess:** Finally, $\mathcal{F}_1$ outputs it's result c'. If $c' = c$, $\mathcal{G}$ outputs 1(indicating $E = e(g_{q+1}, \tilde{g})$), otherwise outputs 0.

Clearly, if $E = e(g_{q+1}, \tilde{g})$, $\mathcal{F}_1$ can guess c correctly with the probability $1/2 + \varepsilon$. When E is uniformly random and independent element of G_T, the probability that $\mathcal{F}_1$ guesses c correctly is $2/p$. Meanwhile, the probability that $\mathcal{G}$ solves the truncated decision q-ABDHE correctly without $\mathcal{F}_1$'s help is $1/2$. As an result, $\mathcal{G}$ solves the truncated decision q-ABDHE with $1/2 + \varepsilon - 2/p - 1/2 = \varepsilon - 2/p$. This completes the proof of C-IND-CPA secure.

Security of Trapdoor

Theorem 2. *Our BdPEKS scheme is T-IND-CAP secure.*

Proof: The adversary $\mathcal{F}_2$ is assumed to be a malicious outside attacker. We show that $\mathcal{F}_2$ can not distinguish Whether two trapdoors were created by the same keyword.

Firstly, in our scheme, the trapdoor is $T_1 = P_s^v$, $T_2 = g^v \cdot (\beta P_s^{-1})^{\frac{1}{a-h'}}$ ($h' = H(w')$) where v is an random element in Z_p^*. The trapdoor is updated every time due to the difference of v we selected.

Due to the $K_r = a$ is kept secret from $\mathcal{F}_2$, the $\mathcal{F}_2$ can not known $(\beta P_s^{-1})^{\frac{1}{a-h'}}$. In fact, let $\beta = g^k$ ($k \in Z_p^*$ is some unknown value), then $T_2 = g^v \cdot (\beta P_s^{-1})^{\frac{1}{a-h'}} = g^{\frac{k-b}{a-h'}+v}$. With v is randomly selected from Z_p^*, T_2 is an random element in G. Thus T_2 is independent of keyword w' from $\mathcal{F}_2$'s view. As a result, our scheme satisfies the trapdoor indistinguishability.

3.2   Our Enhanced dPEKS Scheme (EdPEKS)

Base on the BdPEKS scheme, we construct an enhanced dPEKS scheme (EdPEKS). Our EdPEKS scheme has stronger security. Especially, the EdPEKS scheme can resist inside keyword guessing attacks from the untrusted server if the sender's identities are kept secret from cloud server. The EdPEKS scheme is constructed as follows.

Let G, G_T be multiplicative cyclic groups of prime order p. Let $H_0: \{0,1\}^* \to Z_p^*$ and $H_1: \{0,1\}^* \to G$ be two hash function.

- **Setup:** Take two multiplicative cyclic groups G, G_T with prime order p, a bilinear map e, this algorithm generates public parameters $\mathcal{PP} = (p, G, G_T, g, e, H_0, H_1)$, where $g \in G$ is a generator of G. Additionally, let $S_{id} \in \{0,1\}^*$ be the sender's identity.
- **KeyGen** $(\mathcal{PP})$: Taking a, b and $g \in \mathcal{PP}$ as input, this algorithm outputs the receiver's public key and private key $P_r = g^a$ and $K_r = a$, and the server's public key and private key $P_s = g^b$ and $K_s = b$.
- **dPEKS** (P_r, P_s, S_{id}, w): Taking $\mathcal{PP}$, P_r, P_s, S_{id} and a keyword w as input, the sender chooses a random $u \in Z_p^*$ computes the dPEKS ciphertext as follows:

$C=(C_1,\ C_2,\ C_3)=\big(e(H_{id},P_s)^u,\ e(P_s,P_s)^u,\ P_r^u\cdot g^{-uh}\big)$
where $H_{id}=H_1(S_{id})$ and $h=H_0(w)$.

- **Trapdoor** $(K_r,\ P_s,\ S'_{id},\ w')$: Taking $K_r=a$, P_s, S'_{id}, a keyword w' and a random $v\in Z_p^*$ as input, the receiver computes the trapdoor of w' as follows:

$T=(T_1,T_2)=(P_s^v,g^v(H'_{id}P_s^{-1})^{\frac{1}{a-h'}})$, where $H'_{id}=H_1(S'_{id})$ and $h'=H_0(w')$

- **dTest:** Taking the dPEKS ciphertext C and trapdoor T, the server performs searching operation by checking $C_1=C_2\cdot e(C_3,T_2^bT_1^{-1})$. If this equation holds, it returns 1; Otherwise returns 0;

3.2.1   Correctness

The correctness of the EdPEKS scheme can be verified by the following equation.

With the trapdoor $T_1=P_s^v$, $T_2=g^v(H'_{id}P_s^{-1})^{\frac{1}{a-h'}}$ and the dPEKS ciphertext $C_1=e(H_{id},P_s)^u$, $C_2=e(P_s,P_s)^u$, $C_3=P_r^u\cdot g^{-uh}$, the server can compute:

$$e(C_3,T_2^bT_1^{-1})\ =\ e(P_r^ug^{-uh},(H'_{id}P_s^{-1})^{\frac{b}{a-h'}})\ =\ e\big(g^{u(a-h)},H_{id}^{'\frac{b}{a-h'}}\big)e\big(g^{u(a-h)},$$
$$g^{\frac{-b^2}{a-h'}}\big)$$

Clearly, if $H'_{id}=H_{id}$ and $w'=w$, the equation $C_1=C_2\cdot e(C_3,T_2^bT_1^{-1})$ holds.

3.2.2   Seacurity Analysis

In this section, we analysis the security of EdPEKS scheme.

Theorem 3. *Our EdPEKS scheme is the dPEKS ciphertext indistinguishable secure.*

Proof: Firstly, in EdPEKS scheme, the dPEKS ciphertext $C_3=P_r^u\cdot g^{-uH_0(w)}$. Clearly, it is identical with the C_3 of Basic dPEKS scheme. If the adversary (the server or a outside attacker) can break the C-IND-CPA security of EdPEKS scheme, there exist an adversary can break the C-IND-CPA security of BdPEKS scheme.

Secondly, although the receiver may generate a trapdoor T, $P_s^{\frac{1}{a-H_0(w')}}$ and $g^{\frac{1}{a-H_0(w')}}$, he cannot perform a test since the server's private key K_s is kept secret from him. Therefore, the EdPEKS scheme is C-IND-CPA secure even if the adversary is receiver.

Theorem 4. *Our EdPEKS scheme is trapdoor indistinguishable secure.*

Proof: In EdPEKS scheme, the trapdoor $T=(P_s^v,g^v(H'_{id}P_s^{-1})^{\frac{1}{a-H_0(w')}})$. Clearly, the only difference between the trapdoor of EdPEKS scheme and the trapdoor of Basic scheme is that the β is replaced by H'_{id}. With the same analysis of theorem 3.2, it's easy to see that the EdPEKS scheme is also T-IND-CPA secure.

3.2.3   Inside KGA Analysis

As stated in [14], the inside KGA works as follows. Given a valid trapdoor, the server chooses an appropriate keyword from the keyword space and then uses it generate a dPEKS ciphertext. With his private key, the server can test whether the keyword matches the trapdoor. Since the keyword space is small, the *guessing-then-testing* procedure is efficient to find a correct keyword.

In our EdPEKS scheme, the dPEKS ciphertext is $\left(e(H_{id}, P_s)^u, e(P_s, P_s)^u, P_r^u \cdot g^{-uH(w)}\right)$. The EdPEKS scheme is secure against inside KGA due to the following reasons.

(1) It is easy to see that the server cannot obtain the sender's identity H_{id} from $e(H_{id}, P_s)^u$ even if he holds K_s and the trapdoor T.
(2) The server cannot obtain H_{id} from $T_2 = g^v \cdot (H'_{id}P_s^{-1})^{\frac{1}{a-H(w')}}$ since the receive's K_r is kept secret from him.
(3) The server cannot perform a test for a valid trapdoor if he has not the dPEKS ciphertext.

As a result, to launch KGA, he must guess the appropriate keyword and identity to computes a dPEKS ciphertext. With the space (including the identity space and the keyword space) becoming larger, the *guessing-then-testing* procedure is inefficient.

4 Performance Analysis

We analyze the performance of our schemes in terms of dPEKS ciphertext, the trapdoor and computation cost. This analysis includes a comparison between the other schemes.

Let P_t and E_t be the computational cost of a bilinear pairing operation and an exponentiation (or multi-exponentiation) over a bilinear group, respectively. Let l_G, l_{G_T}, l_p and l_H be the size of an element in G, G_T, Z_p^* and the hash value, respectively. Briefly, the size of dPEKS ciphertext and trapdoor denote ZC, ZT. In addition, the computation cost of trapdoor, ciphertext and test denote TrC, CiC and TeC.

In the Basic dPEKS scheme, by caching $e(\beta, g)$, $e(g, g)$, generating dPEKS ciphertext (C_1, C_2, C_3) does not need the pairing operation. Thus generating (C_1, C_2, C_3) only needs two exponentiations in G_T and one multi-exponentiation in G. Similar, in EdPEKS scheme, generating (C_1, C_2, C_3) need one pairing operation, one exponentiation in G_T and one multi-exponentiation in G. In Basic dPEKS scheme and EdPEKS scheme, generating the trapdoor need one exponentiation and one multi-exponentiation in G.

The Table 1 shows that only [16] and our EdPEKS scheme can resist inside KGA. Compared with others, our schemes are efficient.

Table 1. A comparison of various schemes

Schemes	ZC	ZT	TrC	TeC	CiC	Outside KGA	Inside KGA
[15]	$l_G + l_H$	$2l_G$	$2E_t$	$P_t + 2E_t$	$P_t + 2E_t$	Yes	No
[3]	$l_G + l_H$	l_G	E_t	$P_t + E_t$	$P_t + E_t$	No	No
[16]	$2l_G$	$2l_G + 2l_p$	$2E_t$	$2P_t + 2E_t$	$2E_t$	Yes	Yes
[14]	$3l_G + 2l_{G_T} + l_s$	$l_G + l_p$	E_t	$4P_t + 3E_t + t_v$	$3P_t + 6E_t + t_s$	Yes	No
[13]	$2l_G + l_{G_T}$	$2l_G$	E_t	$3P_t + E_t$	$P_t + 4E_t$	Yes	No
BdPEKS	$l_G + 2l_{G_T}$	$2l_G$	$2E_t$	$P_t + E_t$	$3E_t$	Yes	No
EdPEKS	$l_G + 2l_{G_T}$	$2l_G$	$2E_t$	$P_t + E_t$	$P_t + 3E_t$	Yes	Yes

5   Conclusion

In this paper, we proposed two dPEKS scheme, namely BdPEKS scheme and EdPEKS scheme. In BdPEKS scheme, we prove that the dPEKS ciphertext is C-IND-CAP secure without random oracle. Our BdPEKS scheme is secure against outside keyword-guessing attacks. The BdPEKS scheme is efficient because it only need multiplication and exponentiation to create a dPEKS ciphertext or a trapdoor. Under the original framework of [2], it is not possible to construct an dPEKS (PEKS) secure against inside KGA. To solve this problem, we proposed an enhanced dPEKS scheme (EdPEKS). With the sender's identity are kept secret from server, the EdPEKS scheme is secure resist inside KGA. In our EdPEKS, the trusted third party is removed. Both security analysis and compare results showed that the EdPEKS scheme is secure and efficient.

Acknowledgements. This study is supported by the National Natural Science Foundation of China (No. 61370203) and the Research Foundation of Education Bureau of Sichuan Province (12ZB348), China.

References

1. Song, D.X., Wagner, D., Perrig, A.: Practical techniques for searches on encrypted data. In: Proceedings of 2000 IEEE Symposium on Security and Privacy, S&P 2000, pp. 44–55. IEEE (2000)
2. Boneh, D., Boyen, X.: Efficient selective-ID Secure identity-based encryption without random oracles. In: Cachin, C., Camenisch, J.L. (eds.) EUROCRYPT 2004. LNCS, vol. 3027, pp. 223–238. Springer, Heidelberg (2004). https://doi.org/10.1007/978-3-540-24676-3_14
3. Baek, J., Safavi-Naini, R., Susilo, W.: Public key encryption with keyword search revisited. In: Gervasi, O., Murgante, B., Laganà, A., Taniar, D., Mun, Y., Gavrilova, M.L. (eds.) ICCSA 2008. LNCS, vol. 5072, pp. 1249–1259. Springer, Heidelberg (2008). https://doi.org/10.1007/978-3-540-69839-5_96
4. Yau, W.-C., Heng, S.-H., Goi, B.-M.: Off-line keyword guessing attacks on recent public key encryption with keyword search schemes. In: Rong, C., Jaatun, M.G., Sandnes, F.E., Yang, L.T., Ma, J. (eds.) ATC 2008. LNCS, vol. 5060, pp. 100–105. Springer, Heidelberg (2008). https://doi.org/10.1007/978-3-540-69295-9_10
5. Xu, P., Jin, H., Wu, Q., Wang, W.: Public-key encryption with fuzzy keyword search: a provably secure scheme under keyword guessing attack. IEEE Trans. Comput. **62**(11), 2266–2277 (2013). IEEE
6. Fang, L., Susilo, W., Ge, C., Wang, J.: A secure channel free public key encryption with keyword search scheme without random oracle. In: Garay, J.A., Miyaji, A., Otsuka, A. (eds.) CANS 2009. LNCS, vol. 5888, pp. 248–258. Springer, Heidelberg (2009). https://doi.org/10.1007/978-3-642-10433-6_16
7. Gu, C., Zhu, Y.: New efficient searchable encryption schemes from bilinear pairings. IJ Netw. Secur. **10**(1), 25–31 (2010)
8. Jeong, I.R., Kwon, J.O., Hong, D., Lee, D.H.: Constructing PEKS schemes secure against keyword guessing attacks is possible? Comput. Commun. **32**(2), 394–396 (2009)

9. Liu, Q., Wang, G., Wu, J.: An efficient privacy preserving keyword search scheme in cloud computing. In: International Conference on Computational Science and Engineering, CSE 2009, pp. 715–720. IEEE (2009)
10. Rhee, H.S., Susilo, W., Kim, H.J.: Secure searchable public key encryption scheme against keyword guessing attacks. IEICE Electron. Expr. **6**(5), 237–243 (2009)
11. Yu, Y., Ni, J., Yang, H., Mu, Y., Susilo, W.: Efficient public key encryption with revocable keyword search. Secur. Commun. Netw. **7**(2), 466–472 (2014)
12. Hu, C., Liu, P.: A secure searchable public key encryption scheme with a designated tester against keyword guessing attacks and its extension. In: Lin, S., Huang, X. (eds.) CSEE 2011. CCIS, vol. 215, pp. 131–136. Springer, Heidelberg (2011). https://doi.org/10.1007/978-3-642-23324-1_23
13. Zhao, Y., Chen, X., Ma, H., Tang, Q., Zhu, H.: A new trapdoor-indistinguishable public key encryption with keyword search. J. Wireless Mobile Netw. Ubiquit. Comput. Dependable Appl. **3**(1/2), 72–81 (2012)
14. Fang, L., Susilo, W., Ge, C., Wang, J.: Public key encryption with keyword search secure against keyword guessing attacks without random oracle. Inf. Sci. **238**, 221–241 (2013)
15. Rhee, H.S., Park, J.H., Susilo, W., Lee, D.H.: Trapdoor security in a searchable public-key encryption scheme with a designated tester. J. Syst. Softw. **83**(5), 763–771 (2010)
16. Jiang, P., Mu, Y., Guo, F., Wang, X., Wen, Q.: Online/offline ciphertext retrieval on resource constrained devices. Comput. J. **59**(7), 955–969 (2015)
17. Gentry, C.: Practical identity-based encryption without random oracles. In: Vaudenay, S. (ed.) EUROCRYPT 2006. LNCS, vol. 4004, pp. 445–464. Springer, Heidelberg (2006). https://doi.org/10.1007/11761679_27

Adaptive Algorithm Based on Reversible Data Hiding Method for JPEG Images

Hao Zhang[1], Zhaoxia Yin[1,2(✉)], Xinpeng Zhang[2], Jianpeng Chen[1], Ruonan Wang[1], and Bin Luo[1]

[1] Key Laboratory of Intelligent Computing and Signal Processing, Ministry of Education, Anhui University, Hefei 230601, People's Republic of China
yinzhaoxia@ahu.edu.cn
[2] School of Communication and Information Engineering, Shanghai University, Shanghai 200072, People's Republic of China
xzhang@shu.edu.cn

Abstract. This paper presents an adaptive reversible information hiding algorithm that can maintain thee JPEG file sizes by using RLC (Run Length Coding) AC coefficient coded for embedding, the key point is to choose the appropriate number of participation to hide information. By calculating the maximum storage capacity of the image at different system, select the appropriate RLC pairs to rotate and embed data. In the extraction stage, by calculating the sequence of the original RLC pairs status, then consult the mapping relationships between the current sequence and the original RLC pairs sequence, we extract the secret message and recover the original image. Test results proved that the proposed method can improve the rate-distortion performance to some extent.

Keywords: JPEG · Reversible information hiding · Run length coding RLC · Adaptive

1 Introduction

Information Hiding [1–3] is the method of using images, audio, video, text and other data carriers to embed additional information, and does not affect the original carrier. Reversible information hiding (RDH) refers to the receiving terminal can completely recover the original carrier after extracting the embedded information. For some special scenarios, such as telemedicine, military image communication, requiring that the original image must be accurately recovered after data extraction. So far, a large number of RDH method has been proposed. However, most methods are based on spatial image.

Today, JPEG is the most widely used image format in daily life, which makes the study of reversible information hiding method of JPEG images has more practical significance [4]. Redundant information in JPEG images has been compressed seriously, which made JPEG images reversible information hiding research more challenging, because not only the amount of embedded information and the quality of the

© ICST Institute for Computer Sciences, Social Informatics and Telecommunications Engineering 2018
J. Wan et al. (Eds.): CloudComp 2016, SPNCE 2016, LNICST 197, pp. 196–203, 2018.
https://doi.org/10.1007/978-3-319-69605-8_18

image with secret information, as two performance indicators, but also the need of controlling the post-embedded JPEG image file size should be focused on.

The quantitative coefficient tables, Huffman tables in the header files of JPEG images can also be used to hide data. For example, in the literature [5], some quantization steps in quantization table are divided by an integer, and the corresponding DCT coefficients are multiplied by the same integer, then the additional data are added on the modified DCT coefficients. This method can obtain high embedding capacity, but with increment of the file size. In the literature [6], data are embedded according to the mapping relationship between the method used Huffman codes and the method didn't use Huffman codes. The literature [7] optimized the mapping relationship in [6]. These two methods are lossless and of course can preserve the file size, but both with relatively low embedding capacity. The embedding capacity in [5] are relatively high, but the file size is not controlled well. In worse cases, the file size increment is up to 10,000 bytes, which is collided with the original purpose of JPEG images that is to compress the image file size for economizing resources. In this paper, we proposed an adaptive algorithm based on a reversible data hiding method for JPEG. With the same length of the secret information, we get the best quality image encryption by determining the best secret information storage format and the most suitable number for the logarithm used in rotating storage secret information RLC, at the same time, we keep the file size and embed data by rotating RLC. In the data extraction stage, by determining the mapping relationships between the states with secret information and the original states, the original image is recovered completely after extracting the secret information completely. Compared with [10], this method performs better in rate-distortion to some extent.

2 Proposed Scheme

In this part, how to hide secret information in the carrier images, receive terminal extract the secret information and recover the original image will be described in detail. By choosing appropriate number of RLC pairs, we can determine the storing format of secret information and the receiver use reverse process to extract information and recover the image. The JPEG encoding [9] and RLC pairs rotation [10] will be described in Sects. 2.1 and 2.2 firstly. Then the procedure of data embedding, data extraction and image recovery are presented in Sects. 2.3 and 2.4.

2.1 The JPEG Encoding

In JPEG encoding, the key that data can be compressed is that DCT coefficients have been quantized. After quantization, many high frequency AC coefficients will be quantized to zero. For the DC coefficients, because there's a great correlation between the adjacent blocks of quantized DC coefficient, so we use the Differential Pulse Code Modulation (DPCM) to the sequence of quantized DC coefficient first. For the AC coefficients, each piece contains many zero-valued coefficients, and many of them are continuous, so we use the Run Length Coding (RLC) to the AC coefficients: first, convert the AC coefficients into one-dimension sequence in Zigzag order, then encode it into a RLC pairs sequence, as formula (1) shown. Finally, we obtain the final code stream by using Huffman encoding.

$$\left\{P_k = \left(r_k, \ v_k\right)\right\}_{k=1}^{L} \tag{1}$$

where L is the number of the nonzero AC coefficients in a block, which means the number of RCLP. v_k is the value of the k_{th} nonzero AC coefficient and r_k is the zero run before v_k.

The RLC pairs sequence of most image blocks will present an obvious law: with the low-frequency RLC pairs, the zero range r is small and the amplitude v is large; with the high-frequency RLC pairs, the zero range r is large and the amplitude v is small.

2.2   RLC Pairs Rotation

The RLC Pairs Rotation mainly use the two characteristics of the RLC pairs sequence mentioned in Sect. 2.1: with the low-frequency RLC pairs, the zero range r is small and the amplitude v is large; with the high-frequency RLC pairs, the zero range r is large and the amplitude v is small.

Specific operation is: suppose there is a RLC pairs sequence in certain length, donate its last four pairs of continuous sequence $p_1 p_2 p_3 p_4$ as the original sequence state S_0, which S_0 is shown as Table 1. Then S_0 is rotated right once by a pair, generating other three sequence states $S_0 \sim S_3$. Next, S_4, reversed from S_0, is rotated in the same way to generate the RLC sequence states $S_5 \sim S_7$. There will be 8 different sequence states $S_0 \sim S_7$ including original sequence state.

Table 1. The 8 kinds of states of RLC pair

States	Sequences	Data	States	Sequences	Data
S_0	$P_1 P_2 P_3 P_4$	000	S_4	$P_4 P_3 P_2 P_1$	100
S_1	$P_4 P_1 P_2 P_3$	001	S_5	$P_1 P_4 P_3 P_2$	101
S_2	$P_3 P_4 P_1 P_2$	010	S_6	$P_2 P_1 P_4 P_3$	110
S_3	$P_2 P_3 P_4 P_1$	011	S_7	$P_3 P_2 P_1 P_4$	111

For each sequence state $s_i (0 \leq i \leq 7)$, the value of r, v in the first two RLC pairs $(r_1, \ v_1)$, $(r_2, \ v_2)$ and last two RLC pairs $(r_3, \ v_3)$, $(r_4, \ v_4)$ are put into Eq. (2) [8] to calculate. Calculate α_i and β_i, then subtract α_i from β_i and we have Δ_i. There will be 8 different $\Delta_i (0 \leq i \leq 8)$ generate by 8 different rotating states. Because of the RLC pairs features mentioned above: the value of $|v_1|$, $|v_2|, r_3$, r_4 will be relatively large, and the value of $|v_3|$, $|v_4|$, r_1, r_2 will be relatively small. In every $\alpha_i (0 \leq i \leq 7)$ and $\beta_i (0 \leq i \leq 7)$, the α in initial status will tend to the maximum, and the β in initial status will tend to the minimum, then the Δ_0 in initial status will be the largest among all $\Delta_i (0 \leq i \leq 7)$. So, when extracting information, confirm the status of $\Delta_{max} = max\{\Delta_i\}_{i=0}^{7}$, then we can extract the secret information and restore the original image successfully.

$$\begin{cases} \alpha_i = (|v_1| + |v_2|) \times (r_3 + r_4 + 2) \\ \beta_i = (|v_3| + |v_4|) \times (r_1 + r_2 + 2) \\ \quad\quad \Delta_i = \alpha_i - \beta_i \end{cases} \tag{2}$$

2.3 Data Embedding

First, we need to determine an appropriate value of nr, based on the length of the secret information. Parameter nr represents the number of RLC pairs being used to hide in each block, and parameter na represents the length of binary bits can be embedded in each block. This method calculates the maximum storage capacity of the image in the quaternary system, octal number system and hexadecimal system (which means rotating 3, 4 and 8 pairs of RLC pairs), and then choose the most suitable system.

When calculating the maximum capacity, the first step in this phase is to pick out the blocks with $L \geq th$. These blocks are defined as Bc blocks. (th is a parameter to decide which block can be chose to be th blocks, and it must be larger than or equal to $nr + 1$ because the first RLC pair of every block will be used to embed mark information and will not be rotating to store secret information. So we can't hide 7 binary number in one block which need 64 RLC pairs rotate) Then we can get the maximum capacity in different na.

For selected na, choose the minimum nr in this na, and $th = nr + 1$. Generally speaking, the current capacity value is the maximum value, but sometimes there will be fluctuations, so after recording the current capacity, expanding nr to get maximum capacity, and choose the maximum of na with principle, this time the maximum capacity will be longer than the length of the cipher text, change the value of nr again to make the capacity slightly longer than the length of the cipher text, we choose to reduce nr.

After determining the nr, we improve the value of th constantly, and finally we get the maximum capacity, which is most closed to the length of the cipher text. This is the nr and th used in the data embedding. Then we confirm the Bc block we need by $L \geq th$.

Second, the last nr RLC pairs on each Bc block are rotated. For instance, when $nr = 4$, whose rotation states are shown in Table 1.

There are eight sequence we got according to the method mentioned previously. For each $\Delta_i (0 \leq i \leq 2nr - 1)$ we can calculate an unique Δ_{max} and then those blocks with Δ_{max} can be picked out as Bm blocks. Among these Bm blocks, we use flag-bit 1 to mark the blocks whose Δ_{max} is in the original states ($\Delta_{max} = \Delta_0$), and these blocks can be chose to embed secret information. Other blocks, meanwhile, are marked with 0 ($\Delta_{max} \neq \Delta_0$). FB is the array to store these flag-bits in order, and LF is the length of FB. Obviously LF equals to the number of Bm blocks.

Third, a data hiding key K (which is the seed chosen manually to generate random number) can be used to generate LF positions randomly to decide the Bc blocks to hide information. The flag-bits in array FB are used to replace the LSBs of variable length integer (VLI) on the first RLC pairs in these LF blocks. Then the needless data in LF array are converted into sequence L_d. L_d is divided into many units with 4 bits in each unit to embed information.

Fourth, according to Table 1, the blocks we got in the second step are rotated according to d. For example, if $d = 010$, S_0 is rotated to S_2, and is rotated to S_5 if $d = 101$.

2.4   Data Extraction and Image Recovery

In this part, we will elaborate on the specific data extraction and image restoration steps.

First: Get the Bc blocks and Bm blocks in the same way described in Sect. 2.3.

Second: By the same data hiding key K, array FB' can be taken from the Bc blocks, then the embedding blocks containing embedded data can be picked out from the FB' array.

Third, for these embedding blocks, each $\Delta_i(0 \leq i \leq 2nr - 1)$ should be calculated and compared to find the position of Δ_{max}, represented as M. Then M is exactly the decimal form of secret information. For example, as shown in Table 1, if the S_M of a marked block is $P_1P_4P_3P_2$, and the Δ_{max} is in the state of $S_2 : P_1P_2P_3P_4$, then the embedded data is 2 in decimal, and is 010 in binary. If the S_M of a marked block is $P_1P_4P_3P_2$, then the embedded data is 5 in decimal, and is 101 in binary. All the extracted data units in binary are concatenated as L'_d.

Finally, the original LSBs of VLI on the first RLC pairs are obtained from L'_d, and put back to the original position. Then the images are recovered perfectly.

It must be said that, the position change of the RLC pairs would not generate any negative effects on encoding and decoding of JPEG image, for we only change the order of RLC sequence, this will not affect the result of Hoffman coding.

3   Experiment Result

The test JPEG pictures are compressed from the standard 512×512-pixel gray picture according to different QF (80). In this paper, we try to analysis the performance of this method from the quality of the picture with secret information, the embedding capacity and the change of the picture before and after the information embedding.

First is the quality of the picture with secret information. Figure 1 shows the original pictures and the pictures with secret information of Lena, Barbara, Baboon and Crowd with PSNR of each picture marked below the picture when $QF = 80$ and the length of secret information $ls = 800\,bits$. As is shown in the Fig. 1, the pictures with secret information perform well in visually, and all the picture with secret information can be recovered in this method. Figure 2 shows the comparison of the performance of rate-distortion between the experimental result in the method this paper proposed and the experimental result literature [10] obtained. Figure 3 shows change of file size in different embedding capacity of four different pictures.

Finally, comparing the method in this paper with literature [10], shown in Fig. 2, the method has obvious advantages with lower embedded capacity. Since the cipher text is converted into high system to store information, the total amount of blocks has more influence on picture. When embedded capacity is high, this method can get the

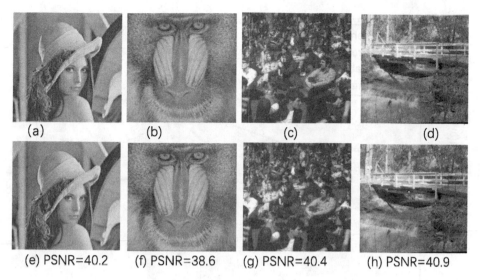

Fig. 1. (a) Lena (original) (b) Baboon (original) (c) Bridge (original) (d) Crowd (original) (e) Lena (with secret information) (f) Baboon (with secret information) (g) Bridge (with secret information) (h) Crowd (with secret information)

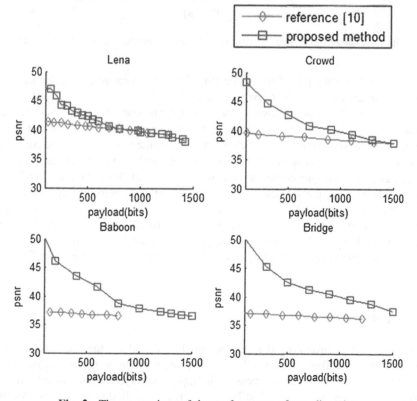

Fig. 2. The comparison of the performance of rate-distortion

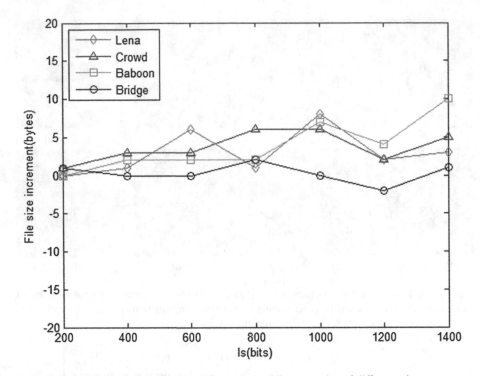

Fig. 3. Change of file size in different embedding capacity of different pictures

same result as literature [10] does, while it can get larger capacity, for the method in this paper can choose more RLC pairs to rotate.

The greatest advantage of this method is that it can keep the size gap between the original picture and the picture with secret information. As is shown in Fig. 3, with different secret information length of different picture, the size change of these pictures is close to zero. It is because in the embedding stage, only the order of the RLC pair is changed, there is no influence on the Huffman coding unit. With the change of flag-bit in the recoding stage, the size change cannot be control to zero, but the change is so small that can be ignored.

At the same time, the security of the picture can be ensured. In the recovery stage, without the hiding key, we cannot got the position of the hiding blocks, even though someone knew the way of extracting, he still cannot got the secret information in the picture.

4   Conclusion

This paper gives a reversible data hiding method based on the adaptive algorithm which can keep the size of the result file in an appropriate range. By converting the binary information into the secret message in appropriate system and embedding it into a series of blocks in the picture. The key point of this method is to find the maximum capacity of storage in different system first, then choose the best number of RLC pairs used to embed information. When the system and the number of the pairs need to be rotate is determined, raise the requirement of the RLC pairs in these blocks can used to embed the secret information gradually to decrease the number of Bc blocks to decrease the capacity of embedding and make it approach the final result. Finally, choose appropriate parameters and finish the secret information hiding.

Acknowledgments. This research work is supported by National Science Fund for Distinguished Young Scholars under Grant No. 61525203, National Natural Science Foundation of China (61502009, 61472235, 61572308).

References

1. Zhang, X., Wang, S.: Efficient steganographic embedding by exploiting modification direction. IEEE Commun. Lett. **10**(11), 781–783 (2006)
2. Filler, T., Judas, J., Fridrich, J.: Minimizing additive distortion in steganography using syndrome-trellis codes. IEEE Trans. Inf. Forensics Secur. **6**(3), 920–935 (2011)
3. Atawneh, S., Almomani, A., Sumari, P.: Steganography in digital images: common approaches and tools. IETE Tech. Rev. **30**(4), 344–358 (2013)
4. Wang, H., Laio, C.: JPEG images authentication with discrimination of tampers on the image content or watermark. IETE Tech. Rev. **27**(3), 244–251 (2010)
5. Wang, K., Lu, Z.-M., Hu, Y.-J.: A high capacity lossless data hiding scheme for JPEG images. J. Syst. Softw. **86**(7), 1965–1975 (2013)
6. Mobasseri, B.G., Berger, R.J., Marcinak, M.P., NaikRaikar, Y.J.: Data embedding in JPEG bitstream by code mapping. IEEE Trans. Image Process. **19**(4), 958–966 (2010)
7. Qian, Z., Zhang, X.: Lossless data hiding in JPEG bitstream. J. Syst. Softw. **85**(2), 309–313 (2012)
8. Ong, S., Wong, K.: Rotational based rewritable data hiding in JPEG. In: Visual Communications and Image Processing (VCIP), pp. 1–6. IEEE (2013)
9. Wallace, G.K.: The JPEG still picture compression standard. Commun. ACM **34**(4), 30–44 (1991)
10. Long, J., Yin, Z., Lv, J., Zhang, X.: Rotation based reversible data hiding for JPEG images. IETE Tech. Rev. **33**(6), 607–614 (2016). https://doi.org/10.1080/02564602.2015.1132014

Efficient Authenticated Key Exchange Protocols for Large-Scale Mobile Communication Networks

Run-hua Shi[(⊠)] and Shun Zhang

School of Computer Science and Technology, Anhui University,
Hefei City 230601, China
shirh@ahu.edu.cn, shzhang27@163.com

Abstract. For secure communications in mobile communication networks, various authenticated key exchange schemes are proposed to provide the remote client authentication and the session key establishment. In these schemes, more considerations are to reduce the costs of remote mobile clients, but not those of the server. However, the server has become a bottleneck in large-scale mobile communication networks. In this paper, in order to relieve the server's load, we presented an efficient authentication protocol with key exchange between the remote client and the server, and then generalized it to a three-party case, in which two remote clients can authenticate each other with the server's help and share a secure session key. Compared with the relevant protocols, the proposed protocols require lower computation and communication costs, and above all, dramatically reduce those of the server. Therefore, the proposed protocols are more practical and suitable for large-scale mobile communication networks.

Keywords: Elliptic curve cryptography · Authentication · Key exchange · Client-server network

1 Introduction

Secure remote client authentication with key exchange over insecure communication channel is an important issue for many applications in client-server networks, especially electronic transactions (e.g., on-line shopping, Internet banking and pay-TV). On the other hand, Mobile communication recently has become more pervasive with the popularity of mobile devices, such as smart phones, handheld game consoles, personal digital assistants, and mobile internet devices, etc. Therefore, client authentication with key exchange for mobile communication environments is becoming the focus of widely attentions.

For mobile devices, to reduce the computation loads, some authenticated key exchange schemes based on elliptic curve cryptosystem (ECC) were proposed [1–3]. As we know, security of ECC is based upon the difficulty of elliptic curve discrete logarithm problem (ECDLP) and elliptic curve Diffie-Hellman problem (ECDHP) [4, 5]. Compared with traditional public key cryptosystems (e.g., RSA [6] and ElGamal [7]), ECC offers a better performance because it achieves the same security with a

© ICST Institute for Computer Sciences, Social Informatics and Telecommunications Engineering 2018
J. Wan et al. (Eds.): CloudComp 2016, SPNCE 2016, LNICST 197, pp. 204–215, 2018.
https://doi.org/10.1007/978-3-319-69605-8_19

smaller key size. For example, 160-bit ECC and 1024-bit RSA have the same security level in practice [8].

However, early remote client authentication schemes on ECC are based on public-key cryptosystem, in which the public key in the system requires the associated certificate to prove its validity and thus clients need additional computations to verify the other's certificate. To avoid the weakness, in 2009, Yang and Chang [9] proposed an identity-based remote user mutual authentication scheme for mobile users using elliptic curve cryptography. However, Yoon and Yoo [10] demonstrated that Yang and Chang's protocol is vulnerable to the impersonation attack and does not provide perfect forward secrecy, and then proposed an improved protocol. Later, He et al. [11] again confirmed that Yoon and Yoo's protocol does not provide perfect forward secrecy yet and fails to achieve forward secrecy. In addition, they also pointed out that a special hash function called MapToPoint function which is used to map an identity information into a point on elliptic curve is required in the previous protocols. To improve the efficiency, they presented a new remote user authentication protocol without the MapToPoint function [11]. Subsequently, there appeared more improved protocols of authenticated key establishment for client-server networks [12–16].

The above two-party authenticated key exchange (2PAKE for short) schemes can achieve two secure goals of mutual authentication and key exchange between the remote client and the server. However, these schemes are infeasible to establish a secure session key between any two remote clients in client-server networks. For this, there appeared some three-party authenticated key exchange (3PAKE for short) schemes to provide mutual authentication and key establishment between two remote clients with the help of the server. In 2009, Yang and Chang [17] proposed an efficient identity-based 3PAKE scheme to improve the security of Chen et al.'s scheme [18]. In 2010, Tan [19] demonstrated that Yang and Chang's 3PAKE protocol is vulnerable to the impersonation and parallel attacks, and proposed an improved scheme. However, Nose [20] pointed that Tan's scheme suffers from the impersonation attack and the man-in-the-middle attack. Later, He et al. [21] pointed out that Yang et al.'s scheme and Tan's scheme are also based on the public key infrastructure (PKI), and then the users need additional computations to verify the other's certificate. Therefore, He et al. proposed an improved identity-based 3PAKE scheme to improve these drawbacks. Furthermore, Chou et al. [22] again pointed out that a user cannot verify the correctness for his/her private key in these schemes mentioned above, and then proposed two authenticated key exchange schemes with private key confirmation. However, Farash and Attari [23] showed that Chou et al.'s 2PAKE scheme is vulnerable to the impersonation attack and the key-compromise impersonation attack, and their 3PAKE scheme is also insecure against the impersonation attack. To overcome the weaknesses, Farash and Attari presented an improved identity-based 2PAKE protocol using elliptic curves [23]. However, we found that there is still a serious security flaw in the user registration phase of the two schemes [24]: any authorized user can impersonate the server to generate the effective private key of any other unauthorized user.

In existing 2PAKE and 3PAKE schemes for mobile communication environments, the authors always find ways to reduce the computation and communication costs of the remote client/user, such that their respective schemes are feasible to mobile users with limited resources. However, when hundreds of thousands of remote users simultaneously request the server to authenticate their identities and establish the secure session keys, the server's load is very heavy. In fact, the server has becomes a bottleneck in many practical applications for large-scale client-server networks. Therefore, how to reduce the server's load in authenticated key exchange schemes is a practical and important issue.

Most current 2PAKE and 3PAKE schemes are various generalizations of Diffie-Hellman Key Exchange [25], in which two parties fair complete the same computations and communications. However, in the client-server networks, the remote client/user and the server are not peer entities, where the server is trustable. Therefore, there are redundant computations in these authentication schemes. In this paper, we exploited new methods to construct an efficient identity-based 2PAKE protocol, which is especially suitable for large-scale client-server networks. In addition, we extended the 2PAKE protocol to develop a 3PAKE protocol, which allows two remote users to share a secure session key with the server's help. Compared with other relevant protocols, our proposed protocols need lower computation and communication costs, and especially relieve the server's load.

2   Proposed Protocols

2.1   The Proposed 2PAKE Protocol

The proposed 2PAKE protocol includes three phases: Initialization, User Registration, and Mutual Authentication with Key Exchange.

Initialization
The server S generates system parameters as follows:

1. S chooses an elliptic curve equation $E_p(a,b)$ [26] defined on finite field F_p, where p be a large prime.
2. S selects a base point P with the order q over $E_p(a,b)$, where q is a large prime for the security considerations.
3. S random generates its private key $k_S \in_R \mathbb{Z}_q^*$ and computes the corresponding public key $Q_S = k_S P$.
4. In addition, the server chooses a secure hash function, $H : \{0,1\}^* \to \mathbb{Z}_q^*$.
   Then the server publishes these system parameters: $\{p, E_p(a,b), q, P, Q_S, H(\cdot)\}$.

User Registration

1. The user U sends his identity, ID_U, to the server S. Then S checks the authenticity and legality of his identity.
2. After confirming the authenticity and legality of the user, S computes U's private key $k_U = (H(ID_U) \oplus k_S) + H(ID_U)[k_S + (H(ID_U) \oplus k_S)]$.
3. S computes $Q_{ID_U} = (H(ID_U) \oplus k_S)P$ and sends $\{k_U, Q_{ID_U}\}$ to U.
4. After receiving $\{k_U, Q_{ID_U}\}$, U verifies if $k_U P = Q_{ID_U} + H(ID_U)(Q_S + Q_{ID_U})$. If the equation holds, U keeps k_U in secret as his private key.

Mutual Authentication with Key Exchange
In this phase, a user U and the server S authenticate each other and establish a common session key for the later communications. This phase is divided into two rounds which are shown as follows.

Round 1

1. U randomly chooses $r_U \in \mathbb{Z}_q^*$ and $S_U \in \mathbb{Z}_p^*$, and computes $R_U = r_U P$, $V_U = S_U \oplus f_x(r_U k_U Q_S)$ and $h_U = H(ID_U\|S_U\|t_U)$, where t_U is a timestamp that denotes the current time. Please note that $f_x(Q)$ and $f_y(Q)$ denote the x and y coordinates of the point Q, respectively.
2. U sends $\{ID_U, R_U, V_U, h_U, t_U\}$ to the server S.

Round 2

1. After receiving $\{ID_U, R_U, V_U, h_U, t_U\}$, S verifies if t_U is valid. If t_U is not fresh, S aborts the process and sends the failed messages to U; otherwise, he continues to execute the next step.
2. S computes $k_U = (H(ID_U) \oplus k_S) + H(ID_U)[k_S + (H(ID_U) \oplus k_S)]$ and $S_U' = V_U \oplus f_x(k_U k_S R_U)$, where k_S is S's private key.
3. S verifies if $h_U = H(ID_U\|S_U'\|t_U)$. If it is true, S confirms that U is an authorized user; otherwise, he aborts the process.
4. S computes the session key $k_{SU} = H(S_U'\|t_U)$.
5. S computes $MAC_{k_{SU}}(t_U)$ as the response and sends $MAC_{k_{SU}}(t_U)$ to U, where $MAC_{k_{SU}}(t_U)$ denotes Message Authentication Code of the timestamp t_U by the session key k_{SU}.
6. After receiving $MAC_{k_{SU}}(t_U)$, U computes the session key $k_{US} = H(S_U\|t_U)$, and then checks the integrity of $MAC_{k_{SU}}(t_U)$ by the session key k_{US}. U will quit the current session if the check produces a negative result; otherwise, U authenticates the server S and uses k_{US} as the session key with S in future communications.

2.2   The Proposed 3PAKE Protocol

Similarly, the proposed protocol includes three phases: Initialization, User Registration, and Mutual Authentication with Key Agreement. The first two phases are similar to those of the proposed 2PAKE protocol, accordingly. Here, we mainly describe the last phase as follows:

Mutual Authentication with Key Agreement
In this phase, two users A and B authenticate each other with the server S's help and negotiate a common session key for the later communications. Suppose that A and B have obtained their respective private keys, $k_A = (H(ID_A) \oplus k_S) + H(ID_A)[k_S + (H(ID_A) \oplus k_S)]$ and $k_B = (H(ID_B) \oplus k_S) + H(ID_B)[k_S + (H(ID_B) \oplus k_S)]$. This phase is divided into three rounds which are described in detail as follows.

Round 1

1. A randomly chooses $r_A \in \mathbb{Z}_q^*$, and computes $R_A = r_A P$, $V_A = f_x(r_A k_A Q_S)$ and $h_A = H(ID_A||V_A||t_A)$, where t_A is a timestamp that denotes the current time.
2. A sends $\{ID_A, \text{request}\}$ and $\{ID_A, ID_B, R_A, h_A, t_A\}$ to B and S, respectively. The message request denotes a request that A asks B to agree on a session key.

Round 2

1. After receiving $\{ID_A, \text{request}\}$, B randomly selects $r_B \in \mathbb{Z}_q^*$, and computes $R_B = r_B P$, $V_B = f_x(r_B k_B Q_S)$ and $h_B = H(ID_B||V_B||t_B)$, where t_B is the current timestamp.
2. B sends $\{ID_B, \text{response}\}$ and $\{ID_B, ID_A, R_B, h_B, t_B\}$ to A and S, respectively. The message response denotes a response that B accepts A's request.

Round 3

1. After receiving $\{ID_A, ID_B, R_A, h_A, t_A\}$ and $\{ID_B, ID_A, R_B, h_B, t_B\}$, S verifies if both t_A and t_B are valid. If t_A or t_B is not fresh, S aborts the process and sends the failed messages to the users; otherwise, he continues to perform the next step.
2. S computes $k_A = (H(ID_A) \oplus k_S) + H(ID_A)[k_S + (H(ID_A) \oplus k_S)]$ and $k_B = (H(ID_B) \oplus k_S) + H(ID_B)[k_S + (H(ID_B) \oplus k_S)]$. Furthermore, S computes $V_A' = f_x(k_A k_S R_A)$ and $V_B' = f_x(k_B k_S R_B)$.
3. S verifies if $h_A = H(ID_A||V_A'||t_A)$ and $h_B = H(ID_B||V_B'||t_B)$. If both of them are true, S confirms that A and B are all authorized users; otherwise, he/she aborts the process.
4. S computes $h_{SA} = H(ID_A||ID_B||f_x(R_B)||f_y(R_B)||V_A'||t_S)$ and $h_{SB} = H(ID_B||ID_A||f_x(R_A)||f_y(R_A)||V_B'||t_S)$, where t_S is the current timestamp. S sends $\{R_B, h_{SA}, t_S\}$ and $\{R_A, h_{SB}, t_S\}$ to A and B, respectively.
5. After receiving $\{R_B, h_{SA}, t_S\}$, A verifies if t_S is valid. If t_S is not fresh, A aborts the processes; otherwise, A performs the next step.
6. A computes $h_{SA}' = H(ID_A||ID_B||f_x(R_B)||f_y(R_B)||V_A||t_S)$.
7. A verifies if the equation of $h_{SA}' = h_{SA}$ holds. If it holds, A believes that S is the authentic server, and further confirms that B is authenticated by S. Then he/she can obtain the session key shared between A and B by computing $k_{AB} = H(f_x(r_A R_B)||f_y(r_A R_B))$; otherwise, A rejects the transaction.
8. Similarly, after receiving $\{R_A, h_{SB}, t_S\}$, B verifies if t_S is valid. If t_S is not fresh, B aborts the processes; otherwise, B continues to execute the next step.
9. B computes $h_{SB}' = H(ID_B||ID_A||f_x(R_A)||f_y(R_A)||V_B||t_S)$.
10. B verifies if the equation of $h_{SB}' = h_{SB}$ holds. If it holds, B believes that S is the authentic server, and further confirms that A is authenticated by S. Then he/she can obtain the session key shared between B and A by computing $k_{BA} = H(f_x(r_B R_A)||f_y(r_B R_A))$; otherwise, B rejects the transaction.

3   Analysis

We first analyze the security of the proposed protocols against various known cryptographic attacks. The security of our protocols relies on the difficulties of solving Elliptic Curve Discrete Logarithm (ECDL) problem (Given two points P and Q over an elliptic curve $E_p(a, b)$, it is computationally infeasible to find an integer k such that $Q = k \cdot P$) and Elliptic Curve Computational Diffie-Hellman (ECCDH) problem (Given three points P, $a \cdot P$ and $b \cdot P$ over $E_p(a, b)$, it is computationally infeasible to compute a point W such that $W = ab \cdot P$). Then, we give Performance comparisons of some related protocols.

3.1   Security Analysis

In this section, we mainly analyze that the proposed protocols can withstand various related security attacks. In our scheme, since the server is trusted and further all privates are generated by the server's private key, we assume that the server's private key is secure. Otherwise, the whole system will be controlled by the attacker and thus it will not make any sense to again discuss the system security.

Theorem 1 (Replay Attack Resistance). The proposed 2PAKE and 3PAKE protocols can resist the replay attack.

Proof. In the proposed protocols, the receiver can always verify the freshness of the received messages by the freshness of the timestamp t. Furthermore, the timestamp t is embedded in the hashed message (e.g., $h_U = H(ID_U\|S_U\|t_U)$) by the sender, such that it can guarantee the integrity of the timestamp. Therefore, the proposed scheme can resist the replay attack.

Theorem 2 (Known-key security). The proposed 2PAKE and 3PAKE protocols satisfy the known key security. That is, an outsider cannot compute the current session key even he knows some previous session keys.

Proof. In our 2PAKE/3PAKE protocol, the session key $k_{US} = H(S_U\|t_U)/k_{AB} = H(f_x(r_A r_B P)\|f_y(r_A r_B P))$ is obtained by computing a secure hash function. Obviously, the session key depends on the short-term secret $S_U/(r_A, r_B)$, instead of the long-term secret $k_U/(k_A, k_B)$. Furthermore, each session has different short-term secret $S_U/(r_A, r_B)$, which is/are randomly generated. Thus the current session key is independent of the previous session. That is, an outsider cannot compute the current session key even he knows some previous session keys. Therefore, the known-key attack is infeasible for the proposed protocols.

Theorem 3 (Perfect forward secrecy). The proposed 2PAKE and 3PAKE protocols achieve perfect forward security. That is, the compromise of the long-term private keys of both the participating users does not affect the security of the previous session keys.

Proof. In our 2PAKE protocol, in order to successfully compute the session key $k_{US} = H(S_U\|t_U)$, the most critical step is to obtain $k_U k_S r_U P$ and then compute $S_U = V_U \oplus f_x(k_U k_S r_U P)$ rightly. If U's private key k_U is compromised to an attacker, it is still computationally hard for the attacker to compute $k_U k_S r_U P$ based on the difficulty of solving ECCDH Problem since he does not know k_S and r_U. Similarly, in our 3PAKE protocol, even if the private keys, k_A and k_B, of users A and B, are compromised to an attacker, it is also computationally hard for the attacker to compute $r_A r_B P$ based on the difficulty of solving ECCDH Problem since he does not know r_A and r_B. Therefore, the proposed protocols can provide perfect forward secrecy.

Theorem 4 (Key-compromise impersonation resistance). The proposed 2PAKE and 3PAKE protocols provide resistance to key-compromise impersonation attack. That is, even though the remote user's long-term private key is compromised, an adversary, who obtained the private key, cannot masquerade the other user or the server and obtain the resulting session key.

Proof. In our proposed protocols, the participant authentication mainly depends on if the sender/receiver can compute $k_U k_S r_U P$ rightly. Even if the remote user U's private key k_U is compromised to an attacker, it is still computationally hard for the attacker to compute $k_{U'} k_S r_{U'} P$ or $k_U k_S r_U P$ without knowing $\{k_S, k_{U'}\}$ or $\{k_S, r_U\}$, where $k_{U'}$ and k_S are the private keys of the other user U' and the server, respectively. That is, even though the remote user U's long-term private key is compromised, the attacker cannot masquerade the other user U' or the server to obtain the resulting session key. Therefore, the proposed protocols can resist key-compromise impersonation attack.

Theorem 5 (Unknown key-share resistance). The proposed 2PAKE and 3PAKE protocols provide resistance to unknown-key share attack.

Proof. A party A believes the key is shared with another party B, and a party C believes the key is shared with A. The above condition is called unknown key share. Our proposed 2PAKE/3PAKE schemes can obviously withstand the unknown-key share attack because the user's identity is authenticated by the server S.

Theorem 6 (Mutual authentication). The proposed 2PAKE and 3PAKE protocols achieve the property of mutual authentication.

Proof. In our 2PAKE protocol, the server S authenticates the remote user U by computing $S'_U = V_U \oplus f_x(k_U k_S R_U)$ and verifying if $h_U = H(ID_U || S'_U || t_U)$ holds, that is, the server S authenticates the user U by checking if he/she knows the private key, $k_U = (H(ID_U) \oplus k_S) + H(ID_U)[k_S + (H(ID_U) \oplus k_S)]$. In turn, the user U authenticates the server S by comparing the received $MAC_{k_{SU}}(t_U)$ to the result computed by him/herself, because the server S is the only one who can recover S_U from V_U and then computes the session key k_{SU} and $MAC_{k_{SU}}(t_U)$. Similarly, in our 3PAKE protocol, two users A and B authenticate the server S by checking if he can rightly compute $f_x(k_A k_S R_A)$ and $f_x(k_B k_S R_B)$ from their respective sent messages, and then authenticate each other by the help of the trusted server S who authenticates A and B by verifying their respective private keys.

In addition, our proposed protocols can provide the confirmation of the user's private key, which doesn't rely on the digital signature technology. Though the authors in References [22, 23] claimed that their protocols could provide the confirmation of the user's private key, there is a serious security flaw in their respective protocols [24]:

any authorized user can impersonate the server to generate the effective private key of any other unauthorized user, because it can't guarantee the integrity of the public information, Q_{ID_U}. In our protocol, we do not embed Q_{ID_U} into a hash function to ensure its integrity. Otherwise, it will increase the costs of the server, because he has to again compute $Q_{ID_U}(Q_{ID_U} = (H(ID_U) \oplus k_S)P)$ to obtain the user's private key in the mutual authentication phase. Here, we introduce two items of $H(ID_U) \oplus k_S$ in the equation of generating the user's private key, and ensure the equation has obvious architectural features, such that it is infeasible to modify Q_{ID_U} and successfully pass the user's check. To sum up, the good features in these two schemes are still hold in our scheme, and further we can cover the shortage of the impersonation attack.

3.2   Performance Comparisons

We have analyzed the security of the proposed protocols in the above section. Furthermore, we give security comparisons of our protocols and other related works, as shown in Tables 1 and 2.

Table 1. Security comparisons for 2PAKE protocols

	He et al.'s protocol [11]	Islam and Biswas's protocol [15]	Yoon et al.'s protocol [12]	Chou et al.'s protocol [22]	Farash and Attari's protocol [23]	Our 2PAKE protocol
Mutual authentication	Provided	Provided	Provided	Provided	Provided	Provided
Known-key security	Provided	Provided	Provided	Provided	Provided	Provided
Forward secrecy	Provided	Provided	Not provided	Provided	Provided	Provided
Private key confirmation	Not provided	Not provided	Not provided	Insecure	Insecure	Secure
Impersonation attack	Insecure	Secure	Secure	Insecure	Secure	Secure
Key-compromise impersonation attack	Secure	Secure	Secure	Insecure	Secure	Secure
Unknown-key share attack	Secure	Secure	Secure	Secure	Secure	Secure
User registration	Secure	Secure	Secure	Insecure	Insecure	Secure

In addition, we evaluate the performance of our proposed protocols in terms of the computation and communication costs, and list performance comparisons for 2PAKE protocols and 3PAKE protocols in Tables 3 and 4, respectively. Same as References [22, 23] we assume the timestamp length is 16-bit, the size of p used in the ECC is 160-bit, the digest message size of hash function (e.g., SHA-1) or message authentication

Table 2. Security comparisons for 3PAKE protocols

	He et al.'s protocol [21]	Tan's protocol [19]	Yang and Chang's protocol [17]	Chou et al.'s protocol [22]	Our 3PAKE protocol
Known-key security	Provided	Provided	Provided	Provided	Provided
Forward secrecy	Provided	Provided	Provided	Provided	Provided
Private key confirmation	Not provided	Not provided	Not provided	Insecure	Secure
Impersonation attack	Secure	Insecure	Insecure	Insecure	Secure
Key-compromise impersonation attack	Secure	Secure	Secure	Insecure	Secure
Unknown-key share attack	Secure	Secure	Secure	Secure	Secure
Parallel attack	Secure	Secure	Insecure	Secure	Secure
User registration	Secure	Secure	Secure	Insecure	Secure

code is 160-bit, and the identity size is 80-bit. Please note that there are some wrong evaluations in References [22, 23]: the size of a point on the ECC is 320-bit, not 160-bit, since the size of p used in the ECC is 160-bit; the size of the cipher text of the symmetric encryption/decryption is the same size of the plain text, not 128-bit. To estimate and compare the computation costs, we define the following notations: $PM, PA, H, MAC, Hp, I, E(n)$ and $D(n)$ are the time complexity of elliptic curve scalar point multiplication, elliptic curve point addition, one-way hash function, message authentication code, map-to-point hash function, modular inversion, symmetric encryption for n-bit plain text and symmetric decryption for n-bit cipher text, respectively.

According to Tables 1, 2, 3 and 4, the proposed protocols have some good advantages as follows:

(1) The proposed protocols can withstand all related security attacks.
(2) The proposed protocols are identity-based authentication protocols with key exchange using ECC.
(3) The proposed protocols can provide the confirmation of the user's private key, where the cost of the private-key confirmation is lower than that of general digital signature.
(4) The proposed protocols require lower costs in both communication and computation complexity. Especially, the costs of the server in proposed protocols are lowest in all relevant protocols.

Therefore, the proposed protocols are more practical and suitable for large-scale mobile communication networks.

Table 3. Performance comparison for 2PAKE protocols

	Communication costs	Computation costs	
		User	Server
He et al.'s protocol [11]	1152 bits	$3PM + 2H + 2MAC$	$3PM + 3H + 2MAC + 1I$
Islam and Biswas's protocol [15]	1440 bits	$3PM + 2PA + 4H$	$4PM + 2PA + 1Hp + 4H$
Yoon et al.'s protocol [12]	1072 bits	$3PM + 2PA + 5H$	$4PM + 2PA + 1HP + 5H$
Chou et al.'s protocol [22]	1232 bits	$3PM + 3H$	$3PM + 5H$
Farash and Attari's protocol [23]	1232 bits	$3PM + 4H$	$3PM + 6H$
Our 2PAKE protocol	896 bits	$2PM + 2H + 1MAC$	$1PM + 3H + 1MAC$

Table 4. Performance comparison for 3PAKE protocols

	Communication costs	Computation costs	
		User	Server
He et al.'s protocol [21]	2464 bits	$3PM + 3H$	$2PM + 6H + 2I$
Tan's protocol [19]	4224 bits	$4PM + 1E$ (816) + $1D$(816)	$2PM + 2E$ (816) + $2D$(816)
Yang and Chang's protocol [17]	3680 bits	$5PM + 1E$ (640) + $1D$(640)	$2PM + 2E$ (640) + $2D$(640)
Chou et al.'s protocol [22]	2464 bits	$3PM + 2H$	$2PM + 8H$
Our 3PAKE protocol	2464 bits	$3PM + 3H$	$2PM + 6H$

4   Conclusion

In this paper, we presented two efficient authentication protocols in client-server networks, where one provides mutual authentication and key exchange between the remote user and the server, and the other achieves mutual authentication and key exchange between any two remote users with the help of the server. Compared with the relevant protocols, the proposed protocols obtain higher efficiencies, and especially relieve the burden of the server. Therefore, the proposed protocols are more practical and more suitable for large-scale mobile communication networks.

Acknowledgement. This work was supported in part by the National Natural Science Foundation of China (61173187, 11301002), Natural Science Foundation of Anhui Province (1408085QF107), Talents Youth Fund of Anhui Province Universities (2013SQRL006ZD), 211 Project of Anhui University (17110099).

References

1. Abi-Char, P.E., El-Hassan, B., Mhamed, A.: A fast and secure elliptic curve based authenticated key agreement protocol for low power mobile communications. In: Proceedings of the 2007 International Conference on Next Generation Mobile Applications, Services and Technologies, pp. 235–240. IEEE, New York (2007)
2. Chen, Z.G., Song, X.X.: A distributed electronic authentication scheme based on elliptic curve. In: Proceedings of the Sixth International on Machine Learning and Cybernetics, pp. 2179–2182. IEEE, New York (2007)
3. Jiang, C., Li, B., Xu, H.: An efficient scheme for user authentication in wireless sensor networks. In: Proceedings of 21st International Conference on Advanced Information Networking and Applications Workshops, pp. 438–442. IEEE, New York (2007)
4. Miller, V.S.: Use of elliptic curves in cryptography. In: Williams, H.C. (ed.) CRYPTO 1985. LNCS, vol. 218, pp. 417–426. Springer, Heidelberg (1986). doi:10.1007/3-540-39799-X_31
5. Koblitz, N.: Elliptic curve cryptosystem. Math. Comput. **48**, 203–209 (1987)
6. Rivest, R.L., Shamir, A., Adleman, L.: A method for obtaining digital signatures and public key cryptosystems. Commun. ACM **21**(2), 120–126 (1978)
7. ElGamal, T.: A public key cryptosystem and a signature scheme based on discrete logarithms. IEEE Trans. Inf. IT **31**, 469–472 (1985)
8. Hankerson, D., Menezes, A., Vanstone, S.: Guide to Elliptic Curve Cryptography. Springer Professional Computing. LNCS. Springer, New York (2004). doi:10.1007/b97644
9. Yang, J.H., Chang, C.C.: An ID-based remote mutual authentication with key agreement scheme for mobile devices on elliptic curve cryptosystem. Comput. Secur. **28**(3–4), 138–143 (2009)
10. Yoon, E.J., Yoo, K.Y.: Robust ID-based remote mutual authentication with key agreement protocol for mobile devices on ECC. In: Proceeding of 2009 International Conference on Computational Science and Engineering, vol. 02, pp. 633–640. IEEE Computer Society, Washington, DC, USA (2009)
11. He, D., Chen, J., Hu, J.: An ID-based client authentication with key agreement protocol for mobile client–server environment on ECC with provable security. Inf. Fusion **13**(3), 223–230 (2012)
12. Yoon, E.J., Choi, S.B., Yoo, K.Y.: A secure and efficiency ID-based authenticated key agreement scheme based on elliptic curve cryptosystem for mobile devices. Int. J. Innov. Comput. Inf. Control **8**(4), 2637–2653 (2012)
13. He, D.: An efficient remote user authentication and key agreement protocol for mobile client-server environment from pairings. Ad Hoc Netw. **10**, 1009–1016 (2012)
14. Wang, D., Ma, C.G.: Cryptanalysis of a remote user authentication scheme for mobile client-server environment based on ECC. Inf. Fusion **14**(4), 498–503 (2013)
15. Islam, S.K.H., Biswas, G.P.: A more efficient and secure ID-based remote mutual authentication with key agreement scheme for mobile devices on elliptic curve cryptosystem. J. Syst. Softw. **84**(11), 1892–1898 (2011)
16. Karuppiah, M., Saravanan, R.: A secure remote user mutual authentication scheme using smart cards. J. Inf. Secur. Appl. **19**, 282–294 (2014)
17. Yang, J.H., Chang, C.C.: An efficient three-party authenticated key exchange protocol using elliptic curve cryptography for mobile-commerce environments. J. Syst. Softw. **82**(9), 1497–1502 (2009)
18. Chen, T.H., Lee, W.B., Chen, H.B.: A round-and computation-efficient three-party authenticated key exchange protocol. J. Syst. Softw. **81**(9), 1581–1590 (2008)

19. Tan, Z.: An enhanced three-party authentication key exchange protocol for mobile commerce environments. J. Commun. **5**(5), 436–443 (2010)
20. Nose, P.: Security weaknesses of authenticated key agreement protocols. Inf. Process. Lett. **111**(14), 687–696 (2011)
21. He, D., Chen, Y., Chen, J.: An ID-based three-party authenticated key exchange protocol using elliptic curve cryptography for mobile-commerce environments. Comput. Eng. Comput. Sci. **38**, 2055–2061 (2013)
22. Chou, C.H., Tsai, K.Y., Lu, C.F.: Two ID-based authenticated schemes with key agreement for mobile environments. J. Supercomput. **66**(2), 973–988 (2013)
23. Farash, M.S., Attari, M.A.: A secure and efficient identity-based authenticated key exchange protocol for mobile client-server networks. J. Supercomput. **69**(1), 395–411 (2014)
24. Shi, R.H., Zhong, H., Zhang, S.: Comments on two schemes of identity-based user authentication and key agreement for mobile client-server networks. J. Supercomput. **71**(11), 4015–4018 (2015)
25. Diffie, W., Hellman, M.: New directions in cryptography. IEEE Trans. Inf. Theory IT **22**(6), 644–654 (1976)
26. Yao, A.C.C., Zhao, Y.: Privacy-preserving authenticated key-exchange over internet. IEEE Trans. Inf. Forensics Security **9**(1), 125–140 (2014)

DMSD-FPE: Data Masking System for Database Based on Format-Preserving Encryption

Mingming Zhang[1], Guiyang Xie[1], Shimeng Wei[1], Pu Song[1],
Zhonghao Guo[1], Zheli Liu[1], and Zijing Cheng[2(✉)]

[1] College of Computer and Control Engineering, Nankai University, Tianjin,
People's Republic of China
zeriny123@hotmail.com, xiao.sha.gu.a@163.com,
tunrekg@163.com, wishercat@126.com,
1410587@mail.nankai.edu.cn, tunrekg@163.com,
liuzheli@nankai.edu.cn
[2] State Key Laboratory of Space-Ground Integrated Information Technology,
Beijing Institute of Satellite Information Engineering,
Beijing, People's Republic of China
linuxdemo@126.com

Abstract. The traditional data masking systems cannot provide reversible operations for database, and they will destroy the referential integrity of database. To solve the problems above, we provide a new data masking system based on format-preserving encryption (DMSD-FPE). This paper presents the model of it and highlights the appropriate masking algorithms for different databases. DMSD-FPE could guarantee that the format of cipher text is the same as plain text, and provides reversible operations for databases. Besides, the referential integrity is also kept. Furthermore, the experiments demonstrates that the system is efficient enough to adapt to practical uses.

Keywords: Data masking · Data privacy · Format-preserving encryption

1 Introduction

Nowadays, we all expect the precise mining result from the massive data accumulated in the database. But how to protect the privacy of data becomes a new challenge. As we know, data masking is one of the solutions to this problem, which is a method to protect the privacy of desensitized data for the producing and testing environment. Currently, the public pay more attention on data masking and the application area becomes more than ever before, including the data mining based on privacy- protection in different test environments. For example, the hospital wants to dig out the dependencies between medicines and symptoms from the patient information database for a better treatment. In case of data loss or data leaks when the data is sent to a mining institution, the effective data mining method is needed.

With the increasing demand, requirements for data masking are becoming stricter and stricter. Databases contain much more sensitive information, such as ID number

© ICST Institute for Computer Sciences, Social Informatics and Telecommunications Engineering 2018
J. Wan et al. (Eds.): CloudComp 2016, SPNCE 2016, LNICST 197, pp. 216–226, 2018.
https://doi.org/10.1007/978-3-319-69605-8_20

and address. Thus if the data was not masked in time, serious consequences like data leaks would be caused. Therefore, we must not only protect the sensitive information, ensuring the security of private data, but also meet the test environment and data availability requirements (data mining, statistical analysis, etc.). Meanwhile, for the particularity of data from database, the masking process should also guarantee the referential integrity.

As we know, the method of data masking is similar to that of data publishing, but there are some defects for traditional methods [9, 10]. One method requires to remove the sensitive attributes beforehand, which is unable to fully hold the original information. Another method needs to add redundant data to make it chaos, but the information could never be used as before. These methods are mostly one-way and irreversible masking strategy, which will break the referential integrity of database and can't meet the need for data privacy protection.

In addition to the foregoing methods, encryption is the most effective strategy for the protection of privacy. But encryption usually extends the data, such as AES and 3DES, which will output the ciphertext with the length of specified block size and make the ciphertext not to be stored in the original database anymore. Besides, the readability and usability of data become worse, which means, the data mining algorithms based on these data couldn't be used. Meanwhile, encryption will bring challenges to the database operation for ciphertext. It will destroy some of the operating characteristics of the plaintext, so that common queries and gathering operation are not allowed.

However, the format-preserving encryption (FPE [1–4, 11]) brings a new life to data masking for databases. It is necessary to encrypt the sensitive information of them, without breaking the referential integrity. The ideal way is to ensure that the ciphertext and plaintext have the same format (in the same domain), which is the method of FPE. Our data masking system based on FPE could easily protect data in case of data leaks, and it retains the available characteristic of data. Besides, the masking progress of the system is reversible.

1.1   Contribution

In this paper, we present a data masking system named "DMSD-FPE", which is based on format-preserving encryption (FPE). It adopts some data masking algorithms according to the needs of users. Compared with the traditional data masking methods, our system could keep the formation for different types of data and the referential integrity among data tables in the given database.

2   Our Proposed System

In this section, we will introduce where our system is applied to and how it works. Besides, in the second part, we will detail the system modules and explain the work principle of each module.

2.1 Application Scenarios

In practice, the data masking system is mainly applied in two areas, database backups and data mining.

Database backups: With the development of informatization in productive companies, the formal management of database is needed, such as database backups. If the backup database was stored in the form of plaintext, it would cause the information disclosure, so that data needs to be pre-masked before backing up. However, the data of the Shadow Database (the masked database) need to be decrypted sometimes. Then it requires the data masking process be reversible. Our DMSD-FPE system will be able to meet these needs.

Data mining: When the database holders want to send it to the public for data mining analysis, the important private information may be gotten by the third-party. In case of it, the holders could use DMSD-FPE system to mask the key attributes in advance.

2.2 System Model

The model of DMSD-FPE is shown in Fig. 1. It mainly works between the original database and the shadow one. This system could mask all information in the data tables of original database according to the users' decision, and insert the masked information to both new databases (Shadow Database) and new text files (Shadow Text). The information of shadow database is also available for analyzing and adopting in some types of data mining algorithms. We can get effective mining results both from the original database to the shadow one.

Fig. 1. System model

As shown in Fig. 2, DMSD-FPE includes three modules. Because there are three phases in the data masking system. We describe them with three modules in details as follows:

Setup Module: This module includes Source Database, Target Database and Information of Connection. We can choose the type of database, create target database, select the storage path of target database, and so on.

Rules Module: This module is the core operation part of the system, which sets all the rules for the data masking process. We could set key and algorithm for each data type in it, according to the table name and the attribute name. It mainly includes two components as follows:

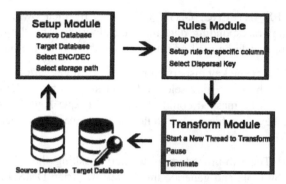

Fig. 2. Module structure of DMSD-FPE.

(1) *Key dispersion*: The DBMS-FPE only assigns one master key, and the encryption key for each column is dispersed via the key dispersal algorithm. This algorithm takes the table name and column name as input, with the dispersal one as output. In order to keep the referential integrity, we need to ensure that the key used for the primary key column and the foreign one is the same. So we must judge the relationship of all the tables first and generate the same key for them if necessary.

(2) *Masking algorithms*: DBMS-FPE will provide the corresponding masking algorithm according to the default data type or the user-chosen one. We will introduce each kind of algorithm in detail in Sect. 3.

Transform Module: In this module, we can start up the data masking process. And the system works in another thread with the masking algorithms chosen by us. After all work is done, the derived data will be imported into the target database via this module.

2.3   Work Flow

Overview. Data masking can be described as applying various basic methods and mixed ones to generate the similar data in the premise of satisfying the data constraints, through analyzing the raw data. Our system implements this process. To further describe this system, we introduce its work flows here:

Database Connecting: According to the type of databases provided by the provider, DMSD-FPE could connect to several common databases, such as SQL Server, Oracle, etc.

Data Analysis and Pre-processing: In order to obtain the structural information and constraints of databases, we should analyze the databases and find out the irrespective disturb. Then we can remove it via data pre-processing, as is called "Denoising". And during the pre-processing, the system could generate the dictionary for the special data masking method (mentioned in Sect. 3.2).

Rules Specifying: This module is to set default masking rules for each column, according to original data types in the database. And also, the users could select the rules (ID_ENC, FFX_INT_ENC, DATE_ENC, etc.) by their own. Finally, DMSD-FPE determines the corresponding data masking algorithms by the decided rules. It requires that the input data be read one tuple to another, so as the output.

Keys Selecting: During the key dispersing process, we'll get various keys for different columns. Therefore, the users may select different keys to mask the columns in one table. Each column to be masked could obtain one unique key. After that, the users need to save those keys in a file, so we could use the same keys to decrypt the data of the masking database directly.

Data Generating: The sub-procedure is to start masking the designated sensitive information tuple by tuple and generate the ciphertext. Then DMSD-FPE will import each ciphertext to a newly-build database (Shadow Database) and a text file (Shadow Text). It's much more convenient to publish or minethe Shadow Database and Shadow Text for effective results.

3   Data Masking Algorithms

In a DMSD-FPE, the core algorithm type is FPE. It mainly includes six kinds of algorithm. In this section, we will focus on the existing data masking algorithms, and introduce some new algorithms for special requirements.

3.1   Data Types and Corresponding Algorithms

In Table 1, there are some common data types and the masking algorithms adopted. We will introduce them in detail as follows.

Table 1. FPE for data types in database.

Data type	FPE schema
Integer	FFX_INT_ENC
Character	FFX_CHAR_ENC
ID number	ID_ENC
E-mail	EMAIL_ENC
Date	DATE_ENC
Items	Mixed schema

Traditional Data Type: For example, the integer [5] adopts FFX_INT_ENC to guarantee that the ciphertext value is within the specified range. The character string [3] stored in the database adopts FFX_CHAR_ENC, and the format of it is the length and storage size.

Expansion Data Type: Some data types, such as ID number, E-mail, Datetime [6] and so on, need to preserve the segment characteristic. So the masking process should base on corresponding algorithm for each of the segments. For instance, an e-mail number consists of a customized string, a symbol "@", a domain name and the suffix. In order to preserve the formation of e-mail number, we could only operate the customized string. Based on the above, we adopt the ID_ENC, EMAIL_ENC and DATE_ENC severally for them.

As for the other special data types of the masking dataset, we call them items, which adopts ITEM_ENC algorithm to do the masking job. This algorithm takes the mixed masking mode, including FFX_INT_ENC and other method for the traditional data type. Let's take the medical data as an example, the ITEM_ENC for it is just an inner substitution method. To preserve the item's format, we should only ensure that the ciphertext belongs to the same dataset as cleartext.

3.2   Implementation Details

To preserve the association rules of the original database and to meet the need of masking sensitive properties, DMSD-FPE mainly adopts six masking methods introduced in 3.1. Here we will introduce the pseudo-code of the main masking algorithms:

(1) Algorithm for Integer

The pseudocode of this algorithm is shown in Table 2. Before masking the integer data, we need to preprocess it. Firstly, we've to check the ASCII table to find out the value of each integer character, and transform the input string into a decimal integer. Secondly, the integer should be divided into two. The right part(R) is transferred to the left. Then we should deal with R through AES algorithm and XOR the result with the left one (L) as the new R'.

Table 2. Pseudocode of FFX_INT_ENC

```
Input:OriginalData, Maxvalue

1:  For   i=1 to 6 do
2:OriginalData→left || right
3:right→Dest_left
4: AES_KEY (right) ⊕left→Dest_right
5: Dest_left    || Dest_right→OriginalData
6:  End for
7: OriginalData→EncryptData
8:  If   EncryptData<Maxvalue
9:    FFX_INT_ENC(EncryptData , Maxvalue)
10: End If
Output:   EncryptData
```

The process above is based on cycle-walking [8], which will be executed for six times all in all. And if the result larger than the maximum value, the transformation will be repeated until it is less than the maximum value.

(2) Algorithm for Character String

The pseudocode of this algorithm is shown in Table 3. In the process of masking the character data, we need to set up a character type dictionary (covering all possible characters). When inputting a string, the program would check up the dictionary to find out the index of each letter and transform the input string into a decimal integer. The rest of the process is similar to FFX_INT_ENC, but the difference is that there is no need to do the cycle-walking.

Table 3. Pseudocode of FFX_CHAR_ENC

```
Input: OriginalData
1:  CharToNumber(OriginalData)→original
2:  For i=1 to 6 do
3:      original→left || right
4:      right→Dest_left
5:      AES_KEY (right)⊕left→Dest_right
6:      Dest_left || Dest_right→original
7:  End For
8:  NumberToChar(original)→EncryptData
Output: EncryptData
```

(3) Special methods

The pseudocode of this algorithm is shown in Table 4. Usually, some special data set has a fixed property, and the masking process can't change the characteristic to the original dataset. It is only the substitution of the existing dataset elements. For example, one product's name should be masked to another product's name.

Flow: In the process of implementing this algorithm, we need to get all the elements of an attribute A and generate a dictionary (Dictionary) of attributes to be queried. Check up the index of element E in the dictionary, and then mask the index to get an index' in a specified range via FFX_INT_ENC. The element in Dictionary whose subscript is index' is the ciphertext A'.

(4) Summary

All of the data masking algorithms mentioned above can preserve the formation of data, and won't influence the availability of data. When we implement different algorithms, we can get different keys through dispersing MK, so that the results are decentralized and the difficulty of cracking is also increased. When returning the mining results, we can also decrypt the data via MK or the key dispersion algorithm.

Table 4. Pseudocode of ITEM_ENC

```
Input: Atrribute A, Originallist
1: Foreach (Table in DataBase)
2:    GetDictionary(Table, A)→Dictionary
3: End foreach
4: For i=1 to Originallist.count do
5:    If Originallist[i]==Dictionary[j] then
6:                         k=FFX_INT_ENC(j,length,
encryptone,maxIndex);
7:        EncryptList.Add(Dictionary[k]);
8:    Else
9:        EncryptList.Add(Dictionary[j]);
10:   End if
11:End for
Output: EncryptList
```

4 Experiment

In this section, we will focus on some details of implementing our data masking system. And also, we'll consider the data analysis, such that evaluate the efficiency of the data masking algorithms.

4.1 Implementation Details

We implement our DMSD-FPE system by Windows C#, an object-oriented programming language. And we implement all of the algorithms through an open kernel API of C++ DLL, called "FPEDLL". As a shared DLL file, it can be invoked by the system program to mask the data. Developers could build other data masking systems based on this DLL with the public interface.

In our Windows Forms application (FPE), we encapsulate five classes totally, including DBFactory, DBOperation, EncryptSelect, DecSelect, ThreadMethod and so on. The functions are as follows:

- DBFactory class: it is used to select the type of database, such as SQL Server, MySql, etc.
- DBOperation class: it contains the operation code of various types of database, including Create, Read, Update and Delete (CRUD).
- EncryptSelect class: it is used to select the encryption method, which calls the encryption algorithms in FPEDLL.
- DecSelectSelect class: it is used to select the decrypting method, which calls the encryption algorithms in FPEDLL.
- ThreadMethod class: it is a class of thread, used to display the progress of encryption and decryption. It contains some data masking process and database operation.

4.1.1   User Interface

The following pictures are the main interfaces of our data masking system, DMSD-FPE, which are shown in Fig. 3.

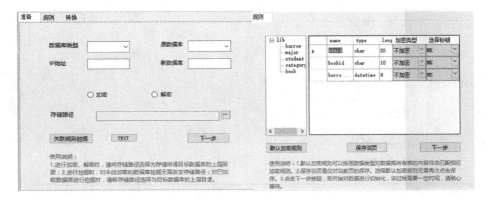

Fig. 3. Interface of DMSD-FPE

The function of the modules in the interface were introduced in detail in Sect. 2.2, and at the bottom of each interface there are some notes to explain the usage of them.

When the users click the Next-Step Button, they should choose whether or not to save the alteration of the current page, which ensures that each action is always right.

What's more, when clicking on the Start Button, the progress bar will show the current processes.

4.2   Efficiency

We performed all of the experiments on Computer of Inter(R) Core(TM) i7-4510U CPU @ 2.00 GHz with Windows10 OS. The efficiency of general data masking algorithms mentioned in Sect. 3 is shown as the follow one (Table 5).

Table 5. Execute time of algorithms

Records number	10	100	500	1000	5000	10000
FFX_INT_ENC	0.0426 ms	0.39420 ms	1.6679 ms	3.3731 ms	17.2152 ms	35.2001 ms
FFX_CHAR_ENC	0.1580 ms	1.4971 ms	6.3412 ms	14.1846 ms	74.9092 ms	137.5970 ms
ITEM_ENC	0.0031 ms	0.1445 ms	3.1749 ms	9.4949 ms	11.7808 ms	13.0087 ms

As shown in Table 5, for the first two encryption algorithm, the execute time has linear relationship with the number of records, which increases exponentially with the number.

However, there is not distinct regularity of execute time for ITEM_ENC algorithm. Because in the process of masking with this algorithm, we need to traverse the items dictionary to find out the index of each item, and the time for each one is actually different according to different location.

As shown in Table 6, the time of data masking is almost not affected by the number of the tables. It only depends on the number of records in the source database, which shows a linear relationship. In addition, the time to create different databases is basically equal, and only becomes more when the number of tables increases.

Table 6. Time of exporting metadata for database tables

Source database		Time-consuming	
Table number	Record number	Data masking	Database creating
1	25	0.4971 s	0.7182596 s
2	25	0.5047 s	0.8073632 s
3	25	0.5091 s	0.8196084 s
1	50	0.9048 s	0.6484303 s
2	50	0.7512 s	0.7388628 s
3	50	0.9063 s	0.7462538 s
1	75	1.3392 s	0.8196084 s
2	75	1.4026 s	0.8816251 s
3	75	1.5477 s	0.7208608 s

5 Conclusion

In this article, we put forward data masking system for database based on FPE. For different types of database we provide suitable masking algorithm according to their shelter needs. We can keep data formats and referential integrity of the database without removing sensitive information at the same time. We implemented this system through experiments. Experiments show that efficiency can meet the needs of practical applications and encryption, moreover, decryption process is reversible.

In order to verify the correctness of this masking system, we still need to use the existing association rule mining and other data mining algorithms to do mining analysis of information for masking database. We look forward to coming to a conclusion, which is the same as the mining result from the original database, to guarantee the correctness of this system.

References

1. Black, J., Rogaway, P.: Ciphers with arbitrary finite domains. In: Preneel, B. (ed.) CT-RSA 2002. LNCS, vol. 2271, pp. 114–130. Springer, Heidelberg (2002). doi:10.1007/3-540-45760-7_9
2. Morris, B., Rogaway, P., Stegers, T.: How to encipher messages on a small domain. In: Halevi, S. (ed.) CRYPTO 2009. LNCS, vol. 5677, pp. 286–302. Springer, Heidelberg (2009). doi:10.1007/978-3-642-03356-8_17
3. Bellare, M., Rogaway, P., Spies, T.: The FFX mode of operation for format-preserving encryption. NIST Submission

4. Hoang, V.T., Morris, B., Rogaway, P.: An enciphering scheme based on a card shuffle. In: Safavi-Naini, R., Canetti, R. (eds.) CRYPTO 2012. LNCS, vol. 7417, pp. 1–13. Springer, Heidelberg (2012). doi:10.1007/978-3-642-32009-5_1
5. Terence, S.: Feistel finite set encryption mode. NIST Proposed Encryption Mode
6. Liu, Z., Jia, C., Li, J.: Format-preserving encryption for datetime. In: Intelligent Computing and Intelligent Systems, vol. 2, Springer (2010)
7. Li, M., Liu, Z., Li, J., Jia, C.: Format-preserving encryption for character data. J. Netw. **7**(8), 1239–1244 (2012)
8. Li, J., Jia, C., Liu, Z.: Cycle-walking revisited: consistency, security, and efficiency. Secur. Commun. Netw. (2012)
9. Espositoa, C., Ficcob, M., Palmierib, F., Castiglionec, A.: A knowledge-based platform for big data analytics based on publish/subscribe services and stream processing. Knowl.-Based Syst. **79**, 3–17 (2015)
10. Yang, J.-J., Li, J.-Q., Niu, Y.: A hybrid solution for privacy preserving medical data sharing in the cloud environment. Future Gener. Comput. Syst. 43–44 (2015)
11. Spies, T.: Format Preserving Encryption. Voltage White Paper

Delay-Tolerant Network Based Secure Transmission System Design

Gang Ming[1] and Zhenxiang Chen[1,2(✉)]

[1] School of Information Science and Engineering, University of Jinan, Jinan, China
czx@ujn.edu.cn
[2] Shandong Provincial Key Laboratory of Network Based Intelligent Computing,
Jinan, China

Abstract. The Internet has been a great success but its architecture
need relatively complete infrastructure construction to implement and
operate. Especially, the situation worsens on resource-limited devices, so
delay-tolerant network was proposed to overcome these disadvantages.
The development of delay-tolerant network provides a new approach to
transmit data but its confidentiality and integrity cannot be guaranteed well. The public-key cryptography provides a feasible mechanism to
protect data. However, the maintenance cost of certificate authorities is
large. Identity-based cryptography allows users to encrypt message with
their identity information. Based on the above-mentioned technologies,
we proposed a secure transmission system based on delay-tolerant network and identity-based cryptography, which does not rely on traditional
key distribution mechanism and simplifies identity verification.

Keywords: Delay-tolerant network · Identity-based cryptography ·
Identity-based encryption · Secure transmission system

1 Introduction

The Internet has been a highly successful architecture and protocol at inter-
connecting communication while operating poorly environments characterized
by long delay path and distributed network location. In addition, the resource
usage for end nodes is unfriendly. Delay-tolerant network (DTN) is an overlay on
top of special-purpose networks including the Internet which can accommodate
long distributions and delays among those networks so that it is fit for embedded
devices communication. Since communications are supposed to store and transmit data among lots of nodes, malicious nodes constructed intentionally may
catch and modify data packets that are not belong to them.

Public-key cryptography (PKC) is a cryptographic system using pairs of keys
which public key may be disseminated widely and private key is only known to
the owner. Certification authority (CA) is introduced for issuing public and
private keys. However, it is almost infeasible to establish such CAs at DTN
due to frequent network partitions and high latency so that the confidentiality

© ICST Institute for Computer Sciences, Social Informatics and Telecommunications Engineering 2018
J. Wan et al. (Eds.): CloudComp 2016, SPNCE 2016, LNICST 197, pp. 227–231, 2018.
https://doi.org/10.1007/978-3-319-69605-8_21

and integrity of data cannot be guaranteed. To handle this problem, we choose identity-based cryptography (IBC) which allows a sender to encrypt a message to an identity without access to a public key certificate.

We designed a secure transmission system by applying DTN and IBC which can deploy on embedded devices to communicate in Internet of Things, Internet of Cars, etc.

2   Related Work

DTN was proposed by Fall [1]. Internet Research Task Force (IRTF) founded Delay Tolerant Networking Research Group (DTNRG)[2] that formulated DTN architecture [3] and bundle protocol specification [4].

In 1984, Shamir proposed a concept of identity-based cryptography [5]. In this theory, users' email or IP address can be used as public key for encryption and signature scheme without managing public key infrastructure. Certificateless public key cryptography (CL-PKC) was proposed by Al-Riyami and Paterson [6] to overcome the disadvantages associated with public key infrastructure (PKI) and identity-based public key cryptography (ID-PKC) which does not require the use of certificates and built-in key escrow of ID-PKC.

Current identity-based encryption schemes are based on bilinear group, but its computational efficiency limits real-world applications. Guo and others [7] proposed Online/Offline IBE (OO-IBE) to reduce encryption time. The application of identity-based cryptography in wireless networks is comprehensive. Shim et al. [8] proposed EIBAS: An efficient identity-based broadcast authentication scheme. A fuzzy identity-based encryption (FIBE) scheme [9] is used for resolving data transmission security problem in Internet of Things (IoT).

3   System Architecture

Our work is based on DTN and IBC. Due to the latency and unstable connection status of point-to-point communication in delay-tolerant network, public key infrastructure is almost unavailable so that we use identity-based cryptography to implement identification of endpoints.

3.1   The Implementation of Delay-Tolerant Network

We implement a simple delay-tolerant network model with libevent, a library that provides asynchronous communication. How to figure the path from source node to destination node aka routing in delay-tolerant network is a critical problem. Traditional routing algorithms cannot accommodate, so modified Dijkstra algorithm using time-varying edge costs [10] is recommended.

Algorithm 1 shows the logic. s is the source node. T is the start time. L is the array returning the cost of the shortest path for all nodes. $G(V, E)$ is the map of DTN. $w(e, t)$ is the cost function. e is an edge from node u to node v.

Algorithm 1. Dijkstra's Algorithm modified to use time-varying edge costs.

Require: G=(V, E), s: source node; t: start time; W(e, t)
Ensure: L;
1: $Q \leftarrow \{V\}$
2: $L[s] \leftarrow 0, L[v] \leftarrow \infty \ \forall \ v \in V \ s.t \ v \neq s$
3: **while** $Q \neq \{\}$ **do**
4:    Let $u \in Q$ be the node s.t $L[u] = min_{x \in Q} L[x]$
5:    $Q = Q \leftarrow \{u\}$
6:    **for** each edge $e \in E$, s.t. $e = (u, v)$ **do**
7:        **if** $L[v] > (L[u] + w(e, L[u] + T))$ **then**
8:            $L[v] \in L[u] + w(e, L[u] + T)$
9:        **end if**
10:    **end for**
11: **end while**

The DTN architecture implements store-and-forward message by overlaying a new transmission protocol called the bundle protocol. When a node receive information, it should judge whether it is receiver or it shall transmit it.

3.2 Key Distribution

We deploy key generation center (KGC) and key privacy authority (KPA) to maintain user register information and issue key (Fig. 1 shows the system). KGC records secret parameter B. KPA provides key distribution and query user information form KGC according to user requests. Calculate key encrypted with secret parameter s and public parameter $P, P_{pub}, H_1, H_2, H_3$ to send to users if identity confirmed as following. The encryption of key and signature is based on type A of pair of curves from PBC library.

$$K = H_3(A \cdot B \cdot P) \tag{1}$$

$$D_{ID} = s \cdot H_1(ID) \tag{2}$$

$$D = DES_k(D_{ID}) \tag{3}$$

Users can get private key D_{ID} as following after receiving encrypted key from KPA.

$$K = H_3(B \cdot A \cdot P) \tag{4}$$

$$D_{ID} = DES_k(D) \tag{5}$$

3.3 Signature Scheme

User generates a random number $K \in Z_q$ and calculates signature R of message M.

$$R = K^{-1}(H_2(M) \cdot P + H_3 \cdot (R) \cdot D_{ID}) \tag{6}$$

Receiver should calculate $\hat{e}(U, V)$ and compare with to verify signature. If (R, S) is a available signature on message M, we will get

$$\hat{e}(R, S) = \hat{e}(P, P)^{H_2(M)} \cdot \hat{e}(P_{pub}, Q_{ID})^{H3(R)} \tag{7}$$

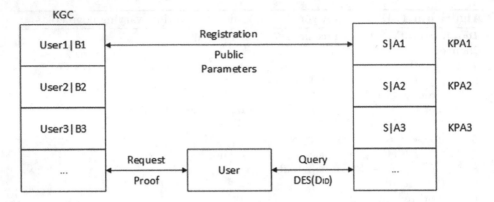

Fig. 1. Key distribution system

3.4   Identity-Based Encryption

An Identity-Based Encryption system (IBE) consists of four algorithms: Setup, Extract, Encrypt and Decrypt. The Setup algorithm generates system parameters and a master key by PKG one time for initializing IBE environment. The Extract algorithm uses the master key to extract a private key when PKG respond a request form users. The encryption algorithm encrypts messages with given identity and system parameters outputting cipher texts. In the end, the decryption algorithm decrypts encoded data using the private key.

4   Evaluation

With the development of IoT, there need a new and secure approach to transmit data. TCP/IP protocol suite, ZigBee and Bluetooth are alternative but their disadvantages are also obvious. ZigBee and Bluetooth are used for short-distance wireless data exchange while TCP/IP performs well at traditional scenes. Our work accommodate distance-varying and frequent network partitions without additional channel resource requirement. We use IBC to ensure the security of data and identities of nodes without construction of PKI reducing the requirement of networks and devices, which keeps DTN light and effective. Therefore, the security of data is also guaranteed.

The system can be applied to anonymity networks like Tor and temporary communication at disaster-affected area. Our system allows users to improve privacy and security with a new architecture avoiding existing monitoring measures. The communication at earthquake zone will break off and the top priority is to recover communication to coordinate rescue efforts. Rescuers can use mobile devices like cellphone to set up simple and secure communication network with our system.

5   Conclusion

DTN is a new type wireless network accommodating asynchronous network to provide interoperable communications between a wide range of networks which may have exceptionally poor and disparate performance characteristics. Our work provides an effective and secure approach to transmit information. However, DTN cannot afford large traffic transmission so it can be only used at discrete and small data exchange. Due to the unstable connection path and status, data delivery speed may be low.

Acknowledgments. This work was supported by the National Natural Science Foundation of China under Grants Nos. 61672262 and 61472164, the Natural Science Foundation of Shandong Province under Grants Nos. ZR2014JL042 and ZR2012FM010, the Shandong Provincial Key R&D Program under Grants No. 2016GGX101001 and the Program for youth science and technology star fund of Jinan No. TNK1108.

References

1. Fall, K.: A delay-tolerant network architecture for challenged internets. In: Proceedings of the 2003 Conference on Applications, Technologies, Architectures, and Protocols for Computer Communications, pp. 27–34. ACM (2003)
2. Delay tolerant networking research group. http://www.dtnrg.org
3. Delay-tolerant networking architecture. https://www.rfc-editor.org/rfc/pdfrfc/rfc4838.txt.pdf
4. Bundle protocol specification. https://www.rfc-editor.org/rfc/pdfrfc/rfc5050.txt.pdf
5. Shamir, A.: Identity-based cryptosystems and signature schemes. In: Blakley, G.R., Chaum, D. (eds.) CRYPTO 1984. LNCS, vol. 196, pp. 47–53. Springer, Heidelberg (1985). https://doi.org/10.1007/3-540-39568-7_5
6. Al-Riyami, S.S., Paterson, K.G.: Certificateless public key cryptography. In: Laih, C. (ed.) ASIACRYPT 2003. LNCS, vol. 2894, pp. 452–473. Springer, Heidelberg (2003). https://doi.org/10.1007/978-3-540-40061-5_29
7. Guo, F., Mu, Y., Chen, Z.: Identity-based online/offline encryption. In: Tsudik, G. (ed.) FC 2008. LNCS, vol. 5143, pp. 247–261. Springer, Heidelberg (2008). https://doi.org/10.1007/978-3-540-85230-8_22
8. Shim, K., Lee, Y., Park, C.: EIBAS: an efficient identity-based broadcast authentication scheme in wireless sensor networks. Ad Hoc Netw. **11**(1), 182–189 (2013)
9. Mao, Y., Li, J., Chen, M., Liu, J., Xie, C., Zhan, Y.: Fully secure fuzzy identity-based encryption for secure IoT communications. In: Computer Standards and Interfaces, vol. 44, pp. 117–121. Elsevier (2016)
10. Jain, S., Fall, K., Patra, R.: Routing in a Delay Tolerant Network, vol. 34. ACM, New York (2004)

An Internal Waves Detection Method Based on PCANet for Images Captured from UAV

Qinghong Dong[1], Shengke Wang[1(✉)], Muwei Jian[1], Yujuan Sun[2], and Junyu Dong[1]

[1] Department of Computer Science and Technology, Ocean University of China, Qingdao, China
i@dongqinghong.com,
{neverme,jianmuwei,dongjunyu}@ouc.edu.cn
[2] School of Information and Electrical Engineering, Ludong University, Yantai, China
syj_anne@163.com

Abstract. As internal wave is a universal geophysical phenomenon in stratified fluids, study of internal wave features in the coastal ocean is one of the most important tasks in physical oceanography. Traditionally, various internal wave detection methods, such as acoustic, optical, electrical based techniques and SAR based technique have been proposed. However, those methods need expensive measuring devices and often face the difficulties of the installation when deployed in the ocean. With the development of machine learning recently, internal wave detection based on computer vision and machine learning becomes a hot topic. In this paper, a framework for internal waves detection based on PCANet which is a feature learning deep network is proposed. First, we collect simulated internal wave images and non-internal wave images, then we give a label to each image to indicate whether it includes internal waves or not. Finally, we train a discrimination model with PCANet and predict new images at the test stage. Experiment results demonstrated the feasibility of the technique for internal wave detection.

1 Introduction

As a significant ocean interior wave phenomenon, internal wave is widespread in the ocean [1]. Internal wave and its side effects have been studied in various aspects since it can significantly affect oceanic current measurements, undersea navigation and antisubmarine warfare operation [2]. It could also affect offshore oil exploration and development. Internal wave is a tough research field in marine areas due to the complexity of its generation mechanisms and the randomness of its space-time characteristic [3].

Traditional internal wave detection methods usually obtain data from the synthetic aperture radar. Internal wave can be mapped on the SAR image due to the sensitivity of SAR data that changes with the small-scale surface roughness [4–6]. It provides users data over a wide range of area. However, practically it is impossible to repeatedly observe the same wave packet over a short period of time.

© ICST Institute for Computer Sciences, Social Informatics and Telecommunications Engineering 2018
J. Wan et al. (Eds.): CloudComp 2016, SPNCE 2016, LNICST 197, pp. 232–237, 2018.
https://doi.org/10.1007/978-3-319-69605-8_22

In this paper, we introduce a new method based on machine learning for internal wave detection. A simple and effective deep learning network PCANet is conducted to train a single frame internal wave detection model. There are five sections in this paper. After the introduction section, the near surface internal waves was introduced in Sect. 2. In Sect. 3, features of learning algorithm with PCANet. In Sect. 4, performance of the model was evaluated by an original dataset collected in the lab. Final conclusions were addressed in Sect. 5.

2 Near-Surface Internal Waves

Internal wave is widely observed in the ocean, particularly in the relatively shallow waters such as Yellow Sea [7]. Internal wave occurs within subsurface layers of marine waters that are stratified due to temperature and salinity variations. Disturbance created within the ocean give rise to these waves, which represent a significant mechanism for transport of momentum and energy within the ocean [8].

Internal wave plays a significant role in maintaining the ocean circulation and global climate. Moreover, internal wave has certain impacts on human activities, such as platform drillings in industry and submarine voyages in military field [9]. Sea water would have strong inertia wave and stress force induced by the massive energy of internal wave, thus could influence human being activities significantly.

3 Internal Wave Features Extraction with PCANet

PCANet is a relatively simple deep learning network, which is easy to train and can be applied in different tasks in computer vision such as face classification and optical character recognition. The basic architecture of PCANet shown in Fig. 1. The training of PCANet has three stages: the first two stages based on PCA and in the last stage, hashing (in order to produce nonlinear output) and histogram used to demonstrate the results [10].

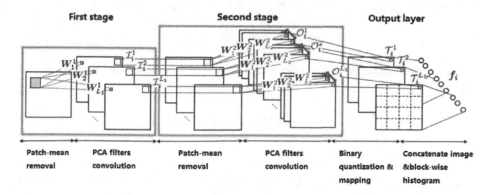

Fig. 1. The structure of the two-stage PCANet

Consider an image with $m \times n$ pixels in size – there are N images in the training set. In each image, a patch of size $k_1 \times k_2$ around each pixel was taken. All the patches were collected, vectored and combined into a matrix of $k_1 \times k_2$ rows and $(m - k_1 + 1) \times (n - k_2 + 1)$ columns.

For example, the i th image I_i, a matrix X_i was obtained, thus the patch mean from each patch was subtracted and get:

$$X = [X_1, X_2, \ldots,] \in R^{k_1 k_2 \times N_c} \tag{1}$$

where c indicates the number of rows of X_i. Then, the eigenvectors of XX^T was obtained, and the ones corresponding to the L_1 maximum eigenvalues as the PCA filters was saved, which can be expressed as:

$$W_l^1 = q_1 (XX^T) \in R^{K_1 K_2}, l = 1, 2, \ldots, L_1 \tag{2}$$

The leading principal eigenvectors capture the main variation of all the men-removed training patches. The first stage was finished at this stage.

At the second stage, a similar process with stage 1 was applied. The input images I_i^l of stage 2 should be:

$$I_i^l = I_i * W_l^1, i = 1, 2, \ldots, N \tag{3}$$

the boundary of I_i is zero-padded so that I_i^l have the same size of I_i, all the patches of I_i^l was collected, and patch mean from each patch was subtracted thus get:

$$Y^l = [Y_1^l, Y_2^l, \ldots, Y_N^l] \in R^{k_1 k_2 \times N_c}, l = 1, 2, \ldots, L_1 \tag{4}$$

in which, the Y^l was combined together as a matrix:

$$Y = [Y^1, Y^2, \ldots, Y^{L_1}] \in R^{k_1 k_2 \times L_1 N_c} \tag{5}$$

After that, the eigenvectors of YY^T, was obtained and the ones corresponding to the L_2 largest eigenvalues as the PCA filters of the second stage was saved.

$$W_\ell^2 = q_\ell (YY^T) \in R^{k_1 k_2}, \ell = 1, 2, \ldots, L_2 \tag{6}$$

At the final stage, for each input image of stage2, the following expression was obtained:

$$T_i^l = \sum_{\ell=1}^{L_2} 2^{\ell-1} H(I_i^l * W_\ell^2), l = 1, 2, \ldots L_1 \tag{7}$$

The function $H(\cdot)$ binaries output results, i.e. the value of the function is 1 for positive inputs and 0 otherwise. For each of the L_1 images T_i^l, $l = 1, 2, \ldots, L_1$ were partitioned it into B blocks, with size of $k_1 k_2 \times B$, and the $2^{L_2} \times B$ histogram matrix in each block ranging from $[0, 2^{L_2} - 1]$ was computed, followed by vectorizing the matrix into a row vector $Bhist(T_i^l)$. Finally, the $Bhist(T_i^l)$ of T_i^l, $l = 1, 2, 3 ..., L_1$ was concatenate as the feature

$$f_i = \left[Bhist(T_i^l), ..., Bhist(T_i^{L_1}) \right]^T \in R^{(2^{L2})L_1 B} \tag{8}$$

As we use the PCANet was used to extract the features of the images of internal waves, and label the normal water surface pictures with 0 and waves pictures with 1. The model parameters of PCANet include the patch size k_1, k_2, the filters number L_1, L_2, the number of stages and the block size for histograms. In the experiments, we resize image into 60×60, patch size 7×7, stage number 2, $L_1 = L_2 = 8$, and the block size 7×7 was set. We extract features from PCANet, and then put it into a linear SVM for classification with the attached labels.

4 Experiments

To verify the feasibility of the technique for internal waves detection, the model was applied on an original dataset collected in the lab. The dataset includes 214 images which are taken by the DJI Drone. During the shooting process, the camera took photos by looking straight down from the belly of the drone over the water surface. First, the drone was hovering over the water surface and photos of clam water surface were taken based on regular intervals. Then the production of waves was simulated and pictures were taken to track the waves. Table 1 shows the sample images of two kinds of sates in different conditions in our dataset. The two states are "Clam water surface" and "simulating the production of waves" with corresponding labels of 0 and 1.

Table 1. Image samples of two kinds of states in different conditions in our dataset

State (Label)	Condition 1	Condition 2
Clam water surface (0)		
Simulating the production of waves (1)		

Then the images were normalized to a resolution of 60*60 pixels to extract features with PCANet model, and training linear SVM classifier to detect the waves. Experiment results indicates that the proposed method has achieved reliable results to detect internal wave. Table 2 shows the accuracy rate of the proposed approach based on the dataset collected by the DJI Drone. Result in the dataset achieves 89% accuracy of detection in gray image on average, and 86.645% accuracy of detection in color image on average.

Table 2. Accuracy rate (%) of the proposed approach on the dataset collected by the DJI Drone

Image format	Condition 1	Condition 2	Average
Gray	84.85	93.15	89.00
Color	82.46	90.83	86.645
Average	83.655	91.99	87.82

5 Conclusions

In this paper, a framework for internal waves detection based on feature learning methods was proposed. The internal wave can be detected successfully by using the PCANet. The experiments demonstrated the feasibility of the technique for internal waves feature detection. Additionally, the result shows that accuracy rate improves with the sample size increasing. It was believed that the experiment can be further improved when larger scale dataset is used.

Acknowledgments. This work is supported by the Natural Science Foundation of China (NSFC) Grants 61301241, 61602229, 61403353, 61501417 and 61271405; Natural Science Foundation of Shandong (ZR2015FQ011; ZR2014FQ023); China Postdoctoral Science Foundation funded project (2016M590659); Qingdao Postdoctoral Science Foundation funded project (861605040008); The Fundamental Research Funds for the Central Universities (201511008, 30020084851);

References

1. Garrett, C., Munk, W.: Space-time scales of internal waves. Geophys. Fluid Dyn. **2**(1), 225–264 (1972)
2. Osborne, A.R., et al.: The influence of internal waves on deep-water drilling. J. Petrol. Technol. **30**(10), 1497–1504 (1978)
3. Zhu, G.: The status and future of research and development of marine environment monitoringtechnology in China. Ocean Technol. (2002)
4. Rodenas, J.A., Garello, R.: Wavelet analysis in SAR ocean image profiles for internal wave detection and wavelength estimation. IEEE Trans. Geosci. Remote Sens. **35**(4), 933–945 (1997)
5. Chen, B., et al.: Internal wave detection and parameter estimation from sar images based on a novel radon transform method. In: International Workshop on Education Technology and Training and 2008 International Workshop on Geoscience and Remote Sensing (2008)

6. Alpers, W.: Theory of radar imaging of internal waves. Nature **314**(6008), 245–247 (1985)
7. Sun, Z., et al.: The influence of internal waves on signal fluctuation in the Yellow Sea. J. Acoust. Soc. Am. **105**(2), 1311 (1999)
8. Chen, C.Y., et al.: An investigation on internal solitary waves in a two-layer fluid: propagation and reflection from steep slopes. Ocean Eng. **34**(1), 171–184 (2007)
9. Rodenas, J.A., Garello, R.: Internal wave detection and location in SAR images using wavelet transform. IEEE Trans. Geosci. Remote Sens. **9**(5), 1494–1507 (1998)
10. Chan, T.H., et al.: PCANet: a simple deep learning baseline for image classification? IEEE Trans. Image Process. **24**(12), 5017–5032 (2014). A Publication of the IEEE Signal Processing Society

Author Index

Printed in the United States
By Bookmasters